LAW AND TORTURE

Contemporary understandings of torture are ruled by a medico-legal duopoly: the language of law (regulating definition and prohibition) and that of medicine (controlling understandings of the body in pain). This duopoly has left little space for contextual conceptualisation – of ideological, emotional and imaginational impulses which function in readily recognising some forms of violence and dismissing others. This book challenges the rigour of this prevailing duopoly. In its place, it develops a new approach to critique the central scripts of 'law and torture' scholarship (around progress, violence, evidence and senses). Drawing on socio-legal and critical-theoretical scholarship, it aims to 'widen the apertures' of the dominant dogmas to their interconnected social, political, temporal and emotional dimensions. These dimensions, the book advances, hold the key to more fully understanding not only the production of torture's definition and prohibition but also its normative contestation – to better grasp whose pain gets recognised and redressed and why.

Ergün Cakal is a researcher at the University of Copenhagen's Faculty of Law and formerly a legal advisor at the Danish Institute Against Torture (DIGNITY). He has worked as an anti-torture lawyer since 2016, focusing on the conceptualisation, prevention and documentation of torture. He holds master's degrees in the sociology of law from Lund University and in international law from the University of Melbourne and a PhD from the University of Copenhagen.

LAW IN CONTEXT

Since 1970, the Law in Context series has been at the forefront of a movement to broaden the study of law. The series is a vehicle for the publication of innovative monographs and texts that treat law and legal phenomena critically in their cultural, social, political, technological, environmental and economic contexts. A contextual approach involves treating legal subjects broadly, using materials from other humanities and social sciences, and from any other discipline that helps to explain the operation in practice of the particular legal field or legal phenomena under investigation. It is intended that this orientation is at once more stimulating and more revealing than the bare exposition of legal rules. The series includes original research monographs, coursebooks and textbooks that foreground contextual approaches and methods. The series includes and welcomes books on the study of law in all its contexts, including domestic legal systems, European and international law, transnational and global legal processes, and comparative law.

Books in the Series

Acosta: *The National versus the Foreigner in South America: 200 Years of Migration and Citizenship Law*
Alaattinoğlu: *Grievance Formation, Rights and Remedies*
Ali: *Modern Challenges to Islamic Law*
Alyagon Darr: *Plausible Crime Stories: The Legal History of Sexual Offences in Mandate Palestine*
Anderson, Schum & Twining: *Analysis of Evidence, 2nd Edition*

Ashworth: *Sentencing and Criminal Justice, 6th Edition*

Barton & Douglas: *Law and Parenthood*

Baxi, McCrudden & Paliwala: *Law's Ethical, Global and Theoretical Contexts: Essays in Honour of William Twining*

Beecher-Monas: *Evaluating Scientific Evidence: An Interdisciplinary Framework for Intellectual Due Process*

Bell: *French Legal Cultures*

Bercusson: *European Labour Law, 2nd Edition*

Birkinshaw: *European Public Law*

Birkinshaw: *Freedom of Information: The Law, the Practice and the Ideal, 4th Edition*

Blick: *Electrified Democracy: The Internet and the United Kingdom Parliament in History*

Broderick & Ferri: *International and European Disability Law and Policy: Text, Cases and Materials*

Brownsword & Goodwin: *Law and the Technologies of the Twenty-First Century: Text and Materials*

Cane & Goudkamp: *Atiyah's Accidents, Compensation and the Law, 9th Edition*

Clarke: *Principles of Property Law*

Clarke & Kohler: *Property Law: Commentary and Materials*

Collins: *The Law of Contract, 4th Edition*

Collins, Ewing & McColgan: *Labour Law, 3rd Edition*

Corrias, *Law and Inhumanity: Dehumanization, Silent Claims and Atrocity Crimes*

Cowan: *Housing Law and Policy*

Cranston: *Making Commercial Law Through Practice 1830–1970*

Cranston: *Legal Foundations of the Welfare State*

Darian-Smith: *Laws and Societies in Global Contexts: Contemporary Approaches*

Dauvergne: *Making People Illegal: What Globalisation Means for Immigration and Law*

David: *Kinship, Law and Politics: An Anatomy of Belonging*

Davies: *Perspectives on Labour Law, 2nd Edition*

Dembour: *Who Believes in Human Rights?: Reflections on the European Convention*

de Sousa Santos: *Toward a New Legal Common Sense: Law, Globalization, and Emancipation*

Diduck: *Law's Families*

Douglas-Scott: *Brexit, Union, and Disunion: The Evolution of British Constitutional Unsettlement*

Dowdle: *Transnational Law: A Framework for Analysis* Dupret: *Positive Law from the Muslim World: Jurisprudence, History, Practices*

Dutta: *A Jurisprudence of Conversations: Law, Life and Feminism in Post-colonial India*

Emon: *Jurisdictional Exceptionalisms: Islamic Law, International Law, and Parental Child Abduction*

Estella: *Legal Foundations of EU Economic Governance*

Fortin: *Children's Rights and the Developing Law, 3rd Edition*
Garnsey: *The Justice of Visual Art: Creative State-Building in Times of Political Transition*
Garton, Probert & Bean: *Moffat's Trusts Law: Text and Materials, 7th Edition*
Ghai & Woodman: *Practising Self-Government: A Comparative Study of Autonomous Regions*
Glover-Thomas: *Reconstructing Mental Health Law and Policy*
Gobert & Punch: *Rethinking Corporate Crime*
Goldman: *Globalisation and the Western Legal Tradition: Recurring Patterns of Law and Authority*
Graber: *The Technosystem of Free Speech: Enriching Fundamental Rights in a Digital Society*
Haack: *Evidence Matters: Science, Proof, and Truth in the Law*
Harlow & Rawlings: *Law and Administration, 4th Edition*
Harris: *An Introduction to Law, 8th Edition*
Harris, Campbell & Halson: *Remedies in Contract and Tort, 2nd Edition*
Harvey: *Seeking Asylum in the UK: Problems and Prospects*
Herring: *Law and the Relational Self*
Hervey & McHale: *European Union Health Law: Themes and Implications*
Hervey & McHale: *Health Law and the European Union*
Holder & Lee: *Environmental Protection, Law and Policy: Text and Materials, 2nd Edition*
Hommes: *The Convention and the Kingdom: How the Netherlands Received the European Convention on Human Rights*
Jackson & Summers: *The Internationalisation of Criminal Evidence: Beyond the Common Law and Civil Law Traditions*
Jeutner: *The Reasonable Person: A Legal Biography*
Kennedy: *Inducing Intimacy: Deception, Consent and the Law*
Kostakopoulou: *The Future Governance of Citizenship*
Kreiczer-Levy: *Destabilized Property: Property Law in the Sharing Economy*
Kubal: *Immigration and Refugee Law in Russia: Socio-Legal Perspectives*
Lewis: *Choice and the Legal Order: Rising above Politics*
Likosky: *Law, Infrastructure and Human Rights*
Likosky: *Transnational Legal Processes: Globalisation and Power Disparities*
Lixinski: *Legalized Identities: Cultural Heritage Law and the Shaping of Transitional Justice*
Loughnan: *Self, Others and the State: Relations of Criminal Responsibility*
Lunney: *A History of Australian Tort Law 1901–1945: England's Obedient Servant?*
Maughan & Webb: *Lawyering Skills and the Legal Process, 2nd Edition*
McGaughey: *Principles of Enterprise Law*
McGlynn: *Families and the European Union: Law, Politics and Pluralism*
Mertens: *A Philosophical Introduction to Human Rights*
Miller: *An Introduction to German Law and Legal Culture: Text and Materials*

Moffat: *Trusts Law: Text and Materials*
Monti: *EC Competition Law*
Morgan: *Contract Law Minimalism: A Formalist Restatement of Commercial Contract Law*
Morgan & Yeung: *An Introduction to Law and Regulation: Text and Materials*
Nash: *British Islam and English Law: A Classical Pluralist Perspective* Ng: *Political Censorship in British Hong Kong: Freedom of Expression and the Law (1842–1997)*
Nicola & Davies: *EU Law Stories: Contextual and Critical Histories of European Jurisprudence*
Norrie: *Crime, Reason and History: A Critical Introduction to Criminal Law, 3rd Edition*
Norrie: *Rethinking Criminal Justice: Punishment, Abolition And Moral Psychology*
O'Dair: *Legal Ethics: Text and Materials*
Oliver: *Common Values and the Public–Private Divide*
Oliver & Drewry: *The Law and Parliament*
Palmer & Roberts: *Dispute Processes: ADR and the Primary Forms of Decision-Making, 1st Edition*
Palmer & Roberts: *Dispute Processes: ADR and the Primary Forms of Decision-Making, 3rd Edition*
Picciotto: *International Business Taxation*
Pieraccini: *Regulating the Sea: A Socio-Legal Analysis of English Marine Protected Areas*
Probert: *The Changing Legal Regulation of Cohabitation, 1600–2010: From Fornicators to Family, 1600–2010*
Qiao: *The Authoritarian Commons: Neighborhood Democratization in Urban China*
Radi: *Rules and Practices of International Investment Law and Arbitration*
Reed: *Internet Law: Text and Materials*
Richardson: *Law, Process and Custody*
Roberts & Palmer: *Dispute Processes: ADR and the Primary Forms of Decision-Making, 2nd Edition*
Rowbottom: *Democracy Distorted: Wealth, Influence and Democratic Politics*
Sauter: *Public Services in EU Law*
Scott & Black: *Cranston's Consumers and the Law*
Seneviratne: *Ombudsmen: Public Services and Administrative Justice*
Seppänen: *Ideological Conflict and the Rule of Law in Contemporary China: Useful Paradoxes*
Siems: *Comparative Law, 3rd Edition*
Stapleton: *Product Liability*
Stewart: *Gender, Law and Justice in a Global Market*
Tamanaha: *Law as a Means to an End: Threat to the Rule of Law*
Taylor: *Fortin's Children's Rights and the Developing Law, 4th Edition*
Tuori: *Properties of Law: Modern Law and After*
Turpin & Tomkins: *British Government and the Constitution: Text and Materials, 7th Edition*

Twining: *General Jurisprudence: Understanding Law from a Global Perspective*
Twining: *Globalisation and Legal Theory*
Twining: *Human Rights, Southern Voices: Francis Deng, Abdullahi An-Na'im, Yash Ghai and Upendra Baxi*
Twining: *Jurist in Context: A Memoir*
Twining: *Karl Llewellyn and the Realist Movement, 2nd Edition*
Twining: *Rethinking Evidence: Exploratory Essays, 2nd Edition*
Twining & Miers: *How to Do Things with Rules, 5th Edition*
Varney: *Disability, Human Rights and Contract Law*
Wan: *Film and Constitutional Controversy: Visualizing Hong Kong Identity in the Age of 'One Country, Two Systems'*
Ward: *A Critical Introduction to European Law, 3rd Edition*
Ward: *Law, Text, Terror*
Ward: *Shakespeare and Legal Imagination*
Watt: *The Making Sense of Politics, Media, and Law: Rhetorical Performance as Invention, Creation, Production*
Wells & Quick: *Lacey, Wells and Quick: Reconstructing Criminal Law: Text and Materials, 4th Edition*
Woodhead: *Caring for Cultural Heritage: An Integrated Approach to Legal and Ethical Initiatives in the United Kingdom*
Yeung and Ranchordás: *An Introduction to Law and Regulation: Text and Materials, 2nd edition*
Young: *Turpin and Tomkins' British Government and the Constitution: Text and Materials, 8th Edition*
Zander: *Cases and Materials on the English Legal System, 10th Edition*
Zander: *The Law-Making Process, 6th Edition*

International Journal of Law in Context: A Global Forum for Interdisciplinary Legal Studies

The *International Journal of Law in Context* is the companion journal to the Law in Context book series and provides a forum for interdisciplinary legal studies and offers intellectual space for ground-breaking critical research. It publishes contextual work about law and its relationship with other disciplines including but not limited to science, literature, humanities, philosophy, sociology, psychology, ethics, history and geography. More information about the journal and how to submit an article can be found at http://journals.cambridge.org/ijc

LAW AND TORTURE

Widening the Apertures from the Doctrinal to the Critical

Ergün Cakal

University of Copenhagen

CAMBRIDGE
UNIVERSITY PRESS

CAMBRIDGE
UNIVERSITY PRESS

Shaftesbury Road, Cambridge CB2 8EA, United Kingdom

One Liberty Plaza, 20th Floor, New York, NY 10006, USA

477 Williamstown Road, Port Melbourne, VIC 3207, Australia

314–321, 3rd Floor, Plot 3, Splendor Forum, Jasola District Centre, New Delhi – 110025, India

103 Penang Road, #05–06/07, Visioncrest Commercial, Singapore 238467

Cambridge University Press is part of Cambridge University Press & Assessment, a department of the University of Cambridge.

We share the University's mission to contribute to society through the pursuit of education, learning and research at the highest international levels of excellence.

www.cambridge.org
Information on this title: www.cambridge.org/9781009719452

DOI: 10.1017/9781009719483

When citing this work, please include a reference to the DOI 10.1017/9781009719483

First published 2026

Vassily Kandinsky, 1913 – *Color Study, Squares with Concentric Circles* / The Picture Art Collection / Alamy

A catalogue record for this publication is available from the British Library

Library of Congress Cataloging-in-Publication Data
Names: Cakal, Ergün author
Title: Law and torture : widening the apertures from the doctrinal to the critical / Ergün Cakal, University of Copenhagen.
Description: Cambridge, United Kingdom ; New York, NY : Cambridge University Press, 2026. | Series: Law in context | Includes bibliographical references and index.
Identifiers: LCCN 2025030963 (print) | LCCN 2025030964 (ebook) | ISBN 9781009719452 hardback | ISBN 9781009719483 ebook
Subjects: LCSH: Torture (International law) | Torture – Law and legislation | Torture victims – Legal status, laws, etc.
Classification: LCC KZ7170 .C35 2026 (print) | LCC KZ7170 (ebook) | DDC 179.7/5–dc23/eng/20250718
LC record available at https://lccn.loc.gov/2025030963
LC ebook record available at https://lccn.loc.gov/2025030964

ISBN 978-1-009-71945-2 Hardback

To Ayşe, Aynur, Charlie, Josie and Sonia

Contents

Figures

Preface

Writing this book emerged out of an indoctrination and its disillusioning fallout. It was a long time in gestation. Seed to fruit, it took eight years. Seeds were sown as a legal advisor at the Danish Institute Against Torture (DIGNITY), where I learned anti-torture doctrine as well as its practice and critique. Experiences as a practitioner led me to pose (rather risky) questions around law's utility and rigidity, which were not dignified in the established 'law and torture' canon. Responses, where offered, were to hold steadfast to faith and to ignore blind spots, biases, habitus and failings. These were neither sensitive to my needs nor satisfactory, to say the least. The idea for the book, as with my fledgling research, was born out of needing to make sense of these questions and failings. Following an age-old recipe, this was an exercise in turning personal troubles into public issues. Some of the ideas presented here would be familiar to those who have meandered through my less doctrinal work. This book represents an attempt to piece together the core ideas in that work, strewn over several articles. It represents them, I hope, in all their connections, with added consideration and exemplification, more coherently and panoramically.

I made clear to whoever listened to my (then) growing profound loss of faith in the law's potency to deliver on its promises – of due recognition and redress towards eradication. There were many at DIGNITY, Lund and Copenhagen universities, within the bounds of my home, hood and beyond, who helped make sense of what was a professional (and personal) crisis – who helped me wield and channel my angst towards the pages before you (and before these). Others' lack of reflexivity and receptivity equally helped fuel my drive. I am glad to have survived and learned to live with the 'compromised circumstances' (I borrow this doublet from dearest Andrew Jefferson, who remains an inspiration). I feel both stronger and frailer for it. The pages to follow might reveal to the reader that my feelings of loss and alienation persist. In their stead, however, a newfound hope in critical thought, the humanities and interdisciplinarity has emerged.

My rupture followed being introduced to and influenced by several strands of scholarship: socio-legal scholarship on state violence, interdisciplinary scholarship on pain, anthropology of violence, feminist phenomenological scholarship on violence and state crime scholarship. These bred a healthy sense of scepticism to think through and against the received doctrinal 'wisdom'. I remember distinct moments when colleagues swivelled on their office chairs to pick out a particular book from their shelves that they thought could offer me solace. Although Tomas Max Martin, Andrew M. Jefferson, Vicky Canning or Toby Kelly might not remember these moments, their imprint is visible on the pages to follow. I thank them for their encouragement and solidarity. I also extend my thanks to the following people: Steffen Jensen, Henrik Rønsbo, Elna Søndergaard, Therese Rytter, Marie Brasholt, Giorgio Caracciolo, Natasa Mavronicola, Annika Lindberg, Darius Rejali, Carmi Lecker, Pau Pérez-Sales, Lutz Oette, Nimisha Patel, Michelle Farrell, Joseph Bernasol, Frederik Rom Taxhjelm, Ylva Lennartsson Hartmann, Jenny Orlando, Silvia Steininger, Ellen Aagaard Marquard and Ezgi Yildiz. There were, then, the countless colleagues working under the threat of torture itself, whom I have chosen not to name. I met you in Armenia, Bangladesh, Egypt, Jordan, Myanmar, Palestine, Sierra Leone, Tanzania, Turkey, Uganda and Ukraine. You generously added to my thinking, perhaps without realising. There were others who took the time to comment directly on an advanced draft of this book; in this regard, I am indebted to Mattia Pinto, Grant Shubin and Vicky Canning. I also thank my editors at Cambridge University Press, and the external reviewers, for their trust and wise guidance throughout this process. Much of this book was shaped during my doctoral research under Mikael Rask Madsen, whose 'macro-management' afforded me the autonomy to engage in side projects such as this book.

I have aimed to capture the ideas and airs of these people in this book. These and other colleagues, past and present, also extended me something of themselves, be it thoughts, walks, warmth, songs, dances, coffees and the occasional puff, to keep me going. This process was also one of finding 'my people' – and I am happy to have found a few. This is not to say that we are all like-minded. Despite the many hands that have helped in penning these pages, what has made it before you represents my own views and vulnerabilities. I am well aware that some of those named might not agree with all of my critiques and conclusions. This book, which I have written in my own time during my doctoral studies, does not represent the position of DIGNITY, to which I returned following an extended absence to pursue a doctorate. I cannot, at the same time, renounce the influence that impressive place has had on me personally and professionally. I have chosen not to please or appease (for the most part). I have not always listened to my colleagues, for better or worse, so they bear no responsibility for the words before you.

It took time, solitude and space to string these ideas together with any semblance of sense. This was all afforded to me by my dears at home. In this regard, I think of Josie, Charlie, Sonia, Tina and Per. Each shouldered and eased my burdens to allow me to stare into space and screen. Josie, I thank you above all for picking me up when I flailed and fell - intellectually, politically, emotionally. The academic space I inhabit, the fights I pick and my obsession with others' suffering have been alienating – no more so than when my mind turns to my mother Ayşe, a peasant from the mountains of the Black Sea turned migrant, oblivious to what I do for a wage. That this work will remain distant to her, written oceans away, means both more and less about the academic ascent it might mark. You are all more important than these ideas, though it might not always have been experienced so by you. So I feel blessed that you indulged my distractions. I am lucky to have and love you.

Usage

Readers should note that I use the terms 'torture's prohibition' and 'torturous suffering' to refer in short to the entire spectrum of state violence prohibited, namely, 'torture', 'inhuman' and 'degrading' treatment (cf. Victoria Canning's 'torturous violence', who focuses on torturous suffering not directly inflicted by the state). As not all legal frameworks refer to 'cruelty', I take it to be covered under the categories of inhuman and degrading treatment. I take the following couplets as effectively synonymous: 'pain' and 'suffering'; 'treatment' and 'punishment'; and 'mental' and 'psychological'. I use 'research' interchangeably with 'scholarship'. I use 'advocates' to refer to legally trained practitioners representing victim-survivors, except where I refer to 'state advocates' and 'adjudicators' to refer to any decision-maker, whether a judge, a committee or a tribunal member. I prefer the term 'victim-survivor', mindful of the different connotations both 'victim' and 'survivor' have in the anti-torture field. Citations accord with OSCOLA with some adjustments for readability, with years and paragraph numbers in caselaw appearing in square brackets and with page numbers indicated with a 'p.'.

Abbreviations

CAT	UN Committee against Torture
CIDT	cruel, inhuman and degrading treatment
CoE	Council of Europe
CPT	European Committee for the Prevention of Torture
CUP	Cambridge University Press
ECHR	*European Convention on Human Rights*
ECmHR	European Commission of Human Rights
ECtHR	European Court of Human Rights
GC	Grand Chamber
IACPPT	*Inter-American Convention to Prevent and Punish Torture*
IACtHR	Inter-American Court of Human Rights
ICJ	International Court of Justice
Istanbul Protocol (IP)	*Manual on the Effective Investigation and Documentation of Torture and Other Cruel, Inhuman or Degrading Treatment or Punishment*
OUP	Oxford University Press
para	paragraph
UN	United Nations

UNCAT	*UN Convention against Torture and Other Cruel, Inhuman or Degrading Treatment or Punishment*
UN HRC	UN Human Rights Committee
UN SRT	UN Special Rapporteur on Torture
USSC	United States Supreme Court

CHAPTER 1

Introduction

> One of the most important ways in which to pulverise revealing relationships is to isolate the event which was the point of departure from the rest of the activity which the event is a part of. In other words, it becomes important, so to speak, to cut the event out of the fabric in which it exists.
>
> Thomas Mathiesen, *Silently Silenced*[1]

THIS PASSAGE HAD NEITHER TORTURE nor law especially in mind when it was penned. Yet it speaks to much of what is to follow, to the failure to situate events in context, whether intentionally or not. In this introduction, I articulate the broader contextual contours of (and for) the anti-torture field. In setting the scene for subsequent chapters, I identify implications and complications which flow from the extent to which context is 'let in' to legal considerations. To be clear, I do not argue that context is wholly absent but that it is selectively present – serving particular ends. I point in directions that pack the potential to enrich 'law and torture' practice and research.

1.1 RECEIVED (AND REPEATED) STORIES

Law and medicine dominate contemporary understandings of torture.[2] Law (especially international human rights law) gives us the words to

[1] Thomas Mathiesen, *Silently Silenced: Essays on the Creation of Acquiescence in Modern Society* (Waterside Press 2004), examines how events are downplayed in public discourse through different but interdependent devices of being individualised, isolated, exceptionalised and normalised.

[2] This is an observation discussed in Andrew M Jefferson, 'Situated Perspectives on the Global Fight against Torture' in Sarah Armstrong, Jarrett Blaustein and Alistair

frame our notions and norms in the form of confident definitions and prohibitions on what is torture, inhuman and degrading and that it is impermissible. The law remains revered as the 'privileged instrument for moral improvement'[3] in interventions and responses to all that we find excessive in the use of state violence. The definition of torture under international law, and its conventional interpretation, has become viewed 'as sacrosanct, often without reference to how narrow it is and instead presented as epistemological fact'.[4] The legal definition has even won out over attempts by doctors to define the reference point for the phenomenon.[5]

Medicine (and increasingly psychology) offers tools to translate, corroborate and 'certify' allegations of torturous suffering in the eyes of the law, that the victim in question, indeed, suffered what they allege to have suffered. This is not altogether unexpected, as medical science is 'positioned as the embodiment of virtue, the triumph of science over superstition where accuracy, certainty and neutrality have replaced expediency and guesswork in healing physical and psychological pain'.[6] This is all we are expected to know. By virtue of their tasks in this effort towards eradication, law and medicine are imbued with a beneficence, that they are well tested and on the side of the well intentioned. We are encouraged to ascribe to their agendas and to trust in their respective and interlocking authorities. This leads us to assume that the broader questions have been resolved, that we have arrived at a consensus on the concept and its

Henry (eds), *Reflexivity and Criminal Justice: Intersections of Policy, Practice and Research* (Palgrave Macmillan 2017), as dominating the discourse but operating at a distance from the realities on the ground. See also Metin Başoğlu (ed), *The Definition of Torture in International Law: An Interdisciplinary Approach* (Oxford University Press 2017), 'Introduction', xxiv.

[3] Samuel Moyn, *The Last Utopia: Human Rights in History* (2010) 211, as quoted in Tobias Kelly, *This Side of Silence: Human Rights, Torture, and the Recognition of Cruelty* (University of Pennsylvania Press 2012) 11.

[4] Victoria Canning, *Torture and Torturous Violence: Transcending Definitions of Torture* (Bristol University Press 2023) 14.

[5] In its 1975 *Declaration of Tokyo*, the World Medical Association defined torture 'as the deliberate, systematic or wanton infliction of physical or mental suffering by one or more persons acting alone or on the orders of any authority, to force another person to yield information, to make a confession, or for any other reason'.

[6] Joe Sim, *Medical Power in Prisons: The Prison Medical Service in England 1774–1989* (Open University Press 1990) ix–x.

corroboration, free of values (except that torture is morally unacceptable). Our means and modes of determining torture (as inhuman and degrading) are thus 'cut out' and abstracted from their social and political contexts, which are largely left out of our view and purview.[7]

With an interest in advancing the identification and eradication of torture through medico-legal means, advocates, academics and adjudicators alike (to have come before me) have devoted and exerted their precious energies and resources to primarily developing legal doctrine. These actors have been given 'the right to define' the categories with which we work.[8] Their authority has been used to promote law as inherently good, devoid of doing wrong when strictly followed – encouraging the celebration of law's by which I primarily mean international human rights law's supposed beneficence in the face of its failings.[9] Many of the arguments directed at the international stand to be amplified against national criminal law, through which the prohibition of torture finds its direct force.[10]

From their liberal standpoint, that is, torture's prohibition has come to represent 'a legal archetype – a provision which is emblematic of our larger commitment to nonbrutality in the legal system [and] our determination to sever the link between law and brutality, between law and terror, and between law and the enterprise of trying to break person's will'.[11] Law, in this schema, remains a benevolent, malleable

[7] I primarily pitch my arguments against the law and peripherally against medicine, but I view the anti-torture field as much wider. A multitude of relevant individual actors populate the field: victim-survivors, police, prison officers, prosecutors, advocates, academics, adjudicators, activists, journalists, therapists, diplomats, detention monitors, ombudspersons, rapporteurs and documentation specialists. These actors normally collaborate, working in institutions as universities, civil society organisations and coalitions, international non-governmental organisations, courts and committees, forensic institutions, national, regional and international preventive mechanisms, ministries (of interior, health and foreign affairs), national human rights institutions and rehabilitation clinics.

[8] David Garland and Peter Young (eds), *The Power to Punish: Contemporary Penality and Social Analysis* (Heinemann 1983) 4.

[9] Lutz Oette, *The Transformation of the Prohibition of Torture in International Law* (Oxford University Press 2024) 141, has also recognised that 'lawyers and others working in the anti-torture movement risk being professionally prone to celebrating the role of law and international standards'.

[10] I am indebted to Mattia Pinto for his invaluable scholarship on this point.

[11] Jeremy Waldron, 'Torture and Positive Law: Jurisprudence for the White House' (2005) 105 *Columbia Law Review* 1681.

and perfectible institution. There is an entrenched assumption in law, as in international law, that it *naturally, necessarily* and *progressively* opposes violence. It is this assumption, based on the 'idea that juridification is automatically associated with progress',[12] that sees precious energies directed towards regulation and litigation. That law represents the negation of violence (with torture only occurring upon the suspension of proper legal precautions) is the predominant view amongst legal practitioners (a position somewhat oblivious to the reality that law aids in both the infliction and inhibition of violence). Why else would we see a perennial proliferation of legal standards, if not because of a fervent belief in law's beneficence?

Such belief in principles and processes is central to the reproduction of any field. In anti-torture work, as more broadly in human rights work, practitioners find it incumbent to espouse the law's more aspirational and remedial qualities in providing for prevention and redress. Accepting this inherited origin story (that which renders law a beneficent bulwark against violence) gives rise to profound implications in how practitioners work in the anti-torture field: ceaselessly seeking to inform norm-setting processes with empirical data; compiling expert evidence on individual victims to submit before courts for full recognition of harms and capacitating colleagues elsewhere to do the same.[13] If only more evidence is brought before the court, if only the judge is made to understand in good faith and be faithful to the letter of the law as strictly as possible, as dictated by rules of interpretation, and so on. This has seen a great energy spent on sharpening and supplementing evidentiary technologies of documentation like the *Istanbul Protocol*.[14] Should a legal regime facilitate torture and impunity, more self-assured legal corrections are prescribed and deployed in terms of definitional tweaks or

[12] Tilmann Altwicker and Oliver Diggelmann, 'How Is Progress Constructed in International Legal Scholarship?' (2014) 25 (2) *European Journal of International Law* 439.

[13] UN Special Rapporteur on Torture (SRT), Report (2020) A/HRC/43/49 [38]: emphasised the 'practical importance of continuing to clarify the fault lines between lawful non-coercive investigative techniques and prohibited coercive interrogation'.

[14] UN Office of the High Commissioner for Human Rights, *Manual on the Effective Investigation and Documentation of Torture and Other Cruel, Inhuman or Degrading Treatment or Punishment* ('Istanbul Protocol') (2022).

otherwise foreclosing the possibility of defences or derogations, to name but a few stock responses. Upon this schema, the dominant duopoly is imbued with the power to autonomously mark an act with a stigma in the face of state interests. The culmination of these efforts is relied on to proceed to eradication – however incrementally. It is this dominant paradigm, which has evaded meaningful scrutiny, to which I speak in this book.

Questions, nevertheless, abound for the curious: How does one make sense of the prevalence of torture despite its near-universal prohibition and condemnation? How are we to see and make sense of law's failings? Thus left out of this medico-legal duopoly is the question of how law and medicine have come to know what they claim to know. Also left out is an account for the exclusions and failings produced through this nexus. The exceptions, rare though powerful, are presented towards reflecting on received stories circulating in the field. In his recent book, for example, prominent practitioner-academic Malcolm Evans observed that UN 'treaty bodies often end up making utterances that are either devoid of context, content or both … some are pitched at so high a level of generality that it is almost impossible to know what they really mean or what their recipients are really meant to do to achieve them'.[15] Elite reflections do not get more damning.

I admit to painting with broad strokes so far. I will come to argue that the medico-legal duopoly, with its exceptions, has not been a harmonious one. There remains a dialectic tension in the anti-torture field,[16] particularly between law and medicine, which continue to struggle for (or contest) the legal construction (interpretation or qualification) of torture. Legal professionals remain key in shaping the selection, complexion and disposition of cases. The judgments and decisions handed down are not always, with the exception of dissents, explicit or reflective about the consternations amongst legal actors. Legal professionals amongst themselves contest narrow and expansive interpretations and resist the demands of non-legal expertise. Health professionals bemoan and begrudge the reductivity espoused by legal professionals.

[15] Malcolm Evans, *Tackling Torture: Prevention in Practice* (Bristol University Press 2023) 8.

[16] In short, the conception of the field foregrounds notions of contestation over interpretive domination and, in turn, the concealment of that contestation through linguistic and symbolic strategies.

Fuelled by the failings of the law to address its blind spots and deliver on its key promises, my own drive led me in the opposite direction – not of *correction* but of *critique*, not to see its further doctrinal development but to urge its disavowal and distrust – towards doing things differently. In understanding how violence is named (and my co-optation in that practice of naming), commitment to critique urged me to 'first settle the question of which framework is naming violence, through what erasures, and for what purpose'.[17] Frames, I too had failed to see, did not neutrally 'exhibit reality, but actively participate[d] in a strategy of containment, selectively producing and enforcing what will count as reality … always keeping something out'.[18] In other words, by being asked to argue and assess state-sanctioned violence by the state's own abstractions,[19] my received frames were left unquestioned unreflectingly. Better understanding my operative frames has unavoidably led me to the humanities and social sciences. In addition to drawing on a wide array of ideas from scholars from those traditions, I have relied heavily on my own experiences and observations as a practitioner-academic. However fraught it might have been to do so, this book has been written partly out of disillusionment, disappointment and despair, and to extend hope to those there now.

Getting a better grip on the everyday objects of 'law and torture', in its conceptual and practical modes, has required a wider (and richer) discourse – with the aid of critical scholarship, which already exists (and in some cases has existed for decades). Prison studies, sociology and anthropology of state-sanctioned violence, law and emotion, state crime scholarship, phenomenological and feminist approaches to violence, histories and medical anthropologies of pain all stand ready to be connected. With a view to this broader scholarship and experience, this book anticipates an additional litany of questions: What explains the conceptual indeterminacies over torture's definition – rendering its evolving interpretation as less than linear? What explains the resistance of state authorities and human rights courts alike to ascribe full value

[17] Judith Butler, *Frames of War* (Verso 2009) 26.

[18] Ibid xiii.

[19] International human rights law is state-centric in its substance and practice.

to scientific evidence of torture's harms? Why are some forms of state violence accepted as inherent and lawful and others not? How equipped are we really to gauge certain suffering, given its supposed unknowability as supposed by theory? For those curious or critically oriented, these are not idle or moot questions.

Responding to these frustrations, the aims of this book will be threefold: (i) to initially identify the doctrinal 'brackets' (limits) of dominant legal scholarship on torture, inhuman and degrading treatment; (ii) to then identify the extra-legal dynamics that are often placed outside these brackets and, therefore, anti-torture practice and research; and (iii) to advance a reflexive and context-sensitive means of practising and researching 'law and torture'. In doing so, this book does not aim to entirely de-centre the law but rather de-centre the privileged judge-centric,[20] liberal-legal and state-deferential positions, which naturalise torture as whatever it is *legally* qualified to be – to politicise the depoliticised.[21] Neither is the aim to de-centre the negative moral value of torture but rather to emphasise its continuity with other harmful state practices born out of police and prisons and beyond (currently shielded but which should be equally and radically scrutinised in anti-torture discourse).

In all, I argue that conventional (medico-legal) constructions of torture, inhuman and degrading treatment, in practice as in research, have evaded serious interdisciplinary engagement and socio-legal examination due to disciplinary bracketing. This is not to say that the figure of the societal is dismissed outright by doctrine: torture is oft-described as 'shocking the conscience' or as causing 'moral outrage' as informed by present social attitudes and structures. Much is left unreflected in the wake of such phrases and adages. What we are left unclear about is whose conscience (is it collective?) and how is that to be constituted and quantified? What can be said with any degree of precision here – theoretically or empirically? Does the legal imagination remain a black box of entangled

[20] For a broader critique on judge-centricity, see Fuad Zarbiyev, 'On the Judge Centredness of the International Legal Self' (2021) 32 (4) *European Journal of International Law* 1139.

[21] In the tradition of Judith Shklar, *Legalism: Law, Morals, and Political Trials* (Harvard University Press 1986).

reasoning and dynamics impervious to clarity and predictability? The 'law and torture' research raising and addressing such questions is fringe and too few. In any case, these are unavoidable entry points for the critically and socio-legally minded.

Through holding 'context as key', I aim to identify vanishing points in what I call 'law and torture' practice and research. I am driven to pushing the field, which stands as my central professional care and concern, from doctrinal to critical considerations. As in previous work, I want to introduce readers to what lies beyond the comforting 'brackets' towards overlooked entry points and resources. Whilst critical scholars have cleared the ground to 'widen the apertures' in important ways,[22] I aim to revisit and revamp the connections made in that work for the newly arrived, resource-poor, *legally* oriented practitioner or researcher. As such, this book offers solace and solidarity to the curious and critically oriented, towards reflexivity and rupture.

1.2 QUANTIFYING LAW'S CONTEXT

> To begin to answer these questions entails putting pain into cultural context, where the experience of the person in pain relates to socially instituted and culturally embedded systems of inclusion and exclusion, along lines of gender, age, class, race and species. ... Pain is only pain where it accords with tacit rules for the acceptable expression or the experience of pain. And to this end, the question of whose pain is authentic is a question of power.[23]

To be sure, torture is more than pain (or, interchangeably, suffering[24]). Pain, however, is a good starting point to explore 'extra-legal'[25] dynamics in this terrain. Those who have previously tended to the nexus of 'law and torture' with adequate curiosity or scepticism will have noted that questions already invoked have been treated with minimal reflection.

22 The subtitle ('widening the apertures') originates from a recurring phrase in Danielle Celermajer, *The Prevention of Torture: An Ecological Approach* (Cambridge University Press 2018), which articulated to me a rigorous and relevant logic at a time of need.

23 Rob Boddice, *Pain and Emotion in Modern History* (Palgrave 2014) 5, 14.

24 Broadly, alternatively: 'harm', 'injury' or 'violence'.

25 The dichotomy between legal and extra-legal is fraught but used as a pedagogical shortcut.

An early triplet already at reading the universal definition of torture might be as follows:[26] What is severe pain? How should we understand its gradations? How much of it ought to legitimately figure in state practices? In answering these as other foundational concerns, context becomes key. Context[27] helps define and, as we'll come to reflect, to distort and deny our experiences and understandings of pain, torturous or otherwise, with our experience also coming to define context. Textual, conceptual and experiential registers (our words, thoughts and feelings), for instance, dictate the expressibility and communicability of pain. This is a dialectical interplay – implicating and intertwining individual, institutional and sociopolitical (micro, meso and macro) processes pertaining to the production of knowledge. I will explain what I mean.

As one scholar on pain has written, 'there is no suffering that does not entail a social appraisal and, by extension, a form of expression linked to cultural guidelines and expectations'.[28] Cultural context is deemed key to ascribing meaning to any experience, yet alone one that entails suffering. Whether we call any form of violence 'torture', 'inhuman' or 'degrading' treatment readily indicates an interplay between the law and its sociocultural, scientific and political aspects. This has led another scholar to observe these categories to 'essentially reflect subjective judgements that are inevitably determined to a significant extent by culturally shaped perceptions of what constitutes severe mental pain or suffering'.[29] Context, cultural as others, remains inescapable. It informs what we come to understand to be legitimate pain and punishment – and, by extension, what lies beyond in what is considered 'torturous'. The law here is entrusted as the proxy for capturing and consolidating these sociocultural and political positions.

How law's actors (namely, its advocates, academics and adjudicators) conceive of torture as informed by those contexts is hazy in reality. Legal actors busy themselves making sense of this context – which most often

[26] UN *Convention against Torture* (1984), article 1.

[27] Lois Presser, *Unsaid: Analyzing Harmful Silences* (University of California Press 2023) 145, takes context to mean the 'circumstances surrounding and impinging on events, actions, and experiences'.

[28] Javier Moscoso, *Pain: A Cultural History* (Palgrave 2012) 56.

[29] Başoğlu (2017) 11.

is left inadequately examined on the face of legal decisions. These actors have primarily drawn on legal standards and medico-legal expertise to make sense of the allegations before them – in assessing the gravity and veracity of suffering as well as to situate that in its extra-legal context. Precedents are dusted off and repeated, standards are identified and similar cases are compared and differentiated. These actors, therefore, have turned the task into something technical – concerned with blinkered assessments of elements such as severe pain, purpose, intent, necessity and officiality. Medico-legal evidence, that which is accepted as 'objective', is an accepted albeit subsidiary aid. This aid, as I will argue, has not convincingly handled this context. At its most impoverished, the law 'pretends to have no history and no context', particularly of its original and operational relationship to violence.[30] Legal instruments, their interpretations, as animated by expert evidence, albeit abundant, have brought us only so far.

Although not always the case nationally[31] or internationally,[32] adjudicators have come to formulaically claim to have examined the relevant context or the 'totality of the circumstances',[33] but this is never as exhaustive as presented. It is selective, and that selection, although it is given the impression of 'totality', magnifies the weight attributed to a normally predetermined finding.[34] There are, in fact, four significant assumptions directing and delimiting the contextual intake of a conventional legal approach: '1) that torture is an issue of detention and interrogation; 2) that political or security detainees are archetypal victims

[30] Bryan S. Turner, *The Body and Society* (3rd ed, SAGE 2008) 2–3.

[31] See *Hutto v. Finney* (1978) 437 U.S. 678, where the USSC first advanced assessing Eighth Amendment cases in the 'totality of conditions'.

[32] Antonio Cassese, 'Can the Notion of Inhuman and Degrading Treatment Be Applied to Socio-Economic Conditions?' (1991) 2 *European Journal of International Law* 143.

[33] References to 'the totality of the acts of aggression and the conditions in which the State deliberately put the inmates' as per *Cantoral-Benavides* [96] and *Castillo-Petruzzi* [197]; 'on the totality of evidence and material', 'having regard to the entire circumstances of the case' per *Ireland v. UK* [1978] ECtHR 5856/72 [167].

[34] A version of this is what Mariana Valverde, 'Theoretical and Methodological Issues in the Study of Legal Knowledge Practices' in Austin Sarat et al (eds), *How Law Knows* (Stanford 2007) 85–86, calls 'exemplary excerpting', the selective appropriation of broader material elsewhere and presented as being representative, with 'a bit that is cut and pasted automatically becomes exemplary'.

of torture; 3) that legal reform is one of the best ways to fight torture; and 4) that human rights monitoring helps to stamp out violence'.[35] In other words, legal actors, whether knowingly or not, privilege and operate on certain assumptions, in terms of where torture is taken to *prevail* (understood to take place, e.g., police and prison cells, during certain situations such as arrest, interrogation and custody), or where it is *assailed* (understood to be redressed, e.g., parliaments, tribunals and courts). These assumptions, in turn, foreground and frame those who are more vulnerable to being tortured, for whom victimhood is relatively readily attainable: men in the control of the state.[36] From this vantage point, the law is evoked and, in turn, advocates and adjudicators are endowed with central functions in torture's eradication: regulation, investigation, litigation and adjudication. Much of this constellation rings true at first glance: naturally, we tend to imagine the suspect being given the third degree in an interrogation room and a human rights judge as surveying the scene with empathetic objectivity. The danger here, however, is that this essentialises and engenders an unthinking reflex about what is and is not torture, who is or who is not tortured.

This is brought into stark relief where the focus is shifted to a protest, the psychiatric institution or the school. Does violence against protestors, patients or pupils evoke the anti-torture paradigm, or are these to be approached from other prisms? Can a state inflict torturous suffering without proximity to the individual, whilst they remain in their home or on the street? How are we to think about the quasi-formal state, the publicly funded corporation entrusted to deliver pain on behalf of the state? Why can poor living conditions, as caused by state policies, not be thought of as torturous? These questions engage our imaginaries of torture, of where it is thought to occur and who is taken to inflict or inhibit it or be subjected to it. These imaginaries can be descriptive (describing how things are) but also prescriptive (representing how things *should* be to count as torture). The reflexive impulse here would be to examine the

[35] Tobias Kelly, 'The Struggle against Torture: Challenges, Assumptions and New Directions' (2019) 11 *Journal of Human Rights Practice* 324, 324.

[36] Alice Edwards, 'The "Feminizing" of Torture under International Human Rights Law' (2006) 19 *Leiden Journal of International Law* 349.

reasons for which the dominant imaginary is constituted as it is or, more pointedly, to examine whether the doctrinal scholarship seeks to serve itself in self-affirming its preponderances. Does this unduly exclude other acts or actors that could reasonably be included? Whether duly or not, the dominant paradigm has 'resulted in limitations in terms of the interventions that are used, the forms of violence that human rights practitioners respond to, and the types of survivors they seek to protect'.[37]

Doctrine to date, to broaden this critique, has been reticent to view torture in its structures (broader conditions, systems or ecologies). Structural conditions are normally backgrounded, 'rather than as an independent force or factor that exacerbates the harm, or as a form of torturous treatment itself'.[38] This is not to say that it never happens. The exception of contextualisation in jurisprudence often serves to underscore the norm. In *Bouyid v. Belgium*, where a police officer's slap on a child's face amounted to degrading treatment, the European Court of Human Rights drew attention to the social significance of the face.[39] There are, to be fair, additional exceptions where doctrinal approaches make important connections between different official actors.[40] The UN Committee against Torture has, for instance, used the notion of 'systematic torture' as per its special inquiry powers (Article 20 of the *UN Convention against Torture and Other Cruel, Inhuman or Degrading Treatment or Punishment*).[41] Article 20 enquiries thus assess systems in their entirety, not individual cases as per Article 1. Numbering only ten to date, these are expansive systematic examinations of a given country.

[37] Kelly (2019) 324.

[38] Başoğlu (2017) 140.

[39] *Bouyid v. Belgium* [2015] ECtHR [GC] 23380/09 [104]: 'A slap to the face affects the part of the person's body which expresses his individuality, manifests his social identity and constitutes the centre of his senses – sight, speech and hearing – which are used for communication with others'.

[40] CAT, Report, A/48/44/Add.1 (1993) [39]. Article 15 of the UNCAT requires that 'any statement which is established to have been made as a result of torture shall not be invoked as evidence in any proceeding'.

[41] Defined by the CAT as being 'of a systematic character without resulting from the direct intention of a Government. It may be the consequence of factors which the Government has difficulty in controlling, and its existence may indicate a discrepancy between policy as determined by the central Government and its implementation by the local administration'.

What is remarkable is that intent is not a strict requirement for a finding of systematic torture. When Brazil was found to have practiced systematic torture, it challenged the finding specifically on this point.[42] Such exceptions, to me at least, prove the general rule.

Doctrinal legal practice and research, beyond these and related exceptions, are yet to adequately *imagine* and *evidence* contextual dynamics (sociocultural, scientific and political) so central to how torture is legally interpreted. At best, these dynamics remain intuitive and implicit. At the most rigid end of the spectrum, the doctrinally committed reject the critical influence of context – holding rather that a judge merely neutrally interprets and applies the law. Whilst doctrinal legal practitioners and researchers might continue to hold that the torturous is simply what a judge says it is, this is an impoverished view without credence to crucial context. Their position effectively denies crucial pieces of the interpretive puzzle. These interpretive practices, despite extensive caselaw, remain complex.

State-sanctioned violence has long been subject to configuration and contestation – in how it is recognised (understood as un/acceptable), regulated (legally limited in part or entirely), redressed (prevented or prosecuted) and substantiated (based on evidence, experience or otherwise). As admitted, context is itself complex and complicated – viewed by law as an element to be tamed and managed. A holistic approach, meanwhile, to understanding the implicated interpretive practices is an imbricated one, nestled and contingent upon one another; the judicial configuration is interrelated to sociocultural, scientific and political contestations around punishment, which take place on the broader field of contestations around pain (see Figure 1.1). Individual advocates and adjudicators operate within such complex collective imaginaries – although this remains background. This premise will read as routine for the social-scientifically inclined, given how widely this is accepted by scholarship.[43]

42 Report on Brazil Produced by the Committee under Article 20 of the Convention and Reply from the Government of Brazil (2009) CAT/C/39/2, 248. Brazil cited *Ireland v. UK* in its defence, arguing that torture required 'special stigma', aggravation and deliberation.

43 See Arthur Kleinman and Joan Kleinman, 'The Appeal of Experience; The Dismay of Images: Cultural Appropriations of Suffering in Our Times' (1996) 125 *Daedalus* 1; Mary-Jo DelVecchio Good (ed), *Pain as Human Experience: An Anthropological Perspective* (University of California Press 1994).

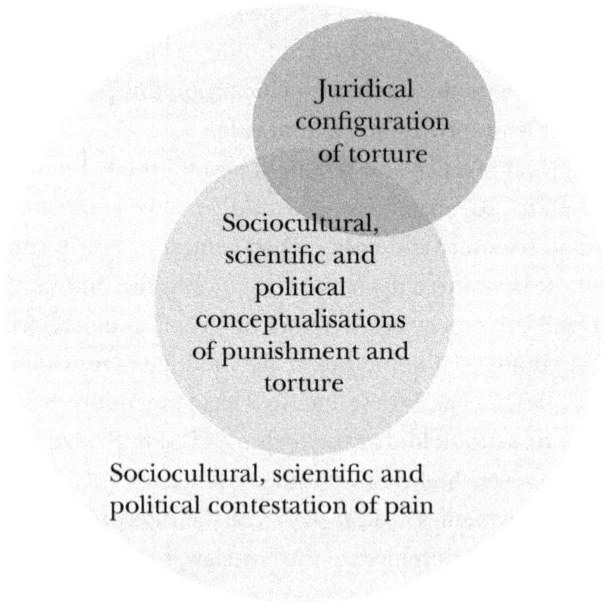

Figure 1.1 Contextual imbrication.

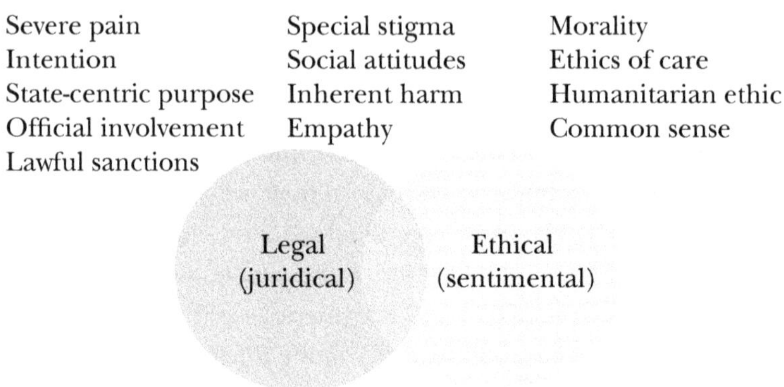

Figure 1.2 Forms.

As an alternative entry point, this exercise can also be viewed as invoking an *ethical* form (see Figure 1.2), as it is, often implicitly, informed by a great range of perennial politically and ethically charged questions, such as how we define and respond to another's suffering and how the nature of state involvement (purpose and intent) aggravates the gravity of

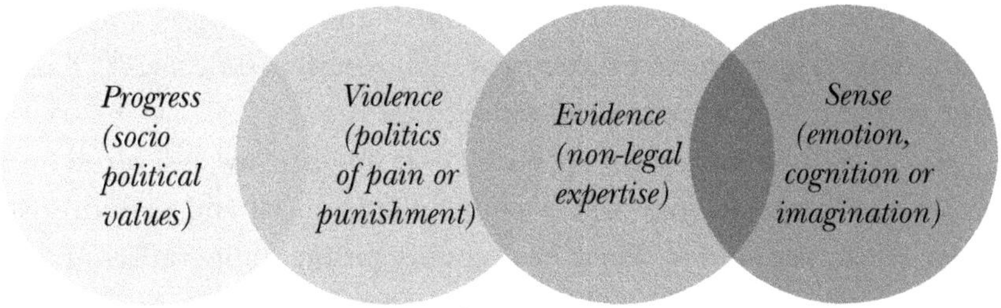

Figure 1.3 Discursive conditionalities, imaginaries and scripts for recognition.

that suffering. The jurisprudence centres on its own definitional elements as listed but has, as will be discussed, often opened itself up to social and ethical concepts such as 'present-day conditions', 'stigma', 'empathy' and 'common sense', to name but a few. These emerge at various points and are codified into legal formulas but are left to operate intuitively and uncritically.

This book canvasses the interplays between legal and extra-legal elements through a critical-theoretical and socio-legal lens. In so doing, it focuses on how pain, punishment and torture are gauged through four thematic entry points – progress, violence, evidence and sense (see Figure 1.3). These are advanced as central to how suffering is both concealed and configured, backgrounded and foregrounded. Each limb represents a part of the puzzle in understanding law's in/ability to engage with its social and scientific context in fully dealing with torturous suffering.

Critical-theoretical approaches, on violence as adjacent phenomena, have concerned themselves with clarifying 'the values and interests that existing ideologies and institutions tend to hide',[44] tending to silences in texts and examining the considerations the law refuses to take into account – namely, the harms that the law quietly renders necessary to *raison d'etat.*[45] Such approaches have brought 'to the surface features that are ignored or unsatisfactorily explained by the prevailing theories' and have opened up 'constructive lines of enquiry

[44] Stephen Bronner, *Critical Theory: A Very Short Introduction* (Oxford University Press 2011) 4–5.

[45] Scott Veitch, *Law and Irresponsibility: On the Legitimation of Human Suffering* (Routledge 2007) 77, 83.

and conceptualisation which may contribute to a more satisfactory understanding of those elements of our experience of law'.[46] This is the orientation I adopt in this book.

I also adopt a socio-legal approach as it tends to law as a social institution, law in its practice and as embedded in social and political contexts (i.e., institutions, doctrines, considerations, imperatives, values and attitudes), in which categories of torture, inhuman and degrading treatment are informed, (re)produced, contested and naturalised. This approach, put differently, anticipates that 'law in practice, whether within the courtroom or far from courts and judges in society, is almost always a jumble of legal and extra-legal discursive elements'.[47] I do so because this approach is developed specifically towards questioning predetermined and positivistic bounds of the law and on the basis of the capacious allowance of empirical and critical lenses – towards an explication and complication of the objects of inquiry.

Unlike doctrinal approaches, a socio-legal approach accepts legal interpretation as contingent on many factors beyond the internal belief systems of law. It takes legal norms as 'shaped within a particular legal system and with reference to an evidentiary record, testimony, legal training and culture, and courtroom procedure [and needing to be] understood with reference to a particular institutional, normative, and sociological context'.[48] The interface between individuals and their institutions, as captured in the problem of agency-structure, is also relevant here in accepting law in its context and accepting legal actors as individuated and acculturated, that behaviour comes to be shaped institutionally and societally.[49] This tension pervades the problems picked on in this book.

[46] Alan Hunt, 'The Critique of Law: What Is "Critical" about Critical Legal Theory?' (1987) 14 (1) *Journal of Law and Society* 5–19.

[47] Michael McCann, David M. Engel and Anne Bloom, 'Introduction' in Anne Bloom, David M. Engel and Michael McCann (eds), *Injury and Injustice: The Cultural Politics of Harm and Redress* (Cambridge University Press 2018) 11.

[48] Emily Kidd White, 'Till Human Voices Wake Us' (2014) 3 *Journal of Law, Religion and State* 201, 208.

[49] Andrea Bianchi and Moshe Hirsch, 'International Law's Invisible Frames: Introductory Insights' in Andrea Bianchi and Moshe Hirsch (eds), *International Law's Invisible Frames: Social Cognition and Knowledge Production in International Legal Processes* (Oxford University Press 2021).

Coming closer to the book's central object of study, that is, torturous suffering, the socio-legally oriented scholarship expectedly pays attention to how 'learned cultural scripts' operate as 'to determine who is and is not a disciplined, law-abiding, reasonable, "responsibilized", and thus justice-deserving person or collective [presenting] another way that conventional morality and social norms often trump or complicate official legal norms in narrative development about injuries'.[50] It foregrounds sociocultural, scientific and political processes and considerations in the construction of suffering, rendering it imperative to look beyond 'pure' legal considerations over 'who gets what, when, how'.[51] This is the overarching puzzle in all that follows.

1.3 ENTRY POINTS: STRUCTURE OF THE BOOK

Despite the weight of the book's title, I do not aim or claim to exhaust the nexus of law and torture. It is, therefore, important at this stage to admit to what this book is not about. I do not write squarely on torture's histories, techniques, impacts, rehabilitation, redress or ethics. To the extent that they appear, I have written instead on how these dimensions have been viewed through the prism of law. While they occasionally appear, I also do not explore torturous suffering inherent in enforced disappearances, the death penalty and arbitrary detention in much depth. These practices, though very much aligned and adjacent to the 'law and torture' practice and research, have spawned distinct practices and research beyond the scope of this book. It is from an international human rights law perspective that I frame my approach, although international humanitarian and criminal law as well as constitutional law also appears. Still, I do not map out prominent anti-torture courts, committees, bodies and mandates and their modes of operation. I have also avoided drawing too heavily on the scholarship examining the US experience post-9/11,[52] as that would have proven redundant. I have

50 McCann et al (2018) 12.

51 Ibid 21.

52 See Lisa Hajjar, *The War in Court: Inside the Long Fight against Torture* (University of California Press 2022) and John T. Parry, *Understanding Torture: Law, Violence, and Political Identity* (University of Michigan Press 2010) for strong scholarship on this front.

also drawn selectively, not systematically, from national experiences elsewhere. I do not squarely critique the related 'unintended' consequences of the criminal law orientation of anti-torture practice, which also problematise the law's relationship to violence. I have left others more skilful to do so.[53] To be sure, much critique as normally directed at human rights practice also applies to anti-torture practice.[54] The reader will find much else absent in what follows, for these and related reasons.

1.3.1 CHAPTER 2: DOCTRINE AND ITS (DIS)CONTENTS. Before I venture to quickly expand on these imbricative entry points, it would serve the discussion to take a step or two back, particularly for the relatively uninitiated reader of anti-torture doctrine. In Chapter 2 ('Doctrine and Its (dis)contents'), therefore, I map the contours of this doctrine, indicating the sources of the questions on which the critique builds. The chapter purposefully identifies doctrinal understandings (inclusions, exclusions, preponderances and assumptions), as focussed on definitions, distinctions, interpretation, contexts and conditions. In so doing, it maps the grounds for my broader claims as well as identifying entry points for their critique in subsequent chapters. I do not aim to rehash the broader discursive debates here. Others, whom I will reference, have done so more astutely.

1.3.2 CHAPTER 3: PROGRESSIVE IMPULSES. The substantive discussion begun in Chapter 2, particularly on interpretation, is continued in Chapter 3 through the prism of progress ('Progressive Impulses'). Collective understandings of state violence, including torture,

[53] Laurens Lavrysen and Natasa Mavronicola (eds), *Coercive Human Rights: Positive Duties to Mobilise the Criminal Law under the ECHR* (Oxford University Press 2020); Karen Engle et al (eds), *Anti-Impunity and the Human Rights Agenda* (Cambridge University Press 2016); Mattia Pinto, 'Historical Trends of Human Rights Gone Criminal' (2020) 42 (4) *Human Rights Quarterly* 729–761; Natasa Mavronicola, 'The Case against Human Rights Penality' (2024) 44 (3) *Oxford Journal of Legal Studies* 535–562.

[54] That it is siloed and training-oriented (framed around single technical issues without due regard for undergirding socio-economic and political drivers), that it is competitive and even cut-throat (that how organisations operate are shaped by dwindling donor funds but increasing demands without due regard for failures, against collective efforts), that it is individualised (addressing select victims, violations and remedies).

are understood to have changed over time, with what was historically conceived as permissible coming to be condemned as reprehensible. Changing understandings of pain and punishment, it is argued, are sociopolitically contingent, with legal assessments of torture too beholden to this broader context. On this register, I chart the broader contours of the central shifts in prevailing social and scientific views, values and knowledge, as channelled or challenged through judges and taken to constitute torture's sociality. This has culminated, I argue, in a script of 'progress' driving the anti-torture field. Advocates, academics and adjudicators have come to conventionally understand the prohibition to 'evolve in response to changes in legal or social concepts'[55] – imbuing the field with a sense of purpose: towards torture's eradication.

The scholarship here has variably but widely conceptualised these collective values, particularly around pain, in references to 'moral sentiment',[56] 'shared imagination',[57] 'compassionate temperament',[58] 'modern sensibility', 'sensibilité',[59] 'humanitarian social imaginary', 'collective conscience',[60] 'public consciousness'[61] and 'sympathies of mankind'.[62] This scholarship has sought to better understand how pain is emotionally, cognitively and socioculturally conceived. These accounts underscore shifting understandings of suffering in collective emotional and ideational imaginaries. Imaginaries, as mentioned, are imbued with teleological drives that promise progress towards a more complete

[55] Humphrey Waldock, 'The Evolution of Human Rights Concepts and the Application of the European Convention on Human Rights' in Paul Reuter (ed), *Mélanges offerts à Paul Reuter: Le droit international: Unité Et diversité* (1981) 547, a former ECtHR judge.

[56] Adam Smith, *A Theory of Moral Sentiments* (Penguin Classics 1759/2009).

[57] Iain Wilkinson, *Suffering: A Sociological Introduction* (Polity Press 2005).

[58] Natan Sznaider, *The Compassionate Temperament: Care and Cruelty in Modern Society* (Rowman & Littlefield 2001).

[59] Lucien Febvre, 'Sensibility and History: How to Reconstitute the Emotional Life of the Past' in Peter Burke (ed), *A New Kind of History and Other Essays* (Harper 1973).

[60] Emile Durkheim, *Division of Labour in Society* (1893) 38–39: 'The totality of beliefs and sentiments common to the average members of a society forms a determinate system with a life of its own. It can be termed the collective or common consciousness'.

[61] Richard Wilson and Richard D Brown (eds), *Humanitarianism and Suffering: The Mobilization of Empathy* (Cambridge University Press 2009) 2.

[62] Iain Wilkinson and Arthur Kleinman, *A Passion for Society: How We Think about Human Suffering* (University of California Press 2018) vii, 22, 42.

humanitarian understanding of and, in turn, response to suffering. There is also much which critiques this teleology – pointing to how states have always protected their violence from serious scrutiny through arguing necessity.[63]

Medical anthropology represents a singularly rich vein of scholarship in this respect. It has offered valuable insights into the sociocultural contingency of pain, as 'influenced by meanings, relationships and institutions', coming to view it as a 'greatly complex knot of bodily, psychological, and philosophical conundrums'.[64] Historical scholarship too takes shifts in sociocultural attitudes and understandings of pain to dictate how pain is 'unpredictable and resistant to standards of measurement', as the body is 'bundled up with confusing social and cultural factors'.[65] The consensus seems to be that far from being 'simply a function of the amount of bodily damage ... the culture in which we have been brought up plays an essential role in how we feel and respond to pain',[66] that it is always subject to 'social appraisal', and best understood as a 'biocultural event'.[67]

Compared to the sophistication in this broader scholarship, how legal actors have determined what counts as social and scientific change around pain and punishment (or otherwise) looks to be left unconvincingly open and uncritically repeated. Ambiguities abound and stand to be better acknowledged. This discussion draws on historical claims and doctrinal concepts including 'present-day conditions'/'attitudes', 'dynamic interpretation', 'progress', 'evolution', 'civilisation', 'democratic values', 'consensus', 'necessity, 'living instrument' and 'legal certainty', which will be put into conversation with law's myths, ethics, sociology of punishment and suffering and governmentality. The fact that not all violence

[63] John Langbein, *Torture and the Law of Proof: Europe in the Ancien Régime* (University of Chicago Press 2006); Michel Foucault, *Discipline and Punish: The Birth of the Prison* (Vintage 1979).

[64] DelVecchio Good (1994) 7; see also Arthur Kleinman et al (eds), *Social Suffering* (University of California Press 1997); Veena Das (ed), *Violence and Subjectivity* (University of California Press 2000); Sara Ahmed, *The Cultural Politics of Emotion* (2nd ed, Edinburgh University Press 2014).

[65] Rob Boddice, *Pain: A Very Short Introduction* (Oxford University Press 2017) 1–2.

[66] Ronald Melzack and Patrick D. Wall, *The Challenge of Pain* (Penguin 1996) 15.

[67] David B. Morris, *The Culture of Pain* (University of California Press 1991) 25–26.

is condemned, for instance, in the name of 'civilisation', necessitates a critical reading of law's claims, leading to ask: What forms of violence has the law historically and progressively recognised and prohibited upon the backdrop of modernity or progress? What is the relationship between social, scientific and legal perspectives on suffering? How contextually bound is the norm against torture, or human rights generally, anyway? The chapter thus comes to problematise law's claims to reflect its sociality and points to devices it deploys (such as 'necessity') to vanish certain forms of violence from justiciability and, in turn, shielding them from scrutiny.

1.3.3 CHAPTER 4: EXCEPTIONALISING SUFFERING. Not all state-sanctioned suffering is considered torture, inhuman or degrading under international law, as that which is assessed to be *inherent, incidental* or *indispensable* to the functioning of the law enforcement apparatus (police and prisons) often passes as lawful. The determination here is a complex threshold- and boundary-drawing exercise. When confronted with the question of the state's violence, human rights advocates and adjudicators appear to accept a predetermined calculus – arguing whether it is *just* or *justified* for the operation of police and prisons. Advocates' and adjudicators' lexicon in the determination of torture claims puts state-centric imperatives first: it is 'violence' when illegitimate (illegal, illogical, unjustified, disproportionate) and 'force' when opposite ('impartial', 'logical', 'measured', 'justified' and 'legitimated' social ends by sociopolitical structures).

These assessments and aspirations have not taken due account of – and have in fact concealed – the broader frameworks in which they operate. This springs not simply from the practitioner but from the framing discourse, and from the state power and self-preserving impulse to denounce any threat to its monopoly as 'unjustified'. The peculiarities in the lexicon, in variably naming violence, are telling here – as concealing as it is revealing of the 'defining framework' in which it is embedded.[68] These associations are tacitly controlled, circulated and communicated in the field. Practitioners' preoccupation with assessing justification

[68] Judith Butler, *The Force of Non-violence: An Ethico-Political Bind* (Verso 2020) 135–136.

(proportionality and necessity) is normally narrowly focused on the individual act, without questioning the *modus operandi* of the broader institution (for instance, should prisons exist?). Whilst justifiability is accepted as a fitting question, that which beckons to what is beyond the brackets is shut down as not justiciable (meaning the 'quality or state of being appropriate or suitable for adjudication by a court'[69]).

That certain forms of suffering will be excluded is a naturalised mode of denial as legitimated through legal processes.[70] Put differently, the law offers 'an acknowledgment that a condition is intolerable, cannot be tolerated, and demands action as a consequence'[71] but can enable, in the absence of such acknowledgement, 'the active toleration of its presence'.[72] The law, criminal law as human rights law, fails on multiple fronts to reflect realities, fundamentally as it 'constitutes a language of governance rather than an authentic response to human suffering' and that the prohibition 'simultaneously outlaws, categorizes, and obscures if not legitimizes, by way of exclusion, forms of direct or structural violence'.[73] On this background, legal protection 'risks being partial, privileging certain experiences and marginalizing others'.[74]

From these points of departure, Chapter 4 delves deeper into the discussion around the torturous suffering inflicted in the name of the state and how that is legitimated ('Exceptionalising Suffering'). The chapter continues to find states to exhibit an existential interest in keeping the legality of some forms of suffering ambiguous and thus deniable (and non-justiciable to the extent possible), given the degree to which state authorities rely on them. Certain methods (solitary confinement, coercive interrogation and life imprisonment) have come to be bracketed away from the prohibition. This evokes the (often effaced) question of the formation of legality and legitimacy of state violence and brings into focus legal concepts such as 'lawful sanctions', 'minimum severity',

[69] Bryan A Garner, *Black's Law Dictionary* (Thomson 2004).

[70] Andrew Trevor Williams, 'Human Rights and Law: Between Sufferance and Insufferability' (2007) 122 *Law Quarterly Review* 132.

[71] Ibid.

[72] Ibid.

[73] Oette (2024) 48.

[74] Ibid 141.

'inherent or incidental', 'discomfort', 'special stigma', 'triviality' and 'necessity'. These stand to be critiqued as being born out of political imperatives to exceptionalise so as to invisibilise and render deniable certain state practices. These categories, as will be argued, have worked to preserve the category of torture as aberrational and nearly unattainable.

1.3.4 CHAPTER 5: SUBSTANTIATING SUFFERING. The recognition of torture is said to be primarily a question of evidence. Law's reliance on medical evidence has thus come to play a significant role. Advocates have busied themselves with setting standards and developing documentation methodologies towards producing compelling evidence for policymakers or adjudicators, before whom torture-related cases or conditions are brought. Yet not all evidence compels recognition, even when according to relevant standards. Why is this so? There are well-established dangers and difficulties involved in documenting torture. These relate to the availability of evidence given its suppression by the state as well as how state violence impacts victims' capacity to preserve evidence, such as memories, but also relate to how the evidence available is *received* when it, against odds, makes it before an institution of potential redress. These difficulties concern how evidence is interpreted and how expertise is credited in how the suffering is recognised or not. This, in turn, brings into focus how the demands for multi- and interdisciplinary collaboration and expertise (particularly medico-legal documentation) have been realised (or not) by advocates and adjudicators.

Upon this background, Chapter 5 ('Substantiating Suffering') trains its attention on evidentiary practices, continuing to ask how law apprehends its world. The discussion reveals that legal actors have had a troubled relation with expert evidence. As with Chapters 1–4, a critical orientation is brought in to explicate law's evidentiary reductivity (manageability of contingency and complexity) – to argue that the law has been unpredictable and unprincipled in how it has registered torture's lifeworld. The pertinent questions here become: How does law interact with the natural and social sciences in the recognition of torture? What types of knowledge and evidence count towards legal recognition? What types are effaced and rendered inadmissible?

1.3.5 CHAPTER 6: SENSING SUFFERING. Bodies and minds are complex and contested spaces, requiring all available to us to imbue them with sense. Pain might be, as Amnesty wrote in the 1970s, 'a common human dominator' as within 'every human being is the knowledge and fear of pain, the fear of helplessness before unrestrained cruelty', even if this is not specific knowledge of being tortured.[75] Yet, all too often, where we do not know enough about another's suffering, we presume and pretend to know where we could instead ask and listen. This is all the more amplified in anti-torture practice and research, which, despite its grassroots origins, are distant from the experience of torture. One account here charges anti-torture professionals as generally 'divorced from the intimate struggles, pain, and trauma experienced by individual humans, focused instead upon reporting and negotiating with governments'.[76] Our abstractions can work against us.

Chapter 6 ('Sensing Suffering') makes it clear that definitions, categories and expertise have not ended interpretive issues. Definitions are disembodied. All forms of violence and suffering, their definition and recognition remain relational in reality, born out of a labyrinthine complexity – in terms of how they are constructed, communicated, filtered and understood. Preconceptions of who is deserving of recognition, the requisites for social identification, moral commitment or collective empathy reveal this to be the case. There is a rich scholarship on pain which underscores the intersubjectivity, complexity and sociocultural contingency of pain. Social science takes suffering to be (inescapably) intersubjectively, textually and sensorially understood – so judicial determinations must also go beyond the technical and doctrinal. The chapter's discussion on temporality continues the theme of sensing. It examines temporal registers in the recognition of torture – exploring the questions: How does time feature and function in juridical understandings of torture? Why does it privilege the event-bound, the spectacular

[75] Amnesty International, *Report on Torture* (1973) 17.

[76] Alexandra S. Moore and Elizabeth Swanson, *Witnessing Torture: Perspectives of Torture Survivors and Human Rights Workers* (Palgrave 2018), 'Prologue', ix. That said, proximity to suffering should not in itself always be seen as aiding anti-torture work. It can also be disenchanting or debilitating to see and hear such experiences – especially when connected to the futility of one's tools.

and the exceptional (over the incremental and invisible)? This discussion on time adds to the kaleidoscopic catalogue of sense-centric registers and reasoning operating in the anti-torture field – illustrating it to be a device of inclusion and exclusion.

The book concludes with a chapter which summarises as to consolidate proposals for reorienting the field in practice and research.

1.4 DISCLAIMER AGAINST DISORIENTATION

Although it might not always be apparent, I have been mindful of you, my reader. This is a book written *about* an area of human rights practice and research ('law and torture'), as it is written *for* its users, whether legally minded or not. There remain, however, unavoidable abstractions, oscillations, connections and conflations which may make for disorienting reading. Some entanglements are embraced and may encumber smooth reading. These relate to both style and substance (aims, arguments, concepts and materials). Although chapters and sections depart from personal–professional vignettes, quotes or cases in foregrounding the questions driving the discussion, readers may find other parts of the text denser and slower. Much has unquestionably been packed into certain sections, where quotes from important sources are strung together. The reader should, where needed, slow down, skip or refer back to the original source (cases or commentaries).

I also anticipate for some readers to readily reject the key concepts I bring together, namely, pain, punishment and torture on 'progress' or the cornucopia of concepts on the 'senses', or concepts which I hold apart, particularly in how they have been sequenced. Despite the separation and sequencing as necessitated for pedagogical reasons, chapters should be viewed as imbricative. Exceptionalising suffering, for instance, involves sociopolitical, evidential and sensorial registers, as discussed in the chapters which follow it. Progressive impulses are similarly complicated by the evidential and sensorial registers and so on. Imagining torture, simply put, is in a dialectical interplay with evidencing torture.

To be clear, this book was written in parallel to my doctoral dissertation on how psychologically oriented practices are downgraded or dismissed through the four-limbed lens as introduced in this book.

As I complete this book, I have started preparing the dissertation for publication with Oxford University Press, entitled *Torture and the Recognition of Psychological Suffering in International Law.* Ideally, the two books should be read consecutively, this then that, as the second book provides an extended and empirical support to what is abstractly argued in the pages before you. This has been an intellectually generative period for me. In the haste to see these ideas surface, and despite care and caution, I may not have been adequately reader-friendly in presentation. I remain, therefore, beholden to your generous reading.

CHAPTER 2

Doctrine and Its (dis)contents

I'VE BEEN REFLECTING ON MY OWN RECEIVED STORIES. During one of my first meetings as a legal advisor at Dignity, a colleague who has since become an anti-torture adjudicator dictated to me that torture, inhuman and degrading treatment were simply what a judge said they were – and 'that's that'. I breathed a sigh of relief – good that that impossible task was out of my inexperienced hands. I better simply 'read up', I thought, and see what these judges had to say. It wasn't long before I came to depend on legal scholars for clarity and coherence about what to make of the harms brought before my desk. Yet, the insights from these experienced doctrinal sources also dried up as they stopped adequately speaking to the complexity and ambiguity that emerged out of my own experience – usually in places where it sounded stupid to invoke these remote juridical authorities.

Doctrine began to leave pressing questions unacknowledged and unaddressed – an early one was 'why mental suffering produced by solitary confinement went overlooked?'. That was more than eight years ago – but my vexed fixation lingers and challenges me in my current practice. Why are we still having these conversations? Why have those to have come before me not done the work to settle the terrain? I can only think this is because the suffering is not static and that the stakes are high – and seem to remain so. The stakes being that of effective recognition and response. That we come to call some experience torturous, inhuman or degrading packs a punch – beyond the conceptual, to the political and in our everyday practice as researchers and practitioners. How have precious energies been directed and depleted in all this time? Have we, having bought into the doctrine's benevolence, simply exerted ourselves to its ends despite its limitations? I fear this to have been so.

> Training in law is training in simplification. It is a trained incapacity to look at all values in a situation, and instead to select only the legally relevant ones … But it is, through its simplifications, a primitive system.[1]

The legally oriented (be it the advocate, academic or adjudicator) have long tended to the intersection of 'law and torture' – from promoting its use in pre- and early modern Europe as a lawful means of extracting evidence eventually to its universal definition and prohibition in the twentieth century. As torture techniques, and understandings of the harms they inflict, have not proven static, the legally oriented have continued to dominate. Their powers and privileges are all too evident in setting and interpreting standards, helping configure thresholds of state violence as acceptable (or not), distinguishing between prohibited categories, determining the minutiae of definitional elements and prescribing programmes for prevention. Common across this extensive history is the question, as determined by the legally oriented, of how the violence of the state should or should not be understood and used. The current doctrinal position, as deferential to international human rights law, resolutely holds law as antithetical to torture, that law is solely concerned with torture's prohibition and eradication, not its perpetuation.

The prevailing point of departure on torture conventionally looks to the universal definition as found in the *UN Convention against Torture and Other Cruel, Inhuman or Degrading Treatment or Punishment* (UNCAT) over and above similar prohibitions[2] and definitions[3] in international law.

[1] Nils Christie, *Limits to Pain* (1981) 57.

[2] The prohibitions include *Universal Declaration of Human Rights*, 10 December 1948, Article 5; *United Nations International Covenant on Civil and Political Rights*, Article 7; *European Convention on Human Rights*, Article 3; *American Convention on Human Rights*, Article 5; *African Charter on Human and Peoples' Rights*, Article 5; *Arab Charter on Human Rights*, Article 8; *United Nations Convention on the Rights of the Child*, Article 37; *United Nations Convention on Persons with Disabilities*, Article 15; *Geneva Conventions* (GC), Common Article; GCI, Article 12, GCII, Article 12, GCIII, Articles 17 and 87, GCIV, Article 32 (prohibition of biological experiments); GCI, Article 50, GCII, Article 51, GCIII, Article 130, GCIV, Article 147; *Rome Statute for the International Criminal Court*, Article 8 (2) (a).

[3] UN *Declaration on the Protection of All Persons from Being Subjected to Torture and Other Cruel, Inhuman or Degrading Treatment or Punishment* (1975), UNGA res 3452 (XXX), Article 1; OAS, *Inter-American Convention to Prevent and Punish Torture*, 9 December 1985, Treaty Series, no. 6, Article 2.

The legally oriented gaze fixes itself on medical evidence of suffering that a certain practice may entail and ends with an argument as to how an international court ought to assess the suffering in applying the definition. The central question, configured and contested, here is about the legitimate uses of violence by the state: from arrest, interrogation and detention to other official institutional (education- and health-related) interventions. The stakes are high for states. Given how closely guarded states are of their coercive means, this discourse has come to generate voluminous academic scholarship, not to mention awareness-raising advocacy, law reform activities, caselaw and grey literature (i.e., civil society reports). This approach has held the legal apparatus, its actors and norms, as the central grounds both for torture's infliction and inhibition; the law, this discourse assumes, has the power to preserve and perpetuate torturous practices or to pre-empt and uproot them.

This (rather lengthy) chapter offers a sweeping survey of the doctrinal scholarship to date, mapping its principles, presumptions and preponderances.[4] This has been the sole inclusion criterion for what is presented. The newly arrived reader can choose to take a deeper dive in the respective works of prominent commentators to more fully appreciate the aims and assumptions of doctrinal scholarship.[5] In this chapter,

[4] Doctrine is the 'dominant, conventional, liberal, and positivistic scholarship, manned and maintained by the founding and sustaining institutional figures of the UNCAT-oriented framework [and] as a legal methodology which takes existing legal sources (legal principles and instruments) as its focus and as its material, towards developing principally legal solutions', per Ergun Cakal, 'Law and Torture: Contemporary Legal Scholarship on Torture, from the Doctrinal to the Critical' (2023) 25 (5) *International Community Law Review* 397, 400.

[5] Manfred Nowak et al (eds), *The United Nations Convention against Torture and Its Optional Protocol: A Commentary* (2nd ed, OUP 2019); Manfred Nowak and Elizabeth McArthur, 'The Distinction between Torture and Cruel, Inhuman or Degrading Treatment' (2006) 16 *Torture*; Nigel Rodley and Matt Pollard, *The Treatment of Prisoners under International Law* (3rd ed, OUP 2011); Malcolm Evans, 'Getting to Grips with Torture' (2002) 51 *International and Comparative Law Quarterly*; Ahcene Boulesbaa, *The UN Convention on Torture and the Prospects for Enforcement* (Nijhoff 1999); Steven Dewulf, *The Signature of Evil: (Re)Defining Torture in International Law* (Intersentia 2011); J Herman Burgers and Hans Danelius, *The United Nations Convention against Torture: A Handbook on the Convention against Torture and Other Cruel, Inhuman, or Degrading Treatment or Punishment* (Nijhoff 1988); Malcolm Evans and Jens Modvig (eds), *Research Handbook on Torture: Legal and Medical Perspectives on Prohibition and Prevention* (Elgar 2020).

I cut to the core, outlining a catalogue of concepts in constant (not always explicit) circulation in anti-torture practice and research. In doing so, I ask questions that I aim to pick up on in the rest of the book, with respective discussions coming to critique these grounds. To start with, I draw attention to the precision pursued by the legally oriented – a precision which has proven elusive. Identifying the questions routinely asked by doctrinal scholars, I hold, also assists in identifying questions that are overlooked or foreclosed and rigorously examined in the subsequent chapters.

The chapter is divided into (2.1) definition and distinction, (2.2) interpretation and (2.3) discontents. These are represented, indicatively not exhaustively, as the focal points central to understanding doctrinal drives. I foreground what I have called the 'discontents', the contexts and conditions challenging or conventionally excluded by doctrine. These relate to the disconnections made by doctrine between specific acts and systemic factors, individual perpetrators and their institutions. The chapter concludes with a discussion on the possible implications as arising.

2.1 DEFINITION AND DISTINCTION

> Torture is a notoriously slippery subject at every step of defining, documenting, diagnosing, recognising, and prosecuting it.[6]

Torture's definition, prevention and prohibition seem settled at first glance: absolute, evolutive, universal yet context-sensitive and as evoking both negative (to refrain) and positive (to prevent) obligations on states. Torture's prohibition has a long history and pedigree, powerfully confirmed to be a part of customary international law and as a peremptory norm.[7] The universal definition as fixed and found in Article 1 of the UNCAT authoritatively defines torture as an *intentional, purposeful* and *official* act causing *severe* pain. It excludes *lawful* sanctions. Broader

[6] Tobias Kelly, 'Recognizing Torture: Credibility and the Unstable Codification of Victimhood' in Steffen Jensen and Henrik Rønsbo (eds), *Histories of Victimhood* (University of Pennsylvania Press 2014) 141.

[7] *Questions Relating to the Obligation to Prosecute or Extradite (Belgium v. Senegal)*, Judgment, ICJ Reports, 2012, p. 155 [99]; *A v. Bosnia and Herzegovina*, CAT/C/67/D/854/2017 [2.13].

contours of responsive processes are thus equally settled, as entrusted to the remit of law and legal actors. Before broaching its exclusions, the following pages will first canvass the core preponderances in doctrinal approaches to defining and delimiting torture from all else. I discuss these through three sections: *painful*; *intentional and purposeful*; and, *official and lawful*. I then turn to diverse approaches to categorising torture from the inhuman and degrading (in 'Distinction').

2.1.1 PAINFUL. The core yet most obscure element in the definition of torture is that of 'severe pain' (alternatively suffering, damage, impact, harm and injury). It sits at the core because 'it is not possible to define torture without reference to "pain or suffering"'.[8] Scholars nevertheless decry that the element is 'virtually impossible',[9] 'opaque at best',[10] 'very much a matter for debate'[11] and 'not susceptible to precise gradation'.[12] I agree. Pain, to be sure, is not self-announcing nor easily shared, and we are not given clues as to what severe pain looks like at least in the definition. This might also be because pain is more in the realm of 'behavioural sciences' than those legal.[13] In fact, the leading proponent of the international legal framework, Amnesty International, knew full well the difficulties in this terrain. Predating the UN *Declaration on Torture* in 1975, it found 'good reason why the concept of torture resists precise and scientific definition; it describes human behaviour, and each human being is unique, with his own pain threshold, his own psychological make-up, his own cultural conditioning'.[14] So this was always going to be 'site for contestation' between narrow and broad interpretations.[15]

8 Başoğlu (2017), 'Introduction', xxiv.

9 Nigel Rodley, *The Treatment of Prisoners under International Law* (2nd ed, OUP 1999) 98.

10 Natasa Mavronicola, *Torture, Inhumanity, and Degradation under Article 3 of the ECHR: Absolute Rights and Absolute Wrongs* (Hart 2021) 61.

11 Malcolm Evans, 'The Criminalisation of Torture as a Part of the Human Right Framework' (2014) *CRIMEN: Casopis za Krivicne Nauke* 139.

12 Hernan Reyes, 'The Worst Scars are in the Mind: Psychological Torture' (2007) 89 *International Review of the Red Cross* 896.

13 Başoğlu (2017), 'Introduction', xxiv.

14 Amnesty International, *Report on Torture* (1973) 29.

15 Waldron (2005) 1696.

Here is what can be said with some confidence about how this element has featured and functioned since its inscription at the core of torture's definition: that torture requires *severe* pain trains attention on the intensity of the pain caused to an individual; it is a measure of the gravity (intensity, seriousness, degree or level) of the wrong done; and it is used to identify a certain degree of pain as recognisable as torturous, differentiating and holding it out from just *any* pain. So, one is not encouraged to recognise just any pain as torturous and worthy of redress. That torturous pain needs to be severe does not necessarily dispose of the task.[16] This is primarily because it is understood to be open-ended, a combination of subjective and objective understandings, contingent on an individual's profile and vulnerabilities, including but not limited to age, gender and health. Its plural nature recognises that it can be produced through a multitude of means and modes: physical or mental, short or prolonged, single or cumulative, whether through action or inaction.[17]

Who can optimally determine what is severe? To what extent should an individual's own (subjective) assessment inform a legal determination? How much pain is enough? What practices tend to lead to it? What is pain to advocates and adjudicators? How is severity or vulnerability to be gauged? Under what circumstances is severe pain produced? Doctrine does not squarely settle these questions, though there is a presumption that advocates and adjudicators are equipped to adequately apprehend and assess pain in individual cases. In most cases, including in international human rights contexts, this is misconceived. If nothing else, cases with dissenting opinions prove that assessing severity is difficult and divisive.[18] Advocates and adjudicators may (and often do) fail to fully engage with these questions.

[16] Some drafters had unsuccessfully argued for the word 'extreme' in its stead to which I return in Chapter 4.

[17] The element of severe pain has been read into all authoritative prohibitions of torture, including the *Inter-American Convention to Prevent and Punish Torture*, which is understood as not having codified the element. Whilst I also once simply accepted that severity was absent, a close reading of the caselaw of the Inter-American Court of Human Rights (IACtHR) reveals that severe pain has been a requirement, see, e.g., *Bueno-Alvez v. Argentina* [2007].

[18] Look no further than *Ireland v. UK* or *Bouyid v. Belgium* discussed later in the book.

As voluminous as the 'law and torture' research has been, it has also been impoverished especially when it has dealt with the body in pain through and beyond such formulaic prescriptions. Dominant biomedical approaches have failed to offer sufficient solace here, which too have drawn criticism for 'tend[ing] to miss many of the subjectively lived dimensions of the body in pain as well as the complex ways in which it is situated, experienced and produced in cultural, social, political and historical contexts'.[19] Neither is there a scientifically rigorous means of ensuring that state-sanctioned violence does not reach the threshold of severe pain – as will be discussed in Section 3.2. While pain may be explained away as 'never a good frame for objective inquiry',[20] it is incumbent on legal actors to embrace its complexities. As pain cannot be directly shared, it requires articulation and translation.

Through doctrinal discussions, attention is often diverted from key realities, thwarting emphatic engagement – with questions as 'how the punishment hurts, how it feels, the suffering and the sorrow' not *always* afforded adequate consideration.[21] Precedents taken as common knowledge have instead led to positions that 'we "just know"' the pain certain practices entail, without a need for deeper reflection.[22] Empirically and critically viewed, the answers come to depend on the observers' imagination and, truth be told, guesswork albeit in a 'reasoned and patterned manner'.[23] Much is packed into the imagination, including social, cultural and political values. These difficulties defeat doctrinal understandings – a defeat not commonly admitted. Discretion afforded to adjudicators to introduce and apply open-ended supplementary concepts (such as vulnerability and powerlessness) has proven problematic in practice. Their rhetorical force has disguised the reinforcement of stereotypes, selecting, essentialising and pathologising victimhood to authoritatively determine the frames of recognition (that women,

[19] Lisa Folkmarson Käll (ed), *Dimensions of Pain: Humanities and Social Science Perspectives* (Routledge 2013) 2.

[20] Paul W. Khan, *Sacred Violence: Torture, Terror, and Sovereignty* (University of Michigan Press 2008) 26.

[21] Christie (1981) 15.

[22] Evans (2023) 42.

[23] Kelly (2012) 68–69.

children and the older suffer more easily, and that men are relatively more resilient).

As any emphasis on subjectivity invites doubt, however, advocates and adjudicators have generally avoided dealing with concepts that risk bringing in such doubt and indeterminacy. For one prominent scholar, the reluctance in speaking to differences in the characteristics of victims is taken to have strengthened the anti-torture struggle but simultaneously to have 'obscured, or risks obscuring, differential exposure to and experiences of torture'.[24] The reluctance is acutely identified where otherwise responsive human rights courts have dismissed racial dimensions of state violence.[25] In practice, the impulse has been to set thresholds of recognition under torture's prohibition as exceptionally high. Not 'simply' severe (whatever that is taken to mean) but 'extremely' severe (serious, considerable and grave).[26] In effectively demanding extreme and otherwise explicit suffering (namely, physical spectacles), high thresholds have served as a means to deal with pain's obscurity – questions raised about its gravity and causality. There emerges thus an impulse to use the level of pain as a differentiator (aggravator) between torture and other categories – to set it at the 'apex' of the pyramid, to attribute a 'special stigma' and to reserve it for 'the worst of the worst'. This calls into question political (or policy) considerations beyond that which exists on the face of the convention(s). It is to such considerations that this book, particularly Chapter 3, seeks to speak.

To be fair, context is not entirely avoided by doctrinal scholarship. In grappling with questions raised, the legal understanding of pain has resorted to additional notions not found on the face of the definition: relativity, objectivity and vulnerability. These serve to somewhat structure the open-textured nature of pain, offering clues as to how to

[24] Oette (2024) 95.

[25] As has occasionally happened at the ECtHR. In *A.P. v Slovakia* [2020] ECtHR 10465/17, for example, the majority were not convinced that racism had anything to do with the beating of a Roma minor, which a minority of judges cautioned as 'setting an excessively high threshold for the Court to address the merits of complaints under article 14' (discrimination) urging for the Court to 'not shy away from the substance of allegations of racial discrimination' in future cases.

[26] See Ergun Cakal, 'Assessing (and Making Sense of) Severity: Conceptualising and Contextualising Torture's Core' (2022) 91 *Nordic Journal of International Law* 284–309.

approach the body *in* pain *in* society. Pain's relativity accords with prominent non-legal approaches to pain.[27] Pain is universal but also individual, as it is subjectively experienced, 'deeply entrenched with cultural, historical, political, social and symbolic meaning that both situates it in a specific time and place'.[28] That pain is relative to individual factors of age, gender and health is a long-established and oft-cited principle in anti-torture jurisprudence. It formulaically appears in the phrase drawing in considerations of 'duration of the treatment, its physical or mental effects and, in some cases, the sex, age and state of health of the victim'.[29] This effectively means that 'the same act by a perpetrator may cause intense suffering to the former, but inconsequential discomfort to the latter'.[30] This will be returned in Chapter 6.

What about culture – perhaps, the most complex prism of sense making for the victim-survivor? The same goes for culture. Culture is often asserted but not consistently included in all legal assessments, at least explicitly. In its 1973 'Report on Torture', Amnesty weighed in as follows (worth quoting at length):[31]

> The question arises whether or not what constitutes torture is culturally determined and can vary from culture to culture. On this issue the distinction may usefully be made between 'physical' and 'mental' torture.

[27] Dennis Turk and Ronald Melzack (eds), *Handbook of Pain Assessment* (Guilford Press 1992) xi: 'A number of cultural, economic, social, demographic, and environmental factors, along with the individual's personal history, situational factors, interpretation of the symptoms and resources, current psychological state, as well as physical pathology, all contribute to the response to the question "How much does it hurt?"'.

[28] Käll (2013) 1.

[29] *Ireland v. UK* [1978] ECtHR 5856/72 [162].

[30] *Prosecutor v. Zlatko Aleksovski* [1999] ICTY, IT-95-14/1-T, Trial Judgment [56].

[31] International criminal law, through the UN International Criminal Tribunal on the Former Yugoslavia (ICTY), boldly ventured into this terrain to explicitly point to 'the specific social, cultural, and religious background of the victims' per *Limaj v. Prosecutor* [2005] ICTY, IT-03-66-T, Trial Judgment [730–731]. The genocidal context in which the torture took place would have enabled this articulation as compared with the less systematic nature of violations before other international institutions. Vera Piovesan, 'The Mind's Eye: The Invisibility of Culture in Individual Criminal Responsibility' in Mark Drumbl and Caroline Fournet, *Sights, Sounds, and Sensibilities of Atrocity Prosecutions* (Brill 2024), argues that international criminal law is largely reticent to engage the notion of culture.

> The physiology of the human nervous system is the same for all human beings regardless of race, climate or culture. In general the effect of physical torture such as beating, electro-shock, near-drowning, sleep deprivation and drugs will be the same on any human system. Although cultural conditioning can have remarkable effects on resistance to pain, as for example in the case of religious firewalkers, the result of the infliction of pain against the victim's will would seem to be universal at the physiological level.
>
> Mental or psychological torture, on the other hand, can be different, for it usually depends on the value system of the victim for its effect. Some values, such as the protection of children, might be universal for reasons deeper than culture, but values like religion are culturally determined. To make a Moslem fall to his knees and kiss the cross can be a humiliation and torture for him, while the same act for a Christian would not be. What is universal is the prohibition of torture; the means of infliction of pain might vary from culture to culture, the prohibition of torture is universal.

Although certain reactions such as fear in the face of danger might be understood as universal, is there not a cultural contingency to how they are experienced by individuals? The question of culture has met some reluctance amongst advocates and adjudicators as it exposes the assessment of suffering to the claim that an individual can be rendered more or less susceptible to the same treatment. Culture, as with all else subjective, has generally been viewed with scepticism, potentially as bringing in a dangerous relativity, indeterminacy or an unmanageability to legal processes. It is criticised for legitimating (not that the argument is not already being made) sweeping cultural arguments against victims (even if relativism is more faithful to the reality of suffering than universalism).[32] If we are to accept the risk that states will use cultural differences in justifying abusive practices, how are cultural differences, then, to be factored into assessments of pain, if at all?

[32] To lean on the cultural context, or rather the social consequences, in 'locating' suffering is in itself an interesting practice. I am thankful for Grant Shubin for adding to my thinking on this point in illustrating how certain rape cases involving female victims have often focussed on their tarnished place in their community through an emphasis on 'humiliation' and 'stigmatisation', which is not necessarily been the case for the (rare) male victim.

There is also the question of jeopardising the absolute nature of torture's prohibition, should it become so radically dependent on the profile of the victim beyond their age, gender and health. The risk, to put it simply, could be to essentialise what suffering means to different ethnic groups, reifying stereotypes.[33] As with the question of culture, the notion of resilience can also be evoked here. Resilience, as one scholar has argued, 'may impose supernatural coping mechanisms on communities struggling with adversities, romanticize them as exemplary in enduring injustices, obscure their humanity, and normalize (structural) violence they continue to experience or reduce its severity'.[34] Whilst resilience may serve to counter pathologising all victims as broken and bent, it may also have the unintended consequence of expecting much too much from them.[35]

What is gradually becoming clear is that language, its concepts and categories, has proven inadequate in articulating the nature of severe pain – particularly in legal contexts. There is an inherent complexity in understanding how humans experience pain, which is not precisely scientifically measurable – drawing on social, cultural and political factors contingent on time and place. The subjectivities inhering in a full appreciation of pain have simply not fitted well with legal impulses for measurability, manageability and objectivity – with states strategically playing into these ambiguities. States, for instance, have pointed to how suffering, in question during adjudication, was 'beyond the evaluation of the law enforcement authorities and could not be objectively measured, as it related to psychological aspects, such as the emotions and personalities of the individuals concerned'.[36] It is this supposed 'subjectivity' that scares advocates and adjudicators into the grounds of 'objectivity' (however reductive or scientifically shaky these grounds actually are). That is to say, speculations disguised as objectification can be identified in these interpretive exercises, with the assessment of pain often reduced

[33] E.g., Muslim men are often attributed with a fear of dogs, which is not universally true.

[34] Malaka Shwaikh, 'Beyond Expectations of Resilience: Towards a Language of Care' (2023) 17 *Global Studies Quarterly* 1–13.

[35] Ergün Cakal, 'An "Aptitude for Isolation": Using Resilience in Dismissing the Suffering of Solitary Confinement' (2025) *Nordic Journal of Human Rights.*

[36] *Akhiyadova v. Russia* [2008] ECtHR 32059/02 [82].

to opinion. Such guesswork might well be inherent[37] but must be identified and reckoned as being so.

Seemingly on such grounds, adjudicators occasionally admit that 'it may well suffice that the victim is humiliated in his own eyes, even if not in the eyes of others'.[38] That 'all persons under the control of the police or a similar authority, are in a situation of vulnerability'[39] or 'that custodial police interrogation, by its very nature, isolates and pressures the individual … that even without employing brutality, the "third degree" or other specific stratagems, custodial interrogation exacts a heavy toll on individual liberty and trades on the weakness of individuals'[40] do not necessarily lead to the recognition of a violation. Whilst these look to lead to progressive recognition, interpretation has nevertheless maintained the impulse to check the subjective (individual reaction) against the objective (collective reaction). Not having genuinely parted with guesswork disguised as objectivity, adjudicators continue to insist that there are situations 'objectively' and 'inherently' painful regardless of age, gender and health. Yet, these have led to precedential understandings that a select few methods, notably electrocution, falanka and rape, are always (automatically) torture.[41] Claims to objectivity also hold other methods, such as incommunicado detention, prolonged solitary confinement and enforced disappearance, as at least amounting to inhuman treatment. These operate as presumptions, acting as welcomed shortcuts in a complex terrain, for advocates and adjudicators in processing cases involving such practices.

The question of such shortcuts brings in another implicit point of discretion and discussion: is it the nature of the act or its impact that should

[37] Eyal Weizman, *The Least of All Possible Evils* (Verso 2017) 3 argues that 'mere humans must of course guess, speculate and hedge their risks as they proceed towards the future as the blind leading the blind. It is for this reason that they ceaselessly seek to develop and perfect all sorts of technologies and techniques that might allow them to calculate the effects of violence and might harness its consequences'.

[38] *Tyrer v. UK* [1978] ECtHR 5856/72 [31].

[39] *Bouyid v. Belgium* [2015] ECtHR [GC] 23380/09 [107].

[40] *Dickerson v. United States* 530 US 428 (2000) [435].

[41] That rape is always torture needs to be qualified as not all in the wake of these groundbreaking ECtHR and ICTY decisions have been categorised as torture. Many cases from the international tribunals for Yugoslavia, Rwanda and Sierra Leone prosecuted rape as inhuman treatment or outrages on the person. I thank Grant Shubin for bringing this to my attention.

matter most? Should it matter that the victim of electrocution, falanka or rape (understood to always inflict torturous suffering) proved resilient and did not themselves describe their own suffering as severe? To opt for the impact would be to always require evidence of consequences. To opt with the nature of the act (notwithstanding impact) would only require showing that it happened. Why does this matter? It might matter if these select methods start to represent the pinnacle of a pain hierarchy, the likes against which emerging or previously unrecognised practices are compared and contrasted and, in doing so, potentially downgraded or dismissed. Relatedly, the notion that a vulnerability is a common experience, in fact, may even serve to heighten the burden in the legal search for specific vulnerability – a discussion expanded on in Chapter 4. In all, these presumptions and principles are offerings of pragmatism in short supply but should nevertheless be approached with some scepticism given that they flex with procedural and political demands made of them. I will return to problematise the points introduced in these last two paragraphs in the discussion in Chapters 5 and 6.

As the more critically framed discussions in Chapters 3 and 6 will attest, time is also an implicit component here that warrants explication and complication. Whilst 'no rigid durational requirement is built into the definition',[42] it is not immediately clear how different temporal registers shape recognition of pain's gravity – or causality with intent or purpose. The definition does refer to 'an act' but does not exclude multiple acts or delimit its time frame. An interpretive discretion is afforded to set limits.[43] A wide range of related notions has been used in the course of interpretation: duration, repeated, permanent, cumulative, combined, long-lasting, continuous and composite. That torture 'may be committed in one single act or can result from a combination or accumulation of several acts, which, taken individually and out of context, may seem harmless [with the] period of time, the repetition and various forms of mistreatment and severity should be assessed as a whole'[44] is a rare

42 *Prosecutor v. Naletilic and Matinovic* [2006] ICTY Appeal Judgement [300].

43 Notably, the French translation of the UNCAT definition, refers to 'aiguës' (or acute) rather than 'severe' – revealing a focus on the short term not the chronic.

44 *Prosecutor v. Krnojelac* [2002] ICTY Trial Chamber Judgement [182].

extended explication in the jurisprudence. It being an exception begs questions of how time features and functions where it is not otherwise similarly elaborated in legal texts.

Putting all this together, whilst sitting at the core of anti-torture doctrine, pain presents a perennial point of ambiguity and complexity – not lending itself to precise measurement. It is socioculturally, biologically and politically constructed and contingent. Yet, this should not mean that the examination of pain is exhausted. Non-legal scholarship, historical, medical, psychological and social scientific, offers rich explorations of pain – which rarely feature on the surface of the jurisprudence and relevant legal scholarship – which will be further drawn in the following chapters.

2.1.2 INTENTIONAL AND PURPOSEFUL. Doctrinally taken to prove less complex, I now turn to the interrelated elements of intention and purpose. As with severe pain, these are also devices for drawing thresholds. These however work explicitly to bind torture's conception to the state. That these are presented by authoritative commentators as not having resulted in extensive discussion during the definition's drafting is telling. That the drafters and the early commentary took these elements (purpose, intention and official capacity) as uncomplicated is because what they had in mind, namely interrogational torture on political opponents, almost always was purposeful and intentional and implicated the state. It is further telling that the broad consensus was to primarily serve to capture harms of a particular nature: to individual, official, direct and non-accidental actions in the public not the private sphere.

To start with intention, as with much of criminal law, whether an action or inaction is intentional or not serves as an aggravating factor of gravity and culpability. A planned killing, as the common understanding has it, should attract a stronger response than that which is unplanned.[45] For the drafters, this element was included to exclude acts that were 'the result of an accident or of mere negligence'.[46] It acts, in other words, to

[45] This being the essential difference between murder and manslaughter.
[46] Burgers and Danelius (1988) 118.

include planned or reckless[47] actions and inactions as well as to exclude that which is unplanned or accidental. This is occasionally illustrated by the figure of the forgotten detainee, who is 'forgotten by the prison guards and slowly starves to death', whose suffering is accepted to lack 'intention and purpose and, therefore, can "only" be qualified as cruel and/or inhuman treatment'.[48] So on these grounds '[p]urely negligent conduct ... can never be considered as torture'.[49] Beyond differentiating it from negligence, UNCAT drafting history does not afford much attention to intention.[50] The figure of 'forgotten prisoner' has been followed by adjacent devices used to downgrade gravity, including notions of 'poor policies', 'side effects', 'organisational failings' or 'inadequate resources'. The questions begged by these notions are as follows: What qualifies as 'purely' negligent conduct? Can negligence not be intentionally produced through a lack of competency? Can negligence itself not be produced intentionally and purposefully?

Requiring reading the minds of officials for their motives would place the burden unattainably high. Assessing what is intentional necessarily draws, therefore, upon context and circumstance. That a rope, hood, electric cables or a baseball bat is used would indicate that harm was intended. What about a lack of resources to provide for adequate health care, to prevent inter-prisoner violence or to promptly respond to a complaint of domestic violence? This conceivably shifts the focus to inaction and omission. Whilst direct physical beatings would readily indicate intention, what about pain less directly inflicted? The Egyptian prison authorities have, as an illustration, refused medical attention, leading to the deaths of a number of high-profile political prisoners as a standard operating procedure. Was there intent? How could it be proven? What about where the Egyptian prison authorities fail to provide heart medicine to a political prisoner knowing full well that he needs it? Can

47 Recklessness is not often argued. An exception is Juan Mendez and Andrea Nicolescu, 'Evolving Standards for Torture in International Law' in Başoğlu (2017) 244.

48 Gerrit Zach, 'Article 1. Definition of Torture' in Nowak et al (2019) 53; see Nowak (2006) 830.

49 Ibid.

50 Oona Hathaway et al, 'Tortured Reasoning: The Intent to Torture under International and National Law' (2012) 52 *Virginia Journal of International Law* 803.

intentionality be attributed to the 'letting die', to the 'slow death'? The answer should be yes, but these prove to be more difficult to establish than the policeman swinging a bat in the interrogation room.

Another example, across the Egyptian border, to helpfully focus the discussion here is the Israeli State Prosecutor's Office's use of sleep deprivation in the wake of the widely reported 1999 Israeli Supreme Court case.[51] That Office argued that its practice was a permitted 'side effect' of 'prolonged interrogation' and not intentionally used for the purpose of tiring or 'breaking' the detainee.[52] Inaction in both cases, it can reasonably be appreciated, leans more into the contextual, circumstantial, institutional and longitudinal than action: requiring the impact to be traced back over time and place as a culmination of social, political, cultural, legal and economic factors. A focus on action, meanwhile, is conceivably easier to satisfy through assessing individual acts, actors and events. The swing of the baseball bat, we readily think, must have only had one purpose: to harm. As difficult as it might prove, documentation and research must serve to elevate such harms from negligence to wilful neglect, recklessness or intention, to attribute a harmful intention to the environments often taken as background.

Much critique aimed at intention can also be aimed at purpose. The element of purpose too ties torture to state functions, further distancing torture from that which is 'private' and enmeshing it closer to that which is viewed as 'public' (as false as this dichotomy proves in reality). Expressly codified into the universal definition are purposes including obtaining a confession or information, punishment, coercion and intimidation – and any other purposes 'as such'. These purposes, limited to situations where victims are under state control, are an indication of the incentives understood to prevail in the production of torture.[53] Given these connections, commentators have come to advance purpose as the most important differentiator between torture, inhuman and degrading treatment. It is to outright condemn

[51] *The Public Committee against Torture in Israel v. The State of Israel et al* (1999) HCJ 5100/94.

[52] Yuval Ginbar, '"Celebrating" a Decade of Legalised Torture in Israel' (2009) *Essex Human Rights Review* 173.

[53] Burgers and Danelius (1988) 120.

states for using excessive violence towards these anticipated ends. Simultaneously, commentators have also stressed that the element is broad, encompassing much and leaving out little (given readings of the 'as such' clause in the definition) – that it is 'difficult to envisage a realistic scenario of purposeful ill-treatment against a powerless person' that is excluded.[54]

What can be said to be excluded under purpose if anything? Despite the open-endedness, as coded into the term 'as such', obtaining confession or information is purpose *par excellence.* So could it be that observations, that have 'more than 90% of all cases of torture' consist of interrogational torture,[55] in fact reify what is imagined and looked for as purpose? Such statements are after all front and centre of the legal imagination of what torture *should* look like: interrogational and custodial. Adjudicators have, it can be said, proven relatively reticent to freely find purposes of coercion, humiliation and discrimination.[56] Whilst obtaining information or a confession, coercion, punishment and discrimination can never be legitimate purposes to inflict severe pain under the definition, the eminent doctrinal position views the arrest of a suspect, preventing a detainee from escaping, suppressing a riot or protest, self-defence and military force differently.[57]

That purpose follows unambiguous practical incentives, not those less explicable and evident, overlooks real complexities in how officials operate in their institutions. Say, although discriminatory treatment at the hands of the police on the street may be purpose enough, this may well be overlooked as the judicial gaze is preoccupied by narrowly trying to identify the dominant example of extracting a confession. Conversely, this may be a matter of evidence, as of imagination. It is those purposes vertically, proximately and explicitly connected to official actions (as expressed by perpetrators or readily inferred from the context of the interrogation room) that pave the way for a finding of purpose.

[54] UNSRT, Report (2017) A/72/178 [31].

[55] Ibid 34.

[56] Oette (2024) argues how discriminatory aspects of torture have been unduly understudied.

[57] Manfred Nowak, 'What Practices Constitute Torture? US and UN Standards' (2006) 28 (4) *Human Rights Quarterly* 821.

What about when state officials act outside of these purposes – out of boredom or gratification instead? Should these purposes not be traced back to the state? Should intentional official severe pain without a seeming purpose not attract the same condemnation as that with purpose? We can also read that *gratuitous* torture was rejected as an express purpose in UNCAT's drafting.[58] Adjudicators since, it can be reasonably argued, have struggled where an act is not readily proximate (i.e., clear, direct, explicit, rational or readily attributable) to a recognised purpose. The focus is again on the visible, uniform, police and prisons, with similar contexts (health, education and household) added later (though still not holding a prominent place in the imagination).

As with intention, context can also be key to proving purpose. If the Turkish police do not respond to a woman's repeated reports of her husband's death threats and she is ultimately murdered, can a purpose of discrimination be discerned from police inaction?[59] Statistics show that Turkish police have historically not been willing or able to adequately respond to domestic violence, nor were trained or funded by the Turkish government, despite well-established international obligations. Taking this into account, the European Court of Human Rights (ECtHR) did in fact find systemic discrimination in such a case. A discretion is revealed here on acting on context. In a series of subsequent cases,[60] statistics were said not to sufficiently prove systemic discrimination and that the systemic discrimination needed to be connected to the specific claim. In *Volodina v. Russia*, the same court seemed to have advanced the recognition once again by consolidating the jurisprudence towards finding a shifting the burden of proof 'once a large scale structural bias has been shown to exist ... the applicant does not need to prove that she was also a victim of individual prejudice'.[61] Contextualisation again proved crucial in foregrounding the broader discriminatory dynamics, leading to the victimisation and the finding of a purpose of discrimination.

58 Zach, 'Article 1. Definition of Torture' in Nowak et al (2019) 53–54. The use of psychiatry for prolonging confinement was also excluded in the drafting process.

59 *Opuz v. Turkey* [2009] ECtHR 33401/02.

60 *A v. Croatia* [2010] ECtHR 55164/08; *Eremia v. Moldova* [2013] ECtHR 3564/11; *Talpis v. Italy* [2017] ECtHR 41237/14.

61 *Volodina v. Russia* [2019] ECtHR 41261/17.

Intention and purpose are also closely related to a point of possible conflation, as both underscore the ends towards which the perpetrator is motivated. Intention can be differentiated as the *means* (i.e., the intention to inflict pain, a conscious, deliberate act to bring about an impact) for the pursued *end* of extracting a confession (aim, purpose, objective, rationale, desired result and consequence of the confession).[62] As with intention, purpose is not to 'involve a subjective inquiry into the motivations of the perpetrators, but rather must be objective determinations under the circumstances'.[63] This can be circumstantial and contextual but requires adjudicators to be so attentive. Whilst the authoritative commentary does not require that the perpetrator's intention be explicit, as this would disproportionately disadvantage victims, inferring intention from the circumstances or the context can nevertheless difficult to substantiate.

2.1.3 OFFICIAL AND LAWFUL. What of the requirement for official capacity? Does this extend beyond the state functionary in uniform? What about doctors in state hospitals, teachers in state schools, corporate-run prisons, armed fighters financed or guided by state authorities? The principled answer is that official capacity should also attach to those perpetrators working in any capacity with a clear connection to, control or consent of the state. This is captured by the unusual word 'acquiescence' as found in the definition of torture.[64] It is on this score, the definition's state-centricity, that torture necessarily requires a distinct connection to the state, which has led some commentators to argue that the definition has become partly outdated.[65]

Yet another stifled fact is that, whilst the absolute nature of the prohibition rules out explanations and excuses in principle, these conceivably find their way in through notions such as the 'lawful sanctions' and adjacent exclusions (namely, minimum level of severity, necessity and proportionality). These are not squarely admitted, particularly in the doctrinal 'law and torture' practice and research. These are left

62 Mendez and Nicolescu (2017) 244.

63 CAT, General Comment 2 (2008) [9].

64 Ibid 15.

65 Manfred Nowak, 'Can Private Actors Torture?' (2021) 19 *Journal of International Criminal Justice* 415, 419.

to the technicalities of legal interpretation. No additional guidance is expressly provided by the UNCAT as to how 'inherent', 'incidental' and 'lawful' are to be defined.[66] This has attracted occasional criticism and caution since the clause's codification as a 'monstrosity',[67] being 'rather vague and open'[68] and as presenting potentially a 'bypass'[69] or 'a serious loophole for governments'.[70] An authoritative commentary on the UNCAT argues that the lawful sanctions clause 'must simply be ignored' for lack of clarity.[71] This argument, however, is (for reasons unknown) not directed at severe pain, which too is widely held out as vague.[72] The 'lawful sanctions' clause is, I argue, a rather useful prism to view what states have not wanted to be included in torture's definition. The oft-cited example is the resistance advanced by Islamic countries in seeking to exclude their established practices of amputations and lashings sanctioned under sharia law.[73] It extends to much more.

[66] And more fundamentally, there is no reference point for what 'inherent' is. As the law has hardcoded CIS-men into its imagination, it is open to argue that 'inherent' might reflect those experiences overlooking others. I thank Grant Shubin for bringing this to my attention.

[67] Chris Ingelse, *UN Committee against Torture: An Assessment* (2001) 216.

[68] Chris Ingelse, 'The Committee against Torture: One Step Forward, One Step Back' (2000) 18 *Netherlands Quarterly of Human Rights* 307, 311.

[69] The records of the UN working group on the UNCAT also offer limited insights on the matter. UN Commission on Human Rights Draft Convention against Torture and Other Cruel, Inhuman or Degrading Treatment or Punishment, 'Report of the Working Group' E/CN.4/11367 (5 March 1980), *International Legal Materials*, May 1980, 19 (3), pp. 647–667: The UK representative, Anthony Williams, pointed out that 'to prevent the provisions of the convention from being bypassed, it should not exclude pain and suffering deriving from the use of lawful sanctions' (E/CN.4/1984/SR.33, 5 March 1984 [25]).

[70] Amnesty International, *Torture in the Eighties* (1984) 14.

[71] Nowak and McArthur (2008) 84.

[72] Two articles have examined that the 'lawful sanctions' clause do not offer a critical discussion: Celso Eduardo Faria Coracini, 'The Lawful Sanctions Clause in the State Reporting Procedure Before the Committee against Torture' (2006) 24 (2) *Netherlands Quarterly of Human Rights* 305–318; Anna Karapetyan, 'A Recurring Phenomenon: The Lawful Sanctions Clause in the Definition of Torture and the Question of Judicial Corporal Punishment under International Human Rights Law' (2016) 36 *Polish Yearbook of International Law* 137–161.

[73] Objections by Libya and Saudi Arabia to international criticism soon after the UNCAT came into effect have fuelled this imagination: E/CN.4/1987/13, p. 18: 'Libya informed the [SRT] that flogging and other forms of corporal punishment (like amputation) are established by the Holy Koran so that they form part of the religion and beliefs

In the drafting of the *European Convention on Human Rights,* Denmark argued that there be an explicit exclusion made for forced sterilisation, a practice it was inflicting on indigenous habitants of Greenland, as other Nordic countries were around the same time. Whilst not featuring on the face of the European prohibition of torture, a similar threshold was instantiated by the ECtHR through excluding harms that did not reach the 'minimum severity threshold', understood to be 'discomforts', 'inherent', 'incidental', 'inevitable' or 'unavoidable' in the nature of state practices. The notion of 'discomfort' also pervades domestic torture-related cases, serving as a logic to downgrade. The US Supreme Court has on one occasion ruled that 'the Constitution does not mandate comfortable prisons, and prisons ... persons convicted of serious crimes cannot be free of discomfort'.[74] Although left vague, what 'discomfort' meant was effectively associated with what was necessary or justified. This discussion is returned to in Chapter 4.

2.1.4 DISTINCTION. How does torture differ from the related categories of inhuman and degrading treatment? The UNCAT, importantly, defines and prohibits torture but does not define inhuman and degrading.[75] The *UN Body of Principles* on detention, on the other hand, offers additional clues. The debate on defining inhuman and degrading treatment during the drafting of the UNCAT was shifted to the drafting of these *Principles,*[76] which includes a general clause which deems that

of the population and therefore cannot be altered by deletion or attenuation or be replaced by other man-made penalties or by other internationally approved measures'; E/CN.4/1989/15, p. 18: 'When the [SRT] brought a specific case of flogging to the attention of [Saudi Arabia] and asked for its comment he received the reply that his interpretation of the international law *vis-a-vis* the sovereignty of a State Member of the UN and its judiciary system was entirely unacceptable and hence rejected. This reaction can only mean that according to Saudi Arabia a law sanction once it is recognized as lawful in a national system can never constitute torture'.

74 *Rhodes v. Chapman* (1981) 452 USSC 337.

75 The CAT has tried to avoid differentiating between them, holding that torture is often found with CIDT. Doing so, it has read obligations as explicitly attached to torture to cover CIDT.

76 Hans Danelius, 'The International Protection against Torture and Inhuman or Degrading Treatment or Punishment', in Frank Emmert (ed), *Collected Courses of the Academy of European Law / Recueil des cours de l'Académie de droit européen* (1993), writes that this was a move used in the drafting of the UNCAT.

> 'cruel, inhuman or degrading treatment or punishment' should be interpreted so as to extend the widest possible protection against abuses, whether physical or mental, including the holding of a detained or imprisoned person in conditions which deprive him, temporarily or permanently. of the use of any of his natural senses, such as sight or hearing, or of his awareness of place and the passing of time.[77]

The fuzziness of the distinction, or the 'constructive ambiguity' in avoiding clear delineations,[78] is held by some to broadly discourage states from approaching any category.[79] Overly focussing on *torture* as a category, in any case, is often argued to raise 'the risk of downplaying the significance of ill-treatment which does not cross the higher thresholds of seriousness, despite them all being absolutely prohibited'.[80] Put differently, reserving the harshest condemnation for torture can diminish, whether intended or not, the gravity of orbiting categories falling into 'the trap of thinking that something is "not so bad" because it is "only" inhuman. It is this which can result in the "grey zone" in which torture and ill-treatment can flourish' – though equally prohibited. An undue focus on torture has nevertheless played into a hierarchy as according to one prominent practitioner-academic:[81]

[77] *UN Body of Principles for the Protection of All Persons under Any Form of Detention or Imprisonment* (1988) GA res 43/173, General Clause: 'The term "cruel, inhuman or degrading treatment or punishment" should be interpreted so as to extend the widest possible protection against abuses, whether physical or mental, including the holding of a detained or imprisoned person in conditions which deprive him, temporarily or permanently. of the use of any of his natural senses, such as sight or hearing, or of his awareness of place and the passing of time'. Principle 21 (2) reads: 'No detained person while being interrogated shall be subject to violence, threats or methods of interrogation which impair his capacity of decision or his judgement'.

[78] Tobias Kelly, 'The UN Committee against Torture: Human Rights Monitoring and the Legal Recognition of Cruelty' (2009) 31 (3) *Human Rights Quarterly* 777, 790; see John T Parry '"Just for Fun": Understanding Torture and Understanding Abu Ghraib' (2005) 1 *Journal of National Security Law and Policy* 258: 'creating a separate category for an intentionally narrow set of practices labelled and banned as "torture" only functions to normalise and legitimate the remaining practices that are "not-torture"'.

[79] Evans (2002) 368.

[80] Evans (2023) 4.

[81] Ibid 187, 41.

> The problem is that we too often forget that this is so, or think that things 'falling short of torture', as we understand it, are somehow not so bad. They are *not* 'not so bad': they are just different – bad in a different way – and are just as prohibited. We probably meant to highlight just how terrible had been the treatment which we were describing as torture. And it is difficult to do this without conveying the impression that ill-treatment which is not being called out as torture is, somehow, less terrible, less noteworthy and, perhaps, less serious – whereas in truth what one wants to say is that both are terribly serious in their different ways. It is not a hierarchy. But we are all hierarchically minded, and if it is difficult to fight against this impulse in general, it is certainly difficult to fight against it when encountering the forms of ill-treatment that detainees can be subjected to. We want to highlight the worst we see. But it is vital that this is done in a way that does not reduce the focus on everything else that we see which is equally wrong.

Implicit in torture's exceptionality is the need for evidentiary certainty. That is, finding inhuman treatment 'can be made relatively swiftly and easily', 'whereas a finding of torture merits a more fulsome exploration'.[82] The same practitioner-academic has indicated that torture also dominates the prevention context despite the prohibition equally covering torture, inhuman and degrading, writing that:

> Rather than focus exclusively on the 'apex' which might be represented by the cruelty and barbarity of stigma-bearing purposive torture, there is every reason to focus heavily on the routine, mundane and often shockingly purposeless ill-treatment that characterises the experience of so many of those taken into detention but which, because their suffering is of a different order, tends not to attract the same levels of interest, attention or concern.[83]

Such ambiguity cannot be said to have been either constructive nor effective, as it is inhuman and degrading treatment that states commonly inflict and live with but not torture.[84] This vagueness and uncertainty is

[82] Ibid 35–36.

[83] Ibid 187.

[84] Related debates were foregrounded following the Bush Administration's narrow interpretations in downgrading as to legitimate its torturous practices in its so-called 'war on terror'; see Jeremy Waldron, *Torture, Terror, and Trade-Offs: Philosophy for the White House* (OUP 2010) 280.

problematic where, as another prominent scholar has argued, it offers 'insufficient guidance to potential victims or State authorities as to when force may be used'.[85]

If nothing else, the distinction has generated (and continues to generate) voluminous commentary – arguing as to which element, usually pain or purpose, works as the best differentiator between torture and its orbiting categories. Early understandings took the difference between the categories to pivot on pain – that torture required aggravated (or additional) pain compared to inhuman and compared to degrading. This was rationalised on the grounds that torture attracted a 'special stigma' and has been difficult to displace.[86] Pain proving problematic, leading commentators have attempted to shift the point of differentiation to purpose.[87] The most open-ended position is not to singularly pin differentiation on any one element.[88]

Simultaneously, it has become more expansive to hold all categories not as relative, despite shared commonalities, but as qualitatively different.[89] Representing 'connected yet distinctive' harms, all three categories are often found together in reality, 'capable of occurring in combination and independently'.[90] In principle, all categories are absolutely prohibited, which means that there is in fact no real need to draw 'sharp distinctions'.[91] That said, it is also true that certain authorities attach additional obligations for torture than inhuman and degrading

[85] Natasa Mavronicola, 'Güler and Öngel v Turkey: Article 3 of the European Convention on Human Rights and Strasbourg's Discourse on the Justified Use of Force' (2013) 76 (2) *Modern Law Review* 374.

[86] *Ireland v. UK* [1978] ECtHR 5856/72.

[87] Rodley (2002) 489; Evans (2002) 365.

[88] Amnesty International, *Combating Torture: A Manual for Action* (2016) 75–77.

[89] Elaine Webster, *Dignity, Degrading Treatment and Torture in Human Rights Law: The Ends of Article 3 of the European Convention on Human Rights* (Routledge 2018) 4, argues that the effect of referring to 'other forms of ill-treatment' when 'used habitually has been to mask the significance and independent scope of the other forms of treatment as integrated and influential parts of a whole'.

[90] Ibid 21.

[91] UN HRC, 'General Comment No. 20: Article 7' (1992) A/44/40 [4]: it is not 'necessary to draw up a list of prohibited acts or to establish sharp distinctions between the different kinds of punishment or treatment; the distinctions depend on the nature, purpose and severity of the treatment applied'.

treatment. Examining understandings around degradation often proves useful here. It has been accepted by some adjudicators as not strictly requiring severe pain, not requiring the humiliation (to which degradation is closely linked) caused to be more than subjective, and not requiring evidence in all circumstances beyond the testimony of the victim. In a prime example, two boys slapped on the face by the police were found to have been degraded.[92]

It might help the reader to also stay mindful that torture, inhuman and degrading treatment are not remote categories of violations, detached from all other prohibitions, rights and crimes. The physical and psychological integrity of the individual is protected by a whole host of rights, from criminal law assault to the right to privacy and the right to dignified treatment. Whilst such provisions might prioritise different contexts and anticipate a certain type of victim and violation, advocates and adjudicators enjoy a discretion in 'finding a fit'[93] for torturous harm under these related provisions instead.[94] I'll refrain from diving much deeper into this here – suffice as to say that this might lead to more 'sleight of hand' opportunities to downgrade or dismiss the torturous nature of a harm. Instead, I'll turn to the more common question of how the categories should be interpreted relatively as singularly – left open to allow legal actors to flex with emerging circumstances on a case-by-case basis. I do more to unpack this question of distinction in the discussion on the diktats and dynamics of interpretation.

2.2 DIKTATS AND DYNAMICS OF INTERPRETATION

> It is typically states but also actors within the anti-torture movement who are wary of broad interpretations that may weaken the status of the prohibition. ... This tension demonstrates that the prohibition does not

[92] *Bouyid v. Belgium* [2015] ECtHR [GC] 23380/09.

[93] *Taunoa v. Attorney-General* (2004) 7 HRNZ 379 where Young J reasons [274]: 'what happened [regarding the isolation regime] is naturally a better fit with s 23 than s 9'.

[94] By way of an example, the ECtHR has occasionally held psychological coercion by the police to better fit under Article 8 (right to private and family life) instead of Article 3 (prohibition of torture). Article 8 does not exude the same power as Article 3, as it is not absolute and is viewed by some requiring a lower threshold for pain. See, e.g., *Södermann v. Sweden* [2013] ECtHR 5786/08 [84].

> operate in isolation of wider developments in international human rights law. Indeed, it is this very tension that makes the prohibition so dynamic and contested.[95]

Torture, inhuman and degrading treatment are prohibited, absolutely. This means that their prohibition can see no exception, cannot be displaced, derogated, limited, suspended or justified. So, what to some may be to point out the obvious, it is solely the practices interpreted to fall afoul of the prohibition that enjoy this absolute protection.[96] To preserve the prohibition's effectiveness and relevance, the interpretation is expected to keep pace with emerging social understandings in informing state practices not simply on coercive measures but more broadly.[97] A prominent means this premise is given effect is through the doctrine of dynamic interpretation – through which international human rights law presents itself to be linearly, progressively, teleologically oriented, that it 'admits no steps backward'.[98] It has been formulated as rendering legal instruments as 'living' or as 'evolving', and as such needing to be 'interpreted in the light of present-day conditions',[99] to 'consider the changes over time'.[100] Dynamic interpretation of torture's absolute prohibition too articulates a progressive vision, a continuous capture of emergent harms towards broadening protection. It tasks adjudicators

95 Oette (2024) 5.

96 Mavronicola (2021).

97 E.g., on assisted death, abortion, age of criminal responsibility and marriage equality.

98 A.A.C. Trindade, 'Universal Declaration of Human Rights' (UN Audiovisual Library of International Law 2008) 1.

99 *Tyrer v. UK* [1978] ECtHR 5856/72 [31]; Ed Bates, *The Evolution of the European Convention on Human Rights: From Its Inception to the Creation of a Permanent Court of Human Rights* (OUP 2010) 328; *Roger Judge v. Canada*, CCPR/C/78/D/829/1998, 13 August 2003 [10.3].

100 *Right to Information on Consular Assistance in the Framework of the Guarantees of the Due Process of Law, Mexico v. United States* [1999] IACtHR Advisory Opinion OC-16/99, Series A No 16 [114]; see also IACtHR, Advisory Opinion OC-10/89, *Interpretation of the American Declaration of the Rights and Duties of Man*, of 14 July 1989, Series A, n. 10, p. 45 [37]: 'the Court finds it necessary to point out that to determine the legal status of the American Declaration it is appropriate to look to the inter-American system of today in the light of the evolution it has undergone since the adoption of the Declaration, rather than to examine the normative value and significance which that instrument was believed to have had in 1948'.

to consider and respond to 'evolving threats, issues, and practices'[101] and that 'certain acts which were classified in the past as "inhuman and degrading treatment" as opposed to "torture" could be classified differently in future'.[102] The connection between expressions of social values informing excesses of state violence is widely accepted – in practice as research.[103]

At its core, dynamic interpretation is principally a historical exercise, of identifying improvements and advances over time, presented in principle as simultaneously sociocultural as legal, distilled as 'time and change'.[104] It is held to be an exercise involving 'the marrying of past [intentions] and present [purposes] in treaty interpretation' or as concerning 'all shades of casting away or reducing the original or historical meaning attached to a norm in favour of a contemporary reading, i.e., a reading and understanding at the time the interpretation is

101 CAT, General Comment No. 2, CAT/C/GC/2 (2007) [1]; CAT, *Ahmed Harun v. Switzerland*, CAT/C/65/D/758/2016, dissent [4–6]; UN SRT, Report (2020) A/HRC/43/49 [12].

102 *Selmouni v. France* [1999] ECtHR 5803/94 [101]; *R. v. Secretary of State for Health ex p Quintavalle* [2003] UKHL 13 [9] (Bingham), [21–23] (Steyn): the 'meaning of "cruel and unusual punishments" has not changed over the years since 1689, but many punishments which were not then thought to fall within that category would now be held to do so'.

103 *Trop v. Dulles* (1958, p. 101), which concerned the denationalisation of an individual as punishment for desertion, the US Supreme Court (USSC) held that determinations of cruel and unusual punishment must draw their meaning from 'the evolving standards of decency that mark the progress of a maturing society [and] judged not by the standards that prevailed in 1685 [or] when the Bill of Rights was adopted, but rather by those that currently prevail'; 'broad and idealistic concepts of dignity, civilised standards, humanity and decency' (*Estelle v. Gamble* 429 US 97 (1976) at 102–103), 'must be informed by current and enlightened scientific opinion as to the conditions necessary to insure good physical and mental health for prisoners' (*Spain v Procunier* 600 F 2d 189 (1979) 200 [15]), 'whether the punishment prescribed is so excessive as to outrage standards of decency' (*R v Smith* [1987] 1 SCR 1045 [54]), 'without penological justification' (*Gregg v Georgia* (1976) 428 US 153 at 183), characterised 'by contemporary standards of decency' (*Taunoa v Attorney-General* [2007] NZSC 70 at 101); see further on link between national and international law, Eirik Bjorge, 'The Convention as a Living Instrument: Rooted in the Past, Looking to the Future' (2017) 36 (7–12) *Human Rights Law Journal* 243–255.

104 Robert Kolb, 'Evolutionary Interpretation in International Law: Some Short and Less Than Trail-Blazing Reflections' in Georges Abi-Saab et al (eds), *Evolutionary Interpretation and International Law* (Hart 2019) 15.

undertaken'.[105] The notion of 'effectiveness' is also invoked here, required to 'avoid the petrification or stultification of key areas of fundamental rights and freedoms' and 'to adapt to the constant and often dramatic societal changes that have occurred since the instrument was first drafted'.[106] Whilst the logics of 'progress' and 'effectiveness' are found in much of the scholarship in this area, its treatment has been predominantly legal and only loosely social, unpredictably regressive as expansive, and subject to judicial discretion.[107] I take a step or two back in explaining what I mean.

Doctrines, such as dynamic interpretation, afford the law the 'extraordinary elasticity' to adapt to circumstances not originally foreseen.[108] Legal interpretation anticipates and functionalises textual generality in words like 'reasonable', 'negligent', 'unjust' and 'significant', which often 'depend to some extent upon principles or policies lying beyond the rule'.[109] A degree of indeterminacy is doctrinally recognised as inherent in legal rules and precepts. Law, after all, brings together 'certainty and uncertainty, the determinate and what is beyond determination'.[110] In this light, terms such as 'living instrument' and 'present-day attitudes' may be looked upon as necessary phenomenological truncations, by-words and aids for law to sense and feel towards enabling a wider epistemic and empathetic field of vision. Such interpretive elasticity also enables adjudicators to act outside 'law and reason', 'neither as an interpreter meticulously and faithfully applying the rule … nor as a logician bound by the deductive rigor of his "method of realization"'.[111] Accounting for any

[105] Ibid 16.

[106] Nicholas Bratza, 'Living Instrument or Dead Letter: The Future of the European Convention on Human Rights' (2014) *European Human Rights Law Review* 116.

[107] Tulkens (2022) 293: 'the ECtHR ranges between tradition and progress, between protection and the development of human rights, between flexibility and legal certainty'; Fuad Zarbiyev, 'Judicial Activism in International Law – A Conceptual Framework for Analysis' (2012) 3(2) *Journal of International Dispute Settlement* 247: 'As practice shows, recourse to the "object-and-purpose" argument does not necessarily lead to an extensive interpretation. In the same vein, the use of *travaux préparatoires* does not necessarily amount to a conservative interpretation'.

[108] Pierre Bourdieu, 'The Force of Law: Toward a Sociology of the Juridical Field' (1987) 38 *Hastings Law Journal* 814, 827.

[109] Ronald Dworkin, *Taking Rights Seriously* (Duckworth 1977) 27–28.

[110] Peter Fitzpatrick, *The Mythology of Modern Law* (Routledge 1999) 119.

[111] Bourdieu (1987) 827.

anomalies or divergences from the 'correctness' is the notion of 'partial autonomy' (or discretion) enjoyed by actors.[112] This might conceivably lead to a means-to-ends-driven reasoning, where meaning is settled, imposed through power and cloaked in legal devices to exude authority. This discretion is evident in the selection of precedents available to actors, who 'can choose the one most suited to a particular result' and 'to manipulate legal aspirations – to create them in certain cases, to amplify them or discourage them in others'.[113] As such, the law swings between 'flexibility and legal certainty' in realising its ends[114] – arguably questionably.

This is not to say that indeterminacies don't conceptually challenge law and its modes of categorical certitude and recognition. To be sure, the law has a proclivity to hold what is familiar as legible and the new or irregular as illegible. Complexities can vex the law. Foucault's figure of the 'monster' – shorthand for the radically different or unrecognisable subject – lends some theoretical support here. Through the 'monster', Foucault contends that a profound irregularity creates anxiety and 'calls law into question and disables it'[115] because 'it is a legal labyrinth, a violation of and an obstacle to the law, both transgression and undecidability at the level of the law'.[116] Ultimately, he argues, the nature of law is fundamentally called into question and, as such, the '[l]aw must either question its own foundations, or its practice, or fall silent, or abdicate, or appeal to another reference system, or again invent a casuistry'.[117] Some suffering at the hands of the state, like the practice of 'voluntary' isolation in prisons, can be readily invoked here.

Scholarship on legal interpretation anticipates and functionalises textual generality but also rejects too much indeterminacy. The scholarship is split between, on the one hand, holding vagueness as constructively

112 Ibid 826–827. Bourdieu calls this 'partial autonomy … the best measure of his position in the structure of distribution of juridical authority's specific capital'.

113 Ibid 833.

114 Francoise Tulkens, 'Judicial Activism v Judicial Restraint: Practical Experience of This (False) Dilemma at the European Court of Human Rights' (2022) 3 *European Convention on Human Rights Law Review* 293.

115 Michel Foucault, *Abnormal: Lectures at the Collège de France, 1974–1975* (Picador 2003) 64. See also Andrew N Sharpe, *Foucault's Monsters and the Challenge of Law* (Routledge 2010).

116 Ibid 65.

117 Ibid 64.

facilitating the necessary ambivalence to prevent illegal behaviour and the flexibility to deliberate factual scenarios where precise legislation is impossible, and, on the other hand, arguing that these assumptions are overestimated.[118] The law's vagueness is explained as a necessary consequence of its irreducibility (or 'incommensurate multidimensionality' beyond ordering one or more of its dimensions but not its totality).[119] So far, legal indeterminacy, in whichever area of law, looks to be as good as our belief in law's ability to recognise and redress harms.

Caught up in these more general currents of legal interpretation, consistency and specificity in the anti-torture jurisprudence have proven to be in short supply. An indeterminacy has long prevailed in interpreting 'cruel', 'inhuman' and 'degrading' forms of treatment. Each of these words is contestable, given how they each embody 'a normative standard [allowing] different users [to] disagree about the detailed contents of that normative standard'.[120] This account also charges a lack of depth in interpretation, as '[n]o one spends much time reflecting on the predicates that are incorporated' in 'inhuman' and 'degrading'.[121] The blurring between these words has at times been contently perpetuated as erring towards flexibility, 'constructive ambiguity', and at others problematised as among other things lacking sufficient and coherent legal reasoning. A generous doctrinal explanation has it that: 'this is probably inevitable given the intentionally broad scope of the prohibition, the somewhat subjective nature of some forms of suffering, the upward evolution of social expectations over time, and a reluctance by institutions to tie themselves too closely to a set formula given the creativity of authorities in improvising abuses in particular situations'.[122] Glaring inadequacies do abound but are entrusted to dynamic interpretation towards a collaborative reconfiguration in recognising and reacting to changes in the social order – a discussion returned to in Chapter 3.

118 Hrafn Asgeirsson, *The Nature and Value of Vagueness in the Law* (Hart 2020) 1–3.

119 Ibid 2.

120 Jeremy Waldron, 'Vagueness in Law and Language: Some Philosophical Issues' (1994) 82 *California Law Review* 509.

121 Waldron (2010) 287.

122 Nigel Rodley and Matthew Pollard, *The Treatment of Prisoners under International Law* (3rd ed, OUP 2009) 131.

2.3 DISCONTENTS: CONTEXTS AND CONDITIONS

> The Court's unduly narrow definition of punishment blinds it to the reality of prison life ... Where a legislature refuses to fund a prison adequately, the resulting barbaric conditions should not be immune from constitutional scrutiny simply because no prison official acted culpably.[123]

> [L]aw might hold up the promise of clarity, precision and enforcement, but also creates its own limits, abstracting us from the complex ways in which torture is inflicted and experienced on the ground. In doing so, it can bracket torture off from the wider forms of violence within which it is embedded, and thereby limit our ability to understand the causes and consequences of torture.[124]

Torture, inhuman and degrading treatment, as already alluded to, can only be defined with reference to broader framings of sociocultural-political belief and power. To talk about torture is 'not just to talk about pain but to enter into a complex discourse of morality, legality and politics'.[125] Torture's definition, given all its interpretive contingency, has been called a 'universal template' onto which disparate and complex experiences need to be 'fitted'[126] – rendering its use 'unpredictable and erratic' and therefore 'arbitrary'. These interpretive practices 'shape and produce, rather than simply distort, understandings of suffering'.[127] With practitioners coming to insist that for 'a legal violation, there must be a victim, a perpetrator and a remedy',[128] what prevails is individuation and disconnection between actors and factors producing torture. Doctrinal cues force the field to think about the phenomena as discrete categories as constituted by certain elements for the sake of process, which 'erases the overlapping, entangled, and

[123] *Farmer v. Brennan* (1994) 511 USSC 825 per Justice Harry Blackmun.

[124] Kelly (2019) 329.

[125] Stanley Cohen, 'Talking about Torture in Israel' (1991) 6 *Tikkun* 23.

[126] Kelly (2014) 144–158.

[127] Ibid 144.

[128] Kelly (2012) 13; Kenneth Roth, 'Defending Economic Social and Cultural Rights: Practical Issues Faced by an International Human Rights Organization' (2004) 26 *Human Rights Quarterly* 63, has it as 'violation, violator, and remedy'.

messy practice of violence' – particularly how 'torture is practiced and embodied'.[129]

Let's take intention as an example. When combined with evidentiary expedience sought by advocates and adjudicators, intention trains attention on the direct, deliberately decided or desired, explicit and away from circumstantial (indirect, resulting from recklessness, intangible and intrinsic) factors, although equally important for a rendering of intention. The circumstantial can be thought of as consisting of *material* (resourcing as to encourage or discourage), *situational* (provoking, pressuring or providing opportunities) and *ideological* (institutional inscriptions or culture) cues to inflict torturous harm.[130] The element of intention, as other devices, works to obfuscate these complex factors and to isolate individuals from their institutions, untenably placing the institutional logics, conditions and controls beyond doctrinal brackets. Whilst many cases 'downgrade' the wrongfulness of an act from torture to another category based on a lack of intention, a similar logic has also been evident in further downgrading ill-treatment to a non-violation based on a lack of intention.[131] To put this more pithily, 'when intention is built into a legal definition, not finding it is one important way of making responsibility disappear'.[132]

The element of purpose too narrows our imagination of the torturer's motivations, who is also simultaneously conceived as sadistic and a bad apple serving personal motive. This broader reading takes torture's 'essence' as being 'the deliberate instrumentalization of the pain or suffering inflicted on a powerless person as a vehicle for achieving

[129] Caitlin Biddolph, 'Queering Crimes of Torture: A (Re)imagining of Torture in International Criminal Tribunal for the Former Yugoslavia Jurisprudence' (2021) 27 (2) *Australian Journal of Human Rights* 382, 382.

[130] Jonathan Luke Austin and Riccardo Bocco, 'Becoming a Torturer: Towards a Global Ergonomics of Care' (2016) 98 (3) *International Review of the Red Cross* 859–88.

[131] Mavronicola (2021) 136, 89, analyses the words 'treatment' and 'subjected' (as used in Article 3) as conceivably indicating direct rather than structural orientations. She uses *Tanase v. Romania* [2009] ECtHR 62954/00 [123] as a case study of undue emphasis on intentionality, where the ECtHR held that 'bodily injuries and physical and mental suffering experienced by an individual following an accident which is merely the result of chance or negligent conduct cannot be considered as the consequence of "treatment" to which that individual has been "subjected" within the meaning of Article 3'.

[132] Veitch (2007) 108.

a particular purpose, *even if exclusively for the sadistic gratification of the perpetrator*'.[133] 'Gratuitous' is defined as '[d]one, made, adopted, or assumed without any good ground or reason; not required or warranted by the circumstances of the case; uncalled-for; unjustifiable'.[134] Whilst this is oversimplified *purely* as sadism or psychopathy, it is not so clear-cut. Again, although it denotes a total absence of reason, accounting for institutional conditioning, it could alternatively be understood as 'low on expressive and instrumental motivations'.[135] Remote though it may be from the expressed purposes, it is incumbent on adjudicators to assess how dis/connected a given instance of gratuitous violence is from state function.

The dominant conventional position by way of such disconnections ignores the fact that we all work in institutions. Individuals, especially those working within and through bureaucracies, are deeply embedded and come to embody as resist their institutions. The exclusion of personal or gratuitous violence from the prohibition's purview is a prime example of how law takes its functionaries to be unconditioned,[136] abstracting the individual official from institutional incentives. In other words, state institutions are not associated with incentives such as 'peer pressure, competitive brutality, gendered self-images of toughness, deskilling effects of overreliance of violence … career advancement'.[137] What about 'the maintenance of public order, control of racial, ethnic, and religious minorities, and – critically – domination for the sake of domination (or, if you prefer, for the sake of power)'?[138] Tedium, survival, conformity – it might be that these are also entangled with personal initiative. Yet this 'does not necessarily remove it from the category of crimes of obedience'[139] as long as 'the action is supported by the

[133] UNSRT, Report (2017) A/72/178 [31], my emphasis.

[134] Oxford English Dictionary.

[135] David Bruce, 'Anger, Hatred, or Just Heartlessness? Defining Gratuitous Violence' (2010) 34 *South African Crime Quarterly* 13.

[136] Judith Butler, *Precarious Life: The Powers of Mourning and Violence* (Verso 2004) 66.

[137] Darius Rejali, 'The Field of Torture Today' in Steven Barela et al (eds), *Interrogation and Torture* (OUP 2020) 85.

[138] Parry, 'Just for fun' (2005) 275.

[139] H. C. Kelman and V. L. Hamilton, *Crimes of Obedience: Toward a Social Psychology of Authority and Responsibility* (Yale University Press 1989) 50.

authority structure: as long as the perpetrators believe and have good reason to believe that the action is authorized, expected, at least tolerated, and probably approved by the authorities'.[140] Whilst, according to social scientists, purpose could be presumed from the very nature of state function, implicit in the relational and situational aspects of official duty, this is rejected through doctrinal disconnections between the specific and systemic, individuals and institutions.

Individuals thus do not naturally emerge as or arrive at being predisposed to harming others but are actively (and tacitly) co-opted, compelled, directed, regulated, produced and ultimately come to embody the situational (institutional, social, cultural and political) dynamics in which they are embedded. The state apparatus implements 'policy decisions even as they fragment or eliminate responsibility for them [through which decisions] to impose harsh conditions are made clear in a variety of ways to officials or soldiers on the ground even as responsibility or authorship of those decisions dissipates'.[141] Accordingly, from a bottom-up perspective, the actions of 'street-level' officials (such as police or prison staff) can come to be viewed as inextricably dictated by the state-controlled conditions, settings and framings (material or otherwise) in which they are called to work.

Questioning the element of 'official capacity' more critically similarly serves to unravel doctrine's deceptive simplicity. The key critique has been that characterising any form of violence as private serves to conceal its fit under the definition. Social scientists to have asked who counts as a public official, problematising the self-evident legal conceptualisations, especially in weaker states, find that public authority:[142]

> can be embedded in very different political, economic, and cultural processes that create different forms of legitimacy, different boundaries between the private and the public, and different relationships with the

[140] H. C. Kelman, 'The Policy Context of Torture: A Social-Psychological Analysis' (2005) 87 (857) *International Review of the Red Cross* 126–127.

[141] Parry, 'Just for fun' (2005) 276.

[142] Zahid ul Arefin Choudhury et al, 'Counting Torture: Towards the Translation of Robust, Useful, and Inclusive Human Rights Indicators' (2018) 36 (2) *Nordic Journal of Human Rights* 132–150, 144.

> deployment of violence amongst other things. What counts as a public official can therefore never be taken for granted, either normatively or empirically. Public authority is not a yes/no binary distinction, but a spectrum, with ebbs and flows of intensity and meaning over both time and space. The production and interpretation of indicators around the involvement of public officials therefore need to take into account the slippery nature of public authority.

A fuller understanding of how state violence is produced requires that these narrow conceptualisations be explicated and empirical connections between the individual and institutional be retained – from political to operational decisions as to designing, resourcing and running coercive practices (particularly police and prisons). Disconnecting and distancing specific acts from systemic factors fosters impoverished understandings, serving to delimit agency and to compartmentalise responsibility. It obscures the chains of action and inaction in the infliction of state violence, aiding legitimation. Torture, we know, can be inflicted in any interaction with state – from street to station (so not simply interrogation, though this is central to our imagination). Torture can be slowly, routinely, undramatically inflicted – as opposed to the oft-imagined spectacle. There may be no 'THE torturer', given the 'complex institutional and social relationship(s)' of the state through which torture is instigated and inflicted.[143] Dichotomous understandings of 'personal conduct – easily condemned as perverse, immoral, or disgusting – and the proper, upright conduct of the normal state actor' thus stand to be rejected, for the state co-opts or defines 'our emotions, passions, and perversions, so that a guard who, seemingly on a personal, sadistic whim, strips a prisoner naked and puts him on a leash to be photographed in a position of subservience, simultaneously channels the sovereign power of the state'.[144] There is a complexity to such violence that the law is driven to manage and evade. Exceptions in looking more broadly at context do exist but arguably serve to confirm the norm.

[143] Darius Rejali, 'Ordinary Betrayals: Conceptualizing Refugees Who Have Been Tortured in the Global Village' (2000) 1 (4) *Human Rights Review* 8–25, 9.

[144] Parry, 'Just for fun' (2005) 281.

A more ecological approach, situating the act and actor in their institution, would infer intention from institutional craft, nature and structure, finding it to be implicit and complicit. This shift would have fundamental repercussions for readings as follows:[145]

> Rather than individual discrete acts that might be dismissed as ill-considered, inadvertent, or episodic, institutional settings are by definition configured and arranged environments that their creators have envisioned, implemented, preserved, and chosen not to make more benign. The level of foresight and premeditation required to create such an environment, the level of ongoing knowledge about what transpires inside it, and the willingness to tolerate the negative effects it inflicts on others seem to us to collectively moot the question of whether or not the painful and potentially damaging consequences are 'intended'.

Problematic distinctions emerge between the specific and systematic, the individual and their institution, their agency and structure. This is true in torture's production as much as it is in its interpretation. It is also important to note here that interpretive practices take place between a constellation of actors. It is controlled, contested and configured, not simply naturally or organically occurring. Whilst the authority is conventionally ascribed to judges or their institution as correctly applying the law to a specific case, numerous actors and their material and ideational positions are instrumental in this process. That is, whilst legal decision-makers are conventionally attributed with the central authority in these exercises, what is occasionally overlooked is how they are dependent on a web of a multiplicity of actors such as registry staff and litigating lawyers. Although institutional actors are dependent on external arguments and evidence, the practice and research lack a sensitivity to how institutional actors are variably dependent on such factors. This conceptualising intertwines responsibility with temporality and proximity. That solely those immediately proximate to the victim are understood to be involved in the production and perpetration of torture

[145] Craig Haney and Shirin Bakhshay, 'Contexts of Ill-Treatment: The Relationship of Captivity and Prison Confinement to Cruel, Inhuman, or Degrading Treatment and Torture' 139–78 in Başoğlu (2017) 143.

reveals this blinkered view to be the norm. This is a scenario entertained by the more critical scholarship.[146]

With exceptions aside, doctrine has not tended wholeheartedly to the connections which appear between acts and actors. Connections can be more precisely traced from the community (who may dehumanise and demonise a particular group of the population) to the parliament (who may not allocate sufficient resources to inhibit violence) to the judge (who doesn't think twice about sending an accused to a notorious detention centre) to the police (who may turn a blind eye to torturous practices) and to the very infliction of the torturous harm itself. Knowledge of torturous practices at the hands of the police or prisons does not stop at the court door. Where there is such knowledge, complicity should conceivably flow from official passivity (inaction or disregard). That is to say, those with the discretionary power to divert a potential victim away from such conditions, whether a prosecutor or adjudicator, bear a shared responsibility for any harm ultimately inflicted.

Doctrinal approaches rather prefer to characterise torture as exceptional and aberrational events, as antithetical to the law, caused instead by dysfunctional individuals. Some of this is partly because human rights practice has generally tended to address rights in silos than as interconnected and interdependent – distancing right from right. This has started to change, with a few scholars tending to certain torture's growth conditions such as corruption and poverty,[147] admitting to the limits of doctrine as:[148]

> the very focus on legal interventions, with its underlying faith in the law and legal systems, may fail to tackle structural factors perpetuating violations and impunity, such as inequalities, discrimination and weak or

146 Patricia M. Wald, 'Violence under the Law: A Judge's Perspective' in Austin Sarat and Thomas Kearns (eds), *Law's Violence* (University of Michigan Press 1993) 86: 'when trial judges are presented with evidence of prison conditions that fall markedly below professionally endorsed standards for humane confinement, they should be able to mandate the correction of these conditions, on constitutional grounds if necessary'.

147 Lutz Oette, 'The Prohibition of Torture and Persons Living in Poverty: From the Margins to the Centre' (2021) 70 (2) *International and Comparative Law Quarterly* 307.

148 Lutz Oette, 'Implementing the Prohibition of Torture: The Contribution and Limits of National Legislation and Jurisprudence' (2012) 16 *The International Journal of Human Rights* 717.

> corrupted institutions. Approaches relying predominantly on legal tools must therefore be mindful of their inherent limitations and consider what complementary strategies are likely to make the prohibition of torture more effective.

Speaking even more critically to the status quo of 'law and torture', another critically oriented scholar has advanced a more limited role for law:[149]

> There is a sense that the more complex the law, the more legal game-playing is made possible, and the more the argument shifts towards legal technicalities and away from the causes and consequences of acts of torture. We can keep tinkering with a legal regime, making its provisions more complex, but there comes a point when this becomes counterproductive, if it fails also to take into account the political context within which torture takes place. The point here is not that law is ineffectual, but that it can be effective in unexpected ways. More law does not lead to less violence, and legal regimes, even liberal legal regimes, have historically played an important role in legitimating particular forms of violence.

It is reasonable to say that torture's definition and prohibition say nothing of its practice and production, nothing on its individual and societal impacts. The prohibition fares worse, leaving us 'to proceed on the theory that "we know it when we see it", or that we can recognize this evil using a sort of visceral "puke" test'.[150] Scholars must do more to go beyond doctrine in identifying an individual violator or violation of the prohibition – but rather explicate and explain the sustaining structural frames. As put by another critical scholar, until we do that we will continue to:[151]

> make arguments that are really quite beside the point. We are arguing about the definition of torture (When do we move from 'rough interrogation' to torture?), the usefulness of torture (Does it yield important information?), the political morality of torture (Must we be utilitarians in our political judgments?), and the procedures for torture (Can we juridify torture?).

149 Kelly (2019) 329.
150 Waldron (2005) 1695.
151 Kahn (2008) 11.

These points raise complex questions over how the institutional escapes legal attention. Where is torture thought to occur and under what conditions is it produced? There is nothing concrete on the face of the definition except connection to official capacity. Whilst the emphasis on the institutional may serve to invisibilise the individual, it is ultimately the institution that is the more powerful and thus responsible for the acts of its agents. What is practiced in reality by state agents, whatever the formal policy, is what should come to matter as official, 'the routines they establish, and the devices they invent to cope with uncertainties and work pressures, effectively become the public policies they carry out'.[152] To not adequately resource the law enforcement apparatus to implement a formal policy, for instance, might lead to unreasonable pressures, in light of which certain 'coping mechanisms' might arise. These 'mechanisms' often represent the violent excesses of the state. Whilst there is clearly a danger to downplay the agency of the individual in all this, the opposite has largely been true in torture's prevention and accountability paradigms. Individuals have been abstracted out of their institutions, disaggregated from the chains of complicity in torture's production. Being more receptive to structural conditioning of officials promises to enhance understandings not distort them into apologia. How can doctrinal legal practice and research be reconciled with approaches normally excluded? In the rest of the book, I aim to take first steps.

2.4 CONCLUSION

> [T]orture as a term is a place holder – an abstract word made concrete by the imagination of the reader.[153]

The prohibition of torture, inhuman and degrading treatment is presented as a benevolent institution in its absolute nature, malleable and perfectible through the dynamism of legal actors, functioning solely to combat torture held out as an exceptional aberration. This has served to

[152] Michael Lipsky, *Street-Level Bureaucracy: Dilemmas of the Individual in Public Services* (Sage 1980) xiii.

[153] Sanford Levinson (ed), *Torture: A Collection* (OUP 2004) 27.

depict an archetypal picture of perpetration, drawing torture closer to intentional positive direct actions causing severe harm by state-sponsored actors for a state-centric purpose, as it distances and disconnects harm that which is accepted as central to law enforcement. Doctrinal devices (categories, elements and thresholds) have served to include as much as to exclude, to disconnect, the specific from the systematic, to clarify as to obfuscate the prohibited and permissible. These are variably grounded upon how suffering is *imagined* (linguistically, temporally and spatially perceived and conceived) and *evidenced* (reasoned and substantiated through sense, experience and medical evidence) on the backdrop of broader societal and legal policy considerations (fear of floodgates, resilience and social attitudes). More elements mean more facts to establish, proving increasing burdens and barriers for the victim-survivor.

The doctrine, as canvassed, exudes four distinct traits, which stand to be reconsidered: *definition-centricity* (dominant focus on definitions, distinctions and standards), *adjudication-fixity* (accepting legal processes as the prime site for making sense of torture), *act-specificity* (requiring contained events, victims and perpetrators) and *context-reductivity* (not duly tending to the growth conditions and the broader social, cultural and political aspects). A crucial question stands: if my characterisation holds true, then how do I explain the expansive recognition offered by doctrine? I have met this question, of whether I am not blinded by angst, before: doctrine can only do so much. Yes, I admit to be angst-driven and I have in and following such engagements with doctrinal advocates and adjudicators felt empathetic to the difficulty of their position: that processual and contextual factors were also against them – restraining and conditioning their actions. In all, I return to their individual and institutional discretion to do things differently. This explains the extent to which I have drawn on dissenting opinions where these alternative positions are presented, particularly on the progressive roads not taken.

Framings of a violation of the prohibition, it emerges from this discussion, pivot on a multitude of factors and conditions and the often-oblique process of contestation engenders 'multilayered and often contradictory forms of knowledge about suffering and cruelty'.[154] I will leave others

[154] Kelly (2012) 6.

to discuss the broader (though equally) pressing questions as arising here: Does vagueness operate as a means of protecting juridical capital (keeping advocates and adjudicators in positions of symbolic power production) or as genuinely an acknowledgment of complexity? To what extent is it reasonable to embrace law's ambivalences and indeterminacies? Chapter 3 will instead ask the more pointed questions: 'How can judges identify and reflect the changing views of society when interpreting rights provisions' particularly relating to torturous suffering?[155] How progressive has the interpretation of torture been?

[155] See also Kanstantsin Dzehtsiarou and Conor O'Mahony, 'Evolutive Interpretation of Rights Provisions: A Comparison of the European Court of Human Rights and the U.S. Supreme Court' (2013) 44 *Columbia Human Rights Law Review* 309.

CHAPTER 3

Progressive Impulses

LITTLE DID I KNOW HOW THE SEEDS of disillusionment were being planted in my first days in the field. I was brought in to assist in organising a conference on solitary confinement, consisting of international experts, speaking to the Danish context, where its punitive uses in prison were on the increase. The evidence of the harms inflicted by the practice were incontrovertible. It had even informed the then recently adopted UN Nelson Mandela Rules. Nelson Mandela, no less! The event was a success, much went as expected, prison authorities and policymakers all turned up, genuinely engaged and seemed to react well to the expertise on offer. All transpired as expected, except that nothing changed in the reality of the prisoners in question. The representations made to those in power were given the short shrift. Political considerations, namely tough on crime impulses, overruled. The illusion of progress would take me a step closer to disillusionment. At the end of my first year in the anti-torture field, I asked myself whether I could say that I had prevented a single case of torture. For all the trainings and travels, I could not convincingly tell myself that I had. Whenever I dared to utter these misgivings (which would years later lead to a point of despair), I was met with the figure of the longue durée: that these things took time and that they required a degree of patience.

***

> For a discipline which routinely talks in terms of precedent and prides itself on its long history, the law gives a curiously ahistorical account of itself. Scientists have fashioned their own history likewise, suggesting an unbroken and unproblematic progression from one stage to the next. More than this, their histories project an inevitable progression towards greater and greater rationality.[1]

[1] Carol Jones, *Expert Witnesses: Science, Medicine and the Practice of Law* (1994) 12.

Bulgaria imposed a moratorium on its death penalty in 1990 and, following regular albeit unpredictable public debate, abolished the practice in 1998. Those who were sentenced to and awaiting their death in this period received commutations to life without parole following abolition. Despite its eventual realisation, the abolition of the death penalty remained questioned amongst the public and death row prisoners. And despite the abolition, two death-row-turned-life-without-parole prisoners brought cases against Bulgaria before the European Court of Human Rights (ECtHR), arguing that the long time spent in uncertainty and their detention conditions violated the prohibition of torture. Bulgaria responded with arguments based on time – that progress had been afoot but that it had taken time. In both cases, Bulgaria sought to explain that 'the delay between the moratorium on executions in 1990 and the final abolition of the death penalty in 1998 had been inevitable as the public debate and the evolution of societal attitudes had required time'.[2] The cases connected time and suffering, begging two questions: Should abolition have taken so long?[3] What did this wait mean for the two applicant prisoners?

In separate but mirroring decisions, the Court accepted that 'present-day attitudes in the Contracting States to capital punishment are relevant for the assessment whether the acceptable threshold of suffering or degradation has been exceeded'.[4] Yet, the Court was not drawn in on Bulgaria's 'these things take time' line, preferring another argument based on the passage of time in dismissing the applicants' suffering in awaiting their deaths. The Court, in both cases, assessed that 'initially the applicant must have been in a state of some uncertainty, fear and anxiety as to his future [but that] must have diminished as time went on and as the moratorium continued in force'.[5] Much is read into time here from all sides, the applicants, adjudicators and the state advocate: that

[2] *G.B. v. Bulgaria* [2004] ECtHR 42346/98 [67]; *Iorgov v. Bulgaria* [2004] ECtHR 40653/98 [67].

[3] The more fundamental question, as raised by Mattia Pinto as some of the discussion in this book, is perhaps: 'Are we satisfying ourselves by abolishing things in the law, while we keep them alive by other means (or secretly)?'

[4] *G.B* and *Iorgov* 72.

[5] Ibid 80, a violation of Article 3 was, however, found on the detention conditions.

suffering is made sense of through time, that suffering once intense can abate, that such intensity is shaped by time and place and that progress necessarily takes time. It is the final point from which the discussion at hand departs.

Dominant narratives of international human rights law, as in anti-torture, have taken for granted a one-dimensional future-oriented temporal dimension: a primitive past, an inadequate present and an enlightened future, where promises are realised.[6] Progress is taken to be channelled through shifts in societal sensibilities, understandings of modernity and civility – viewed as implicit in changes in practices: with the iron maiden no longer in use and public squares no longer bearing witness to drawing and quartering. On this register (namely, the disappearance of public and physical punishment), progress appears clear. Such changes in practices of state violence and, in turn, social evaluation are heralded as taking time, marking a temporal *contingency*.[7]

This is borne out in historical and contemporary readings of torture's relationship to law. The prohibition's interpretation is held out as necessarily dynamic, expanding and evolving, needing to keep pace with present-day understandings, practices and conditions. Modern law, especially criminal and human rights law, after all, is presented as a 'story of the progressive elimination of torture'.[8] A narrative of progress is ingrained into how international lawyers look upon their practice, on anti-torture more broadly, expecting it to contribute to sociopolitical advances.[9] Practitioners generally view torture's definition as 'obviously dynamic and evolving all the time',[10] enabling and encouraging them to pitch arguments for expanded recognition under the prohibition of emerging practices and understandings of suffering based on this progressive potential. This necessitates fervent faith in the system.

[6] Fitzpatrick (1992) 40–41; Marie-Benedicte Dembour, *Who Believes in Human Rights? Reflections on the European Convention* (CUP 2006) 35.

[7] For a reliable historical account of torture practices, see Rejali (2007); concurrently, the significance of prohibition of torture – allowing for no derogations due to its absolute nature and constituting one of the handful of peremptory norms under customary international law – is sourced at its historical *constancy*.

[8] Khan (2008) 2–3; 34.

[9] Altwicker and Diggelmann (2014).

[10] Canning (2023) 374.

From time to time, adjudicators have realised this potential to recognise, amongst other practices, the ills of solitary confinement, prisoner transportation, rape, gendered (domestic) violence, sleep deprivation, threats, human trafficking and conversion therapy, to name but a few practices.[11] With law imbued with such a potential to deliver, energies spent on activating established legal processes are redoubled. This premise (or promise) to keep pace has important implications for the anti-torture field: it anoints adjudicators as arbiters of change, tasks anti-torture advocates with building and arguing an evidence-base for change and trusts the legal process to beneficently and dynamically deliver on the promise of progress – in recognising and redressing torture. However it is divined by adjudicators, advocates believe in the power of dynamic interpretation to deliver – hoping (often despite repeated failures) that certain practices would find recognition under torture's prohibition.

Progress becomes problematic, however, when one proceeds to scratch the surface to see that suffering has also been concealed (put into prisons to take a more psychological form). Sidestepping, re-labelling and shape-shifting have been favourite pastimes of states. That prisons are still being built on nineteenth-century values, despite overwhelming evidence of their ineffectiveness, should also give one cause for reflection on this front. Failings in the short term are nevertheless believed to be ironed out in the *longue durée.* Those long in the field seek solace in it, embracing incremental improvements[12] and explaining that it 'can be better to play the long game' but also uncomfortably recognising, if at all, that 'it is a price that others must pay, and that is not a comfortable thought at all'.[13] The culmination of efforts, particularly through established legal means, is relied on to proceed to torture's

[11] Jules Lobel and Peter Scharff Smith (eds), *Solitary Confinement: Effects, Practices, and Pathways toward Reform* (OUP 2019); Ronli Sifris, *Reproductive Freedom, Torture and International Human Rights: Challenging the Masculinisation of Torture* (Routledge 2016); Clare McGlynn, 'Rape, Torture and the European Convention on Human Rights' (2009) 58 *International and Comparative Law Quarterly* 565; Ilias Trispiotis and Craig Purshouse, '"Conversion Therapy" As Degrading Treatment' (2022) 42 (1) *Oxford Journal of Legal Studies* 104; Amnesty, 'Prisoner Transportation in Russia: Travelling into the Unknown' (2017).

[12] Evans (2023) 6: 'after all, it is how all lasting change is achieved'.

[13] Ibid 99.

eradication – however incrementally. Things, this prominent position advances, will simply take time.

Any claim to a tidy linearity, as this chapter will illustrate, proves more rhetorical than real. Despite being long established, torture's interpretation remains a 'difficult, invidious and in some ways an inherently flawed exercise' and as 'fine-grained, ever-shifting and ultimately inconclusive'.[14] Whilst the connection between shifts in social values and recognition of state violence appears self-evident at first glance, there is remarkably little understanding beyond uncritical connections, generalisations and oversimplifications. There is, in all, a need to complicate such reduced linear understandings as evident in legal doctrine – to reassert messiness, regress and stagnancy beyond a simple sense of progress.[15]

To be sure, there are indeed intrinsic connections between pain, punishment and torture, which merit drawing them together. There is also a concurrent risk of slippage here, as these concepts are not synonymous, meaning that there are limitations to this approach.[16] As different societies and scholars, across time and space, have used these concepts (i.e., pain, punishment and torture) to refer to different phenomena, some conflation has been inevitable in the following discussion.[17] I similarly approach the *social*, *cultural* and *political* with broad strokes – taking the social and cultural as relating to the values, beliefs, attitudes, sentiments and all adjacent that exist among a polity, and the political as the interests, incentives, strategies and objectives of state authorities. Whilst entanglements are unresolved on several fronts, I am adamant that treating them together remains generative.

Exploring temporality and sociality, this chapter undertakes this task of complicating the progress narrative as conventionally framed. It

[14] Ibid 4.

[15] Kathryn McNeilly, 'Are Rights out of Time? International Human Rights Law, Temporality, and Radical Social Change' (2019) 28 *Social & Legal Studies* 817–838; Kathryn McNeilly and Ben Warwick (eds), *The Times and Temporalities of International Human Rights Law* (Hart 2022).

[16] I am indebted to Mattia Pinto for pulling me up on this slippage. The errors remain mine.

[17] For instance, drawing and quartering was long thought of as punishment not torture by both societies and scholars – yet I would understand this to be torture from a contemporary perspective.

first explores the link between state violence and social values, how pain and punishment have, respectively, been susceptible to broader socio-cultural values (Section 3.1), a discussion which invites us to consider the impact the emergence of science has had for collective understandings of suffering (Section 3.2). From there, the discussion turns to political considerations in examining the necessity of some state violence (Section 3.3). A discussion of the difficulties abounding in the attempt to better adjudicate progress concludes the chapter (Section 3.4). Several key questions drive the discussion: How do adjudicators gauge the 'zeitgeist' – where do they look? When can one even safely say that there is a shift in social values on a state practice? How does one even reconcile prevailing attitudes calling for harsher responses to crime against the expectations for increasingly progressive attitudes? *Seeds*, towards critically rethinking anti-torture's 'progressive impulses', not *solutions* are offered in what follows.

3.1 SOCIAL SENSITIVITIES

> The law develops as society develops, with new circumstances presenting new 'wrongs' which require new remedies to be developed out of existing ones.[18]

> The local scenes must be understood as the products of broader social processes. The forms of punishment dispensed by the various agents are always inserted in the historical, cultural, and political context that makes them possible. Connecting the two levels – micro and macro, so to speak – is crucial to avoid focusing the explanation on individual conduct or decisions as well as to account for differences across space and time.[19]

However distant histories of torture predating the contemporary struggle might seem, they are useful points of departure in examining the notion of progress. Several important histories on torture have explored the close relationship and purported rupture between law and torture – resulting in the abolition of torture.[20] These confirm that judicial torture,

[18] Richard Nobles and David Schiff, *A Sociology of Jurisprudence* (Hart 2006) 65.

[19] Didier Fassin, *The Will to Punish* (OUP 2018) 80–81.

[20] Page duBois, *Torture and Truth* (Routledge Revivals, 1991/2018); Lisa Silverman, *Tortured Subjects: Pain, Truth, and the Body in Early Modern France* (University of Chicago Press 2001);

what we might now term physical interrogational torture inducing confessions, itself was once a legitimate evidentiary practice in pre- and early modern Europe. When compared to the contemporary, these histories implicitly point to at least one significant conceptual shift: that the concept of torture has expanded to cover the *psychological*, *punitive* and *extra-custodial* (from that which exclusively focussed on the *physical* and *interrogational*). On this rather reduced register, there is clearly evidence of progress.

Whilst these accounts all record that torture was abolished in pre-modern Europe, and that its concept was broadened, they importantly dispute the causes coalescing in its dismantling and disappearance. The case, respectively, built by two of these prominent historical accounts (namely, those of Lisa Silverman and Page duBois), grounds the abolition in shifts in social sensitivities, that cultural (then political, then legal) support waned as the public became more sceptical of torture as a legitimate practice. Silverman presents this thesis as follows (and worth quoting in full):[21]

> Judicial torture was employed not only because it made political and legal sense but also because it made cultural sense. The legal employment of torture is, therefore, an outstanding instance of the way in which legal institutions reflect broader cultural values. Judicial torture possessed not only an institutional logic but also a cultural logic. It made sense not only as a tool of government but also as a form of testimony. As a cultural institution, torture testified both to the meaningfulness of human suffering and the corresponding valuelessness of human volition, and to the intimate connections among pain, truth, and the body.

These developments are framed as more than a debate about 'the nature of legal evidence' but rather one about the 'meaning of human

Langbein (2006); Edward Peters, *Torture* (Penn Press 1996); John H. Langbein, 'The Legal History of Torture' in Levinson (2004) 97. For counter-critique, see Mirjan Damaška, The Death of Legal Torture [Review of Torture and the Law of Proof: Europe and England in the Ancien Régime, by J. H. Langbein] (1978) 87 (4) *Yale Law Journal* 860–884. See also chapter 1 of J.M. Bernstein, *Torture and Dignity: An Essay on Moral Injury* (University of Chicago Press 2015), which treats this listed material philosophically.

[21] Silverman (2001) 7.

experience' and a 'reevaluation of the experience of pain, the uses of the body, and the definition of truth'.[22] So, it is the language of law, in its evidentiary practices and pulses, as coupled with that of social sensitivities that forged towards expanded (and disapproving) understandings of torture.

The adage, after all, has it that 'how society punishes reveals its true character'.[23] As with penal practices, the law has long held itself out to be expressive of sociocultural values – normatively claiming to be a proxy for collectively held beliefs.[24] International law does not differ in its regard, as it is also affected by its broader contexts.[25] Before moving too directly to these connections, it might be an idea to ask: What are even social or cultural values? How can we capture them? Finding this to be an elusive and complicated task, one scholar has defined *culture* as 'a collection of ideas, values, practices, and material objects that are meaningful to a group of people or the entire society, and which allows them to carry out their collective lives in relative order and harmony'.[26] Such *values* are thus viewed as the 'broad guidelines defining what a group considers good, desirable, right, or important [as] express[ing] the ideals of society, as well as of groups of every size'.[27] Social scientific scholarship afield too has taken the social, or the cultural, to 'refer to socially collective beliefs and systems of beliefs that operate as guiding principles in life'.[28] Such values, or beliefs, are 'closely related to the notion of society, a group of people who interact and share a common culture, frequently occupy a particular territorial area'.[29]

A contingency on the sociocultural-political accords with the scholarship on pain. Pain, to be sure, is not solely situated in the body but

[22] Ibid 3.

[23] Austin Sarat (ed), *The Punitive Imagination: Law, Justice, and Responsibility* (University of Alabama Press 2014) 1.

[24] David Garland, *Punishment and Modern Society: A Study in Social Theory* (Clarendon Press 1993) 32.

[25] Mosche Hirsch, *Invitation to the Sociology of International Law* (OUP 2017) 11.

[26] Ibid 6.

[27] Ibid.

[28] Stavroula Tsirogianni and George Gaskell, 'The Role of Plurality and Context in Social Values' (2011) 41 *Journal for the Theory of Social Behaviour* 442.

[29] Hirsch (2017) 6.

also in the world. As Rob Boddice finds, a 'major distinguishing marker of these gradations of humanity was the capacity to feel pain, or degree of sensitivity to pain [with civilization coming] bundled with more pain, since it was in part defined by heightened sensitivity and a closeness to emotional upheaval'.[30] The cultural historical view is that far from being 'simply a function of the amount of bodily damage … the culture in which we have been brought up plays an essential role in how we feel and respond to pain',[31] that it is always subject to 'the variable influx of meaning'[32] and to 'social appraisal',[33] rendering suffering best understood as a 'biocultural event'.[34] This is exemplified by any threat: 'being threatened with a handgun can only be psychologically traumatizing if one knows what a gun is'.[35] Threats, conversely, not only stem from 'external stimuli but also from self-induced pressures, which results from an individual's interpretation of and chosen response to events, both real and imagined'.[36] These individual reactions are connected to and conditioned by the environment. Boddice offers additional clues in writing that

> pain is plastic: it is personal, it is social; it is subjective but formed and alleviated through intersubjective and collective dynamics; it is cultural, insofar as the experience of pain must be learned according to the conceptual framing of the culture in which a person is formed; it is therefore unstable, even in a single individual over the course of life, perhaps even from one moment to the next. Pain is universal only in the meaningless sense that (almost) everybody has experienced something 'painful' at

[30] Boddice (2017) 44, 49.

[31] Ronald Melzack and Patrick D. Wall, *The Challenge of Pain* (Penguin 1996) 15.

[32] David B. Morris, *The Culture of Pain* (University of California Press 1991) 25–26.

[33] Moscoso (2012) 56.

[34] Morris (1991) 'subject to both individual and transpersonal modulation, as variable across social boundaries as other events with mixed biological and cultural significance'. See Boddice (2017) 1–2: 'Pain is unpredictable and resistant to standards of measurement and treatment. It gets bundled up with confusing social and cultural factors'; Boddice (2014) 7: 'The body, in other words, is a cultural body. An individual's physiology is in a dynamic relationship with where it is and what it means to be there'.

[35] Başoğlu (2017) 190.

[36] George Dimitriu, 'Interrogation, Coercion and Torture: Dutch Debates and Experiences after 9/11' (2013) 28 (4) *Intelligence & National Security* 549.

> some point, but it is in fact conceptually plural. I can talk about 'pain' in this general sense, but to do justice to the myriad ways of encountering, enduring, or even celebrating pain, one must examine the conceptual and cultural specificities of different contexts of suffering; one must come to know the signs, symbols, and expressions of situated pains, of 'patients' in their own worlds.[37]

The connection between sociocultural-political contexts, sensitivities to violence and legal content is complex. It may be beyond precise conceptualisation here but not of exemplification, which is easily found. The drafting of prohibition of torture in European human rights law, namely, Article 3 of the *European Convention on Human Rights*, too reads to be grounded in such cultural historical perspectives. These mark torture's 'return' to Europe as 'fortified by many discoveries of modern science'.[38] During this deliberation, the drafting committee invoked the pre-WWII imagination where torture was 'absolutely unthinkable' and 'condemned as an Oriental depravity', and being taught in school that torture 'had been done away with hundreds of years ago, that the world had become civilised, and that, with the development of civilisation, torture had disappeared'. The drafters reminisced that: '[w]e used to go into the museums and see instruments of torture exhibited [and] used to wonder how our ancestors could have been so cruel and so depraved'. In this history, torture's 'return' to Europe is epitomised by Nazi Germany, which was described as having been built upon and having perished in its torture chambers. With 'Nazi atrocities as frame of reference, the drafters set the bar high'[39] – an argument I return to in discussing torture's exceptionality in Chapter 4.

The *travaux* show that such sentiments were shared and met generally positively by the drafters, who urged all to remember 'that barbarism is never behind us, it is underneath us. It is our task to see that it does

[37] Rob Boddice, *Knowing Pain: A History of Sensation, Emotion, and Experience* (Wiley 2023) 204.

[38] ECmHR, 'Preparatory Work on Article 3 of the European Convention of Human Rights' (CoE 1956) DH (56) 6.

[39] Ezgi Yildiz, A Court with Many Faces: Institutional Identities and Interpretive Preferences: The Case of the European Court of Human Rights and the Norm against Torture, PhD thesis, IHEID Geneva ('PhD Thesis') (2016) 214.

not come to the surface'.[40] This thesis gels generally well with scholars of punishment who link the importance of 'civility' with shifting understandings of suffering.[41] That lesser a society was developed (or 'simpler' the society), the higher the intensity involved in its punishment – as reliant on the capital and corporal – and the more developed a society, the lower the intensity of its punishment – as reliant on incapacity through incarceration. Suffering, these scholars stress, is not timeless but contingent on time and place, on social as political associations.[42] Offering helpful linkages between societies and their recognition of suffering, these aim to account for variance in social sensitivities to different forms of violence, discussing societal sophistication or the political necessity of physical violence.[43]

This position also squarely rejects the purely technical and rational ascriptions claimed by modern regimes of penality – purporting to have divorced *passion* from *ration*. Pain and punishment, in other words, remain informed by social sensitivities. To not accept the continuing interplay between passion and ration, as David Garland has put it, would be 'too much a story of smooth evolution and functional adaptation to fit the facts'.[44] Whilst punishment is 'administered by state functionaries' and might be presented in technical terms, for Garland, it remains 'necessarily grounded in wider patterns of knowing, feeling, and acting, and it depends upon these social roots and supports for its continuing legitimacy and operation'.[45] So penality (and, with it, configurations of the torturous) remains *mediated* between passion ('morally toned desire to punish') and ration ('administrative, rationalistic, normalizing concern

40 ECmHR (1956) 6.

41 Norbert Elias, *The Civilizing Process* (Blackwell 2000).

42 Boddice (2007) 108, using hysteria as an example; Rob Boddice, *Pain and Emotion in Modern History* (Palgrave 2014).

43 Iain Wilkinson, *Suffering: A Sociological Introduction* (Polity 2005); Iain Wilkinson and Arthur Kleinman, *A Passion for Society: How We Think about Human Suffering* (University of California Press 2016); Pieter Spierenburg, *The Spectacle of Suffering: Executions and the Evolution of Repression: From a Preindustrial Metropolis to the European Experience* (CUP 1984); Garland (1993); Kleinman et al (1997); Veena Das et al (eds), *Violence and Subjectivity* (University of California Press 2000); Ahmed (2014); DelVecchio Good (1994).

44 Garland (1993) 49.

45 Ibid 21.

to manage') – clashing and contrasting but integral to the social process of punishing.[46]

Garland continues to explore 'passion', that which renders certain forms of punishment as viscerally, socially abhorrent, understood as 'conscionable, tolerable, or "civilised"'. For him, as passion, culture determines 'the contours and outer limits of penality as well as shaping the detailed distinctions, hierarchies, and categories which operate within the penal field', ruling out 'a whole range of possible punishments (tortures, maimings, stonings, public whippings, etc)'[47] as

> 'unthinkable' because they strike us as impossibly cruel and 'barbaric' – as wholly out of keeping with the sensibilities of modern, civilized human beings. This is often experienced as a kind of visceral judgment – one which expresses emotional repugnance rather than rational objection. … Usually this boundary line has the unspoken, barely visible character of something which everyone takes for granted. It becomes visible and obvious, only when some outrageous proposal crosses the line, or else when evidence from other times or other places shows how differently that line has been drawn elsewhere. It is therefore stating the obvious – but also reminding ourselves of something we can easily forget – to say that punishment are, in part, determined by the specific structure of our sensibilities, and that these sensibilities are themselves subject to change.[48]

In exploring a parallel notion behind sociocultural sensibility, Garland zooms out to view the notion of *civilisation* as a 'powerfully evocative concept which has extensive connotations within our culture'.[49] The term 'civilised' has come to be a measure of sociocultural appropriateness of punishment. For Page duBois, as with early calls for abolition, modern torture continues to mark the boundary between the 'civilized' and 'primitive', and as a source of 'comfort to the so-called civilized nations, persuading them of their commitment to humanitarian values, revealing to them the continued barbarism of the other world'.[50] More broadly, notions of civility

[46] Ibid 180.
[47] Ibid 195–196.
[48] Ibid 215.
[49] Ibid.
[50] duBois (1991/2018) 157.

and modernity have also served to introduce a more technical language of reason around state violence exuding 'an illusion of control – claiming to disassociate pain delivery from a level which is impermissible'[51] and implying that 'it could be subdued, modified, and improved'.[52]

In all, formation, moderation and recognition of suffering, whether scientifically or legally, necessarily involve moral, societal and civilisational imaginaries and consciousness. But what of the increasing role of science in societal understandings of suffering? What has been the significance of emerging technologies in how torture is produced or prevented? And to turn it more squarely to the object of study, namely, law and its actors, how if at all has science impacted on legal understandings of torture? Has it aided in the fraught attempts to 'measure what are often incommensurable standards of behaviour'?[53]

3.2 SCIENCE AND SUFFERING

> [M]ethods of inflicting suffering ... have already been overtaken by the ingenuity of modern techniques of oppression. Torture no longer presupposes violence, a notion to which the judgment refers expressly and generically. Torture can be practised –and indeed is practised – developed in multidisciplinary laboratories which claim to be scientific.[54]

> In spite of all the progress we have witnessed, even in our own time, it is not possible for the greatest physician, biologist, or any other scientist to define the exact moment when a hanged person, man, woman, or minor, ceases to feel pain ... But one fact emerges: man has not grown less cruel with the passage of that illusory thing called time, though in many parts of the world he has become a far greater hypocrite than he used to be.[55]

[51] Ergun Cakal, 'Cruelty and Corpo-Reality: Connecting Technologies and Practices Integral to the Infliction and Investigation of Torture' (2022) 14 (3) *Journal of Human Rights Practice* 1021, 1022.

[52] Michael Ignatieff, *A Just Measure of Pain: The Penitentiary in the Industrial Revolution, 1750–1850* (Pantheon Press 1978) 218.

[53] Talal Asad, 'On Torture, or Cruel, Inhuman, and Degrading Treatment' in Arthur Kleinman et al (eds), *Social Suffering* (University of California Press 1997) 286.

[54] *Ireland v. UK* [1978] dissent of Judge Evrigenis.

[55] Charles Duff, *A Handbook on Hanging* (New York Review of Books Classics 1999) xxvi, 3

Scientific methods and language have been instrumentalised both in the infliction and inhibition of torturous suffering.[56] Prominent legal scholars, as early as Jeremy Bentham, have aimed to rationalise, impersonalise as to humanise state violence (or rather punishment) – turning it into 'a science, an objective use of pain by the state'.[57] This has paved the way for a 'sanitization of penal practice and penal language'[58] – with pain, punishment or torture no longer presupposing brutality and physicality, but concealed, denied and deniable. The technical and managerial language of rationality and professionalisation has also aimed to neutralise and remove punishment 'from direct public participation and involvement and have been cast in a form which de-emphasizes their moral content'.[59] Put differently, punishment was supposed to be divorced from social sensitivities (alternatively, ethical, moral or social evaluation) and, instead, increasingly subjected to the technical and professional – with the expert's role growing corresponding to the public's role diminishing.[60]

Despite its inhering social sensitivities, modern uses of state violence have come to self-identify as rational, neutral, natural and inevitable – an inevitability embodying progress and reform – purporting to be ruled by 'expedience', 'reason', 'measure' and 'necessity'.[61] The logic exuded here is characterised by quantifiable (measured and calculated) and qualifiable (purposeful) pain – as opposed to social sensitivities (which are based on uncontrolled passion). The rise of objectivist scientistic impulses is also identified and critiqued in pain scholarship, leading to

> the erasure of subjectivity as useful diagnostic or therapeutic information the importance of patients' testimony about their own experiences of

[56] The frontiers of technology-facilitated torture have reached the use of online communication to deliver torturous threats. See Pau Pérez-Sales and Laia Serra, 'Internet and Communications as Elements for CIDT and Torture: Initial Reflections in an Unexplored Field' (2020) 30 (1) *Torture* 5, and of electric-based technologies, see Omega Foundation and Amnesty International, *Ending the Torture Trade: The Path to Global Controls on the 'Tools of Torture'* (2020).

[57] Garland (1993) 76.

[58] Ibid 235.

[59] Ibid 184–185.

[60] Ibid.

[61] Ibid 46.

> pain, [and when] patients did not fit scientific formulations, it was often deemed that there must be something wrong with the patient rather than something wrong with the science.[62]

Reason, as manifest through such exercises and as already argued, has never been value-free or completely disconnected from social sensitivities. That the International Association for the Study of Pain, a body of experts who advance a definition of pain, itself has changed its standardised definition of pain several times also demonstrates the contextual contingencies here.[63] So, it is not only the discipline of the law that is in conversation with social sensitivities on suffering. Health sciences such as medicine and, later, psychology have also introduced a new language around the body and mind, which have come to inform how society, and in turn the law, looks upon pain. Whilst seemingly unquestionable at first glance, the common currency of psychiatric concepts as post-traumatic stress disorder, genealogical examinations reveal, was only established gradually and with some difficulty.[64]

A study of the concurrent recognition of trauma and the disciplinary authority of psychiatry identifies social sensitivities as central, pointing to 'a moral genealogy running parallel to the scientific development [derived] from the collective process by which a society defines its values and norms, and embodies them in individual subjects'.[65] The authors attribute the change to what they call 'collective sensibilities'[66] – finding that this was far from a 'single, linear path, the journey to establishing trauma as part of the regime of truth emerges as an uncertain, ambiguous process, full of contradictions that say much

[62] Boddice (2023) 111–112. Chapter 5 on 'Substantiating torture', picking up on this point, will attest to the biomedical evidence base on which documentation practices have been developed.

[63] International Association for the Study of Pain, 'IASP Announces Revised Definition of Pain', 16 July 2020, www.iasp-pain.org/publications/iasp-news/iasp-announces-revised-definition-of-pain/

[64] Didier Fassin and Richard Rechtman, *The Empire of Trauma: An Inquiry into the Condition of Victimhood* (Princeton University Press 2009) 160, argue that the 'reality of this suffering [trauma] is of course not new, but the recognition of it certainly is. And does recognition not make it a little more real?'.

[65] Ibid 30.

[66] Ibid.

more about moral and political stakes than they do about clinical and diagnostic issues'.[67] The recognition therefore is 'due not to more refined diagnostic tools, but rather to a narrowing of the gap between the climate of public opinion and the preoccupations of mental health professionals, between the moral economy and medical theory'.[68] A crucial interplay between reason and passion is left unresolved.[69] Whilst social sensitivities may have been displaced in modern regimes, neither are they taken to have disappeared. It might be that they enjoy a reduced immediacy, decreased official accountability *and* distant public knowledge than previously.[70] This has the potential of misinforming the public, distorting the debate and creating indifference in some areas and directing passion towards others.

Far from simply aiding progressive understandings and extending protection, the language of science has also been problematically deployed as obfuscation and objection. A parallel concern in this discussion, the belief in science, medical and psychological, to inform so-called 'humane' state policies, too has similarly legitimated suffering. Prison regulation, purporting to be scientifically informed, has served to invisibilise and artificialise the nature of suffering far from drawing us near to how prisons work and hurt.[71] Health professionals, and here I include medical doctors, psychologists and psychiatrists, have lent their language, authority and expertise to state intelligence apparatuses, from the beginnings of the Cold War to the 'war on terror'.[72] This has varied

[67] Ibid 223.

[68] Ibid 21–22.

[69] Ibid 32. Unpacking Durkheim's view that 'passion is the soul of punishment', Garland notes that passion is 'an emotional reaction which flares up at the violation of deeply cherished social sentiments' and that 'although institutional routines modify these accesses of rage, and strain to use them in a productive way, the dynamic and motivating force of punishment is emotional and unreflecting'– making 'a violation of society's morality [simultaneously] a personally felt outrage against every "healthy" individual'.

[70] Ibid 187.

[71] See Tom Kemp and Philippa Tomczak, 'The Cruel Optimism of International Prison Regulation: Prison Ontologies and Carceral Harms' (2024) 49 (3) *Law & Social Inquiry* 1683; Andrew M Jefferson, 'Prison Reform and Torture Prevention under "Compromised Circumstances"' (2022) 24 (2) *Criminology & Criminal Justice* 413.

[72] Stephen Soldz, 'Fighting Torture and Psychologist Complicity' (2011) 23 (1) *Peace Review: A Journal of Social Justice* 12–20; Peter Suedfeld (ed), *Psychology and Torture* (1990).

from providing oversight of detention regimes, and implicitly approving suffering, to actively designing the environment to disrupt cohesion and communication among detainees and to foster dependence and compliance. Trust in health professionals has been co-opted to appease and ameliorate public perceptions, to attest to the false claim that the pain threshold was being expertly and scientifically controlled to a degree that was 'safe, effective, legal and ethical' – or as 'a series of carefully controlled procedures, sanctioned by rational experts who have the aura of authority that comes with knowledge and credentials'.[73] Whilst the age-old principle of 'do no harm' endures for good reason, it has often faltered under the weight of political demands. So, it is not only the deployment of validated scientific knowledge but also pseudo-science, 'use of the language and even behaviours that bear some resemblance to science but critically without the scientific method and the intellectual commitments that follow from the adoption of the scientific method'.[74]

In focusing on the social and scientific however, a key interlocking part of the puzzle is omitted: the political. The simple connection is that the sociocultural, how a population is sensitised to violence, informs and is informed by the political. Political imperatives are also independently formed and imposed top-down. I now turn to this more squarely in the discussion to follow – arguing that state interests have dominated how the prohibition of torture has come to be understood (conceptually expanded or not).

3.3 POLITICAL IMPERATIVES

> [W]e should be concerned not with law's response to, but with law's involvement in, the commission of harms; we should be concerned not with problems about how law restricts acknowledgment of violations that have already taken place, but about how law actively promotes harms; … not with law's impotence, but with its power.[75]

[73] Alfred McCoy, *Torture and Impunity: The US Doctrine of Coercive Interrogation* (University of Wisconsin Press 2012) 24.

[74] Shane O'Mara, *Why Torture Doesn't Work: The Neuroscience of Interrogation* (Harvard University Press 2015) 30.

[75] Veitch (2007) 95.

Historical counterpoints, as, respectively, advanced by Edward Peters and John Langbein, fundamentally contest the importance of social sensitivities in torture's abolition. These prominent scholars prefer to attribute the abolition and prohibition of torture to *raison d'etat* – that it was no longer required for the evidentiary practice or political survival of the state. Langbein, for instance, writes that 'the explanation for the disappearance of judicial torture is neither publicistic nor political, but juristic'.[76] Peters similarly finds that it was only following the waning of its 'technical and legal underpinnings' that torture 'became at last vulnerable to those logical, moral and social criticisms to which it had for so long been virtually immune'.[77] That it is political necessity (or *raison d'etat*) not civility that affects change is also, respectively, accepted by influential works produced by Michel Foucault and, in the same vein, Darius Rejali and Talal Asad. Foucault, for one, argued that the emergence of a 'non-corporal penality' (which was 'less immediately physical', 'more subtle, more subdued') emerged out of a more 'scientifico-legal complex'.[78] In pointing out that 'it is not on account of some profound humanity that the criminal conceals within him but because of a necessary regulation of the effects of power', Foucault rejected connecting these developments to any notion of civilisation or a humanitarian awakening. The change in punishment was only incidental to any change in the nature or forms of pain delivery. That practices such as irreducible life imprisonment and solitary confinement have long been protected away from torture's purview, given their continued use for states serves to support this position. As Chapter 4 will discuss, the pain from such politically protected practices have thus been waved away through adjectives as inherent, inevitable, unavoidable and lawful.

For Rejali, who similarly documents torturous practices by western democracies, the correlation between democracy (or modernity) and torture, or the premise that 'as societies become civilized and establish vital public spheres, barbaric practices such as torture will

[76] Langbein (2006) 4; Peters (1996) 11.

[77] Peters (1996) 84–85.

[78] Michel Foucault, *Discipline and Punish: The Birth of the Prison* (Vintage 1979) 7–8.

eventually disappear', is misleading.[79] In following Foucault, Rejali similarly advances the argument that there is no necessary *in*compatibility between torture and democracy (or modernity) and that torture is rather integral to and inextricable from *raison d'etat*.[80] Taking Rejali's work as a point of departure, Asad also scrutinises *physical* cruelty's association with the pre-modern and its elimination with the modern. For Asad, we are 'inclined to think that at least in humanizing societies more sorts of inflicted pain come to be considered morally unacceptable with the passage of time'.[81] He characterises these dynamics as not only moving towards progressive recognition but also as regressing and desensitising social sensitivities. Asad's claim here is that certain forms of 'pain-producing behavior that was once shocking no longer shocks – or, if it does, not in the way it did in the past [such as] large numbers of people in prison for more and more kinds of offenses'.[82] Differentiating between pain that is necessary and that which is not is also associated with the 'civilizing mission',[83] Asad finds:

> Clearly, in the cause of moral progress, there was suffering and there was suffering. What is interesting is not merely that some forms of suffering were to be taken more seriously than others but that 'inhuman' suffering as opposed to 'necessary' 'inevitable' suffering was regarded as being essentially gratuitous and therefore legally punishable. Pain endured in the movement toward becoming 'fully human' on the other hand, was seen as necessary because social or moral reasons justified why it must be suffered. … As the idea of progress became increasingly dominant in the affairs of Europe and the world, the need for measuring suffering was felt and responded to with greater sophistication.

[79] Rejali (2007).

[80] Ibid; in his earlier work, Rejali also labels the civilization/enlightenment-as-eradication (that 'as societies become civilized and establish vital public spheres, barbaric practices such as torture will eventually disappear') explanation as 'the humanistic approach' and as implausible and misleading: Darius Rejali, 'How Not to Talk about Torture: Violence, Theory, and the Problems of Explanation' in Martha D. Huggins (ed), *Vigilantism and the State in Modern Latin America: Essays on Extralegal Violence* (Praeger 1991) 127–128.

[81] Talal Asad, 'On Torture, or Cruel, Inhuman, and Degrading Treatment' in Arthur Kleinman (2007) 293–297.

[82] Ibid 297.

[83] Ibid 295.

This has been taken to mean that torture's interpretation, through evocations of necessity, 'retains a culturally-biased core of meaning that derives its substance from the colonial-era mission to civilize the natives'.[84] Such takes link torture's historical use to its current 'statist bias', leading to practices in the preservation of the state as 'more easily tolerated by the human-rights discourse, even as it expands the meaning of "torture" to include mental pain and other types of injuries'.[85] Contemporary perspectives from international relations on the prohibition are too undergirded by a civilisational logic – imbuing violations of the prohibition as a 'taboo' treating breaches of the prohibition as 'open[ing] up the opportunity to rank states as "barbaric" or "uncivilised"'.[86]

Taking torture to mean physically overt interrogational torture, that it needed to have visibly marked its victims, there has indeed been a disappearance for the most part. Yet, condemnation or abolition of torturous suffering, others similarly argue, was far from complete. As Michelle Farrell argues, Foucault's (as others') account inflates the case of abolition and has 'overlooked the reality that torture became "part and parcel" of the disciplinary institutions, even if it had gone somewhat into hiding'.[87] Rather, state violence was to be 'held in check and controlled, and its legitimate use was strictly confined to agents of the state'.[88] Its deliberate and gratuitous uses 'came to be seen as barbaric and uncivilized, the controlled use of violence came to be seen as a sign of progress and civilization'.[89] Accordingly, it has been argued that whilst physical forms of torture were abolished (or at least prohibited), *tortura spiritualis* (and *territio*), meaning 'invisible forms of coercion', remained standard official interrogational practice, and, with it, 'torturous violence

[84] Balakrishnan Rajagopal, *International Law from Below: Development, Social Movements and Third World Resistance* (CUP 2003) 182–183.

[85] Ibid.

[86] Jamal Barnes, *A Genealogy of the Torture Taboo* (Routledge 2017) 13.

[87] Michelle Farrell, 'The Marks of Civilisation: The Special Stigma of Torture' (2022) 22 *Human Rights Law Review* 120.

[88] Jürgen Martschukat and Silvan Niedermeier (eds), *Violence and Visibility in Modern History* (Palgrave Macmillan 2013) 3.

[89] Ibid.

continued to uphold its powerful impact by being transformed into verbal and imaginary forms of violence'.[90]

Abetting and masking a more ideological and strategic exercise adopted to expand evaluative discretion in the service of state power, it would seem unreasonable to think that adjudicators would so readily and benevolently constrain themselves through ceding their discretion to a nebulous phenomenon beyond their control.[91] The question in turn becomes not whether social values enter judicial consideration, certainly implicitly, but to what degree they are weighed. Adjudication is ascribed with the authority to channel as well as change understandings of how torture ought to be defined. In moments of reflection, former international judges have related the difficulty of their work as being pitted between 'tradition and progress ... flexibility and legal certainty',[92] and as being compelled to be more conservative than progressive.[93] Such expediency is amply clear in cases where judges have historically refrained from invoking dynamic interpretation concerning politically charged issues, such as assisted death, abortion, the age of criminal responsibility and marriage equality. Judges are mindful not simply of social but also state demands in determining the boundaries of torture's prohibition.[94] And how well-reflected is society of what happens in its prisons or at the hands of their police? And how well-reflected

[90] Thomas Weitin, 'The Visibility of Torture in Nineteenth-Century Case Study Collections', in Jürgen Martschukat and Silvan Niedermeier (eds), *Violence and Visibility in Modern History* (Palgrave Macmillan 2013).

[91] Although 'the public may accept physical violence as being neither cruel nor excessive, varies between different societies and even between different sections of them' (as argued by John Vorhaus, 'On Degradation Part Two: Degrading Treatment and Punishment' (2003) 31 *Common Law World Review* 65), regressive positions are normally overridden by judges. This was indeed how a South African case weighed in on the question, finding that 'public opinion may have some relevance to the enquiry, but in itself, it is no substitute for the duty vested in the Courts to interpret the Constitution and to uphold its provisions without fear or favour. If public opinion were to be decisive there would be no need for constitutional adjudication' in *S v. Makwanyane* (1995) 3 SA 391 at 431 [88] per Chaskalson J.

[92] Tulkens (2022) 293.

[93] Rudolph Bernhardt, 'Evolutive Treaty Interpretation, Especially of the European Convention on Human' 1999 *German Yearbook of International Law* (2000) 22.

[94] Ezgi Yildiz, *Between Forbearance and Audacity: The European Court of Human Rights and the Norm against Torture* (CUP 2023).

are advocates and adjudicators on the question of sociocultural-political understandings on suffering anyway? How do they approach gauging such values, attitudes and beliefs?

3.4 SUBSTANTIATING PROGRESS, REGISTERING TIME

> [I]s it sufficient for an adjudicator to say that his or her interpretation is evolutionary? Or are there more objective criteria? Is it possible to presume a situation of evolutionary interpretation where no mention is made of it?[95]

Time pervades how pain and progress are constructed. Pain, as can be assumed from the foregoing discussion, is not a timeless phenomenon. That which was not taken as painful in the past may over time come to be perceived as painful and prohibited. What was once held out to be legitimate (e.g., the use of the death penalty) can be rendered illegitimate and torturous as understandings of its harms change over time. Time is there in the life breathed into law's metaphors of 'living' and 'dynamic', that the law is always becoming. It is there in the incremental build-up of practices from which torture's prohibition is identified as a part of customary international law. Time is often rejected as relevant, particularly in holding out torture as a timeless wrong – that it was always wrong according to the laws of nature but that its prohibition was only arrived at and declared with modernity.

The figure of time also frames debates around failures. Rather than fundamentally calling into question institutions, time calls for commitment to 'more resources, minor reforms, better staff, more co-operation from other agencies and so on [pointing] to a future programme in which these problems will be better managed and the institution will reform itself'.[96] Improvements are promised, a more 'humane' future is beckoned, and fundamental questions are avoided. Time is also central to legal constructions of what amounts to torture or inhuman and degrading treatment in how long the suffering is required to be, its imminence and so on (a discussion returned to in Chapter 6). Time is

[95] Gabrielle Marceau and Clément Marquet, 'About the Book' in Georges Abi-Saab and others (eds), *Evolutionary Interpretation and International Law* (Hart 2021) 5.

[96] Garland (1993) 5–6.

simply 'ever-present ... from the macro to the micro ... central to the overarching narratives and conceptual ideas that define this area of law as well as to its everyday practice and implementation in localised settings'.[97] Yet despite its ubiquity, here too, 'time in law is often invisible or taken for granted'.[98]

The conventional presentation of time in international human rights law is that rights, such as the right to be free from torture, inhuman and degrading treatment, are 'always orientated towards the future' with a 'definite linearity dominat[ing] how this area of law is understood and narrated', which 'demonstrates a progressive relationship between the past, present and future'.[99] There are, however, some fundamental challenges to studying how this happens, as social values are 'unobservable', 'inconclusive' and 'difficult to substantiate', solely inferred from 'statements and actions' subject to misreading.[100] Substantiating and attributing progress is similarly elusive in human rights practice. Progress is often superficially equated with a proliferation of reports and norms. Yet, the relationship, as discussed, between social and legal change is unquestionably complex, as 'one does not necessarily nor easily translate into the other'.[101] Such linear correlations are overdetermined and overstated, as corroborated by the abundance of unevenness, ambiguities and anomalies in conventional histories of pain and punishment.[102]

As courts rarely attempt to develop a systematic approach to assessing suffering, so have they failed to consistently and coherently conceptualise the evolving nature of suffering in question in its social, cultural and political registers. There is no consensus on what dynamic interpretation means in international law. Dynamic interpretation, at least as used at the European Court of Human Rights, has been described as unclear and unpredictable, sparsely justified and as 'subjective

[97] Kathryn McNeilly, 'Documents and Time in International Human Rights Law Monitoring: Artefacts, Objects, Things' in Kathryn McNeilly and Ben Warwick (eds), *The Times and Temporalities of International Human Rights Law* (Hart 2022) 85.

[98] McNeilly and Warwick, 'Introduction' in McNeilly and Warwick (2022) 1.

[99] McNeilly (2019) 818.

[100] Garland (1993) 229.

[101] Sharyn Roach Anleu, *Law and Social Change* (Sage Online 2012) 5–7.

[102] Garland (1993) 214.

adhockery'.[103] Ensuring effective protection, it would seem reasonable to argue, requires 'adapting it to the changes that have taken place over time – to changes in society, in morals, in mentalities, in laws, but also to technological innovations and scientific progress'.[104] It is thus held to be informed by progressive not prevailing values. Whilst admitted to be far from an exact science,[105] this has unquestionably been the entry point for judges to assert a 'moral reading'[106] and 'political expediency'.[107] These instances are reactive at best, not proactive, and regressive at worst. Another answer here is that adjudicators, at least those in human rights courts, take international legal standards as representing a consensus, convergence or common ground on particular practices.

Calls to 'objectivise' and to 'scientifically analyse social trends and changes of mentalities' have been made by others.[108] This discussion reveals that there is an enigma in the dogma, as its central concepts reveal a messy oscillation and political contingency upon closer scrutiny. This is arguably even messier in national contexts. Sociopolitical shifts discussed are also recorded an ocean away in the United States. What once applied to an 'injury that requires medical attention or leaves permanent marks', such as 'pillorying, disemboweling, decapitation, and drawing

[103] Alistair Mowbray, 'The Creativity of the European Court of Human Rights' (2005) 5 *Human Rights Law Review* 57, 71; Daniel Moeckli and Nigel White, Treaties as 'Living Instruments' in Dino Kritsiotis and Michael Bowman (eds), *Conceptual and Contextual Perspectives on the Modern Law of Treaties* (CUP 2018) 144; Kanstantsin Dzehtsiarou, 'European Consensus and the Evolutive Interpretation of the European Convention on Human Rights' (2011) 12 *German Law Journal* 1730.

[104] Nicholas Bratza, 'Living Instrument or Dead Letter: The Future of the European Convention on Human Rights' (2014) *European Human Rights Law Review* 116, 120; George Letsas, 'The ECHR as a Living Instrument: Its Meaning and Legitimacy' in Anders Follesdal et al (eds), *Constituting Europe* (CUP 2013) 120; ECtHR, 'Dialogue between Judges: What Are the Limits to the Evolutive Interpretation of the Convention?' (2011).

[105] Bratza (2014) 123.

[106] George Letsas, 'Strasbourg's Interpretive Ethic: Lessons for the International Lawyer' (2010) 27 *European Journal of International Law* 520.

[107] Ezgi Yildiz, 'Interpretative Evolution of the Norm Prohibiting Torture and Inhuman or Degrading Treatment under the European Convention' in Anne Lise Kjær and Joanna Lam (eds), *Language and Legal Interpretation in International Law* (OUP 2022) 313.

[108] Gloria Gaggioli, 'The Strength of Evolutionary Interpretation in International Human Rights Law' in Abi-Saab et al (2019) 114.

and quartering',[109] juridical understandings of 'cruel and unusual punishment' under the Eighth Amendment of the US Constitution are also understood to have comparably expanded.[110] Constitutional interpretations of torture prohibitions, as with the United States' 'cruel and unusual punishments' clause, have seen the formulation of powerful rhetoric

> Time works changes, brings into existence new conditions and purposes. Therefore a principle to be vital must be capable of wider application than the mischief which gave it birth. The [clause] may be therefore progressive, and is not fastened to the obsolete but may acquire meaning as public opinion becomes enlightened by a humane justice.[111]

That this progressive impulse is not delivered upon, particularly in terms of the use of the death penalty, have brought scholars to criticise such pronouncements as a 'sham', in selectively drawing on expert sources in facilitating ends-driven reasoning.[112] Surveys of the US Supreme Court caselaw, taking one example, reveal that it has unpredictably drawn upon history, precedent, statutes, jury verdicts, penal purpose, international and comparative law, social science research and ultimately on the personal opinions of its judges.[113]

There are stark parallels with the death penalty in the United States and the struggle to abolish irreducible life sentences (or life imprisonment without the possibility of parole) in Europe – parallels which aid capture the problems with progress here. The practice of irreducible

[109] *Hudson v. McMillian* (1992) 503 USSC 1 per Justice Blackmun.

[110] Dayan (2011) 182–195; see also Meghan J. Ryan and William W. Berry III (eds), *The Eighth Amendment and Its Future in a New Age of Punishment* (CUP 2020).

[111] *Weems v. United States* (1910) 217 USSC 349, 373 and 378.

[112] Corinna Barrett Lain, 'Lessons Learned from the Evolution of Evolving Standards' (2010) 4 *Charleston Law Review* 661: 'In some cases, the Court considers legislative and sentencing trends in its analysis; in others, it does not. In some cases, the Court considers the views of professional organizations and international opinion; in others, it does not. We are accustomed to seeing the accusation that "evolving standards of decency" is just a cover for the policy preferences of a majority of the Justices [who have used] the doctrine to get where they want to go'.

[113] Dwight Aarons, 'The Abolitionist's Dilemma: Establishing the Standards for the Evolving Standards of Decency' (2008) 6 *Pierce Law Review* 441–467; Matthew C Matusiak et al, 'The Progression of 'Evolving Standards of Decency in U.S. Supreme Court Decisions' (2014) 39 (3) *Criminal Justice Review* 253–271.

life is known to be harmful and ineffective yet prevails across Council of Europe states. The cases brought before international courts, particularly the ECtHR, aiming to challenge the practice under the torture's prohibition illustrate how politically contingent the promise of progress can prove. It was a 2009 dissent that first signalled that the 'time was ripe to make a step forward' in moving against irreducible life sentences.[114] The practice was only ruled as amounting to inhuman treatment in the latter case of *Vinter v. UK*, where it was famously characterised as defeating 'hope'.[115] This was followed by a palpable backlash from the UK, who felt that the Court had overreached. So, when it had to rule on the same question against the same state in *Hutchinson v. UK*, the Court backed down in finding no violation of irreducible life sentences.[116] The precedent of *Vinter* resurfaced in subsequent Chamber cases of *Matiošaitis v. Lithuania*[117] and *Petukhov v. Ukraine (no 2)*.[118] In *Khamtokhu and Aksenchik v. Russia*, however, the Court's Grand Chamber could not identify an international trend to abolish the practice so it did not find a violation.[119] With such experiences at hand, the temporality of international human rights law does indeed look messy. Its characterisation as 'a fundamentally open-ended system which pushes toward a future with no real direction, no promise of any particular result, no guarantee of progress or improvement, but with every indication of inherent proliferation and transformation' rings true on this experience.[120]

Measurement of progress, as these illustrations attest, is 'far from being clear'.[121] Confused claims to the constancy and contingency of torture's prohibition, that it is resistant to time but somehow also *of* its time,

114 *Leger v. France* [2009] ECtHR 19324/02 [16] dissent of Fura-Sandström.

115 *Vinter and ors v. UK* [2013] ECtHR [GC] 66069/09 opinion of Power-Forde.

116 *Hutchinson v. UK* [2015] ECtHR 57592/08, [2017] [GC].

117 *Matiošaitis and ors v. Lithuania* [2017] ECtHR 22662/13 [135].

118 *Petukhov v. Russia (no. 2)* [2019] ECtHR 41216/13 [187].

119 *Khamtokhu and Aksenchik v. Russia* [2017] ECtHR 60367/08, 961/11 [86]. Judge Pinto de Albuquerque dissented to hold the practice as inhuman treatment, arguing he could identify such an 'international trend in favour of abolishing this type of punishment', see separate opinion of Judge Pinto de Albuquerque [25–38].

120 Elizabeth Grosz, *The Nick of Time: Politics, Evolution and the Untimely* (Duke University Press 2004) 26, as quoted in McNeilly (2019) 827.

121 Altwicker and Diggelmann (2014) 428.

presents a paradox or a duality. This contradiction is present in human rights and thus torture scholarship, in simultaneously holding human rights as transcending, as well as contingent to, societal attitudes.[122] There is a malleability and contradictory duality here that is maintained at all costs, an ambiguity that retains an unknowability, imponderability and incommensurability. In being situated in the now, it is of the past as well as the future – sustained by the 'prospect of "perfectibility"'.[123] Present inadequacies are 'portents of their supersession', being part of the people but also transcending them.[124]

Mythologising around such universality obfuscates exceptions. Although difficult to come by, there are notable exceptions to sweeping theories of anti-torture progress, which weave contradictory threads together. In *The Law Is a White Dog*, Colin Dayan focuses, amongst other concealed histories, on the inclusion of non-physical pain under the juridical understandings of 'cruel and unusual punishment' under the Eighth Amendment of the US Constitution. Demonstrating how stuttered expansive recognition has been, Dayan argues that '[c]hronologies of progress are always unreliable, especially when these narratives are told by the free in the name of the bound' – ultimately attributing terms 'decency', 'humane' or 'culture', with the same type of function as 'universal'.[125] Michelle Farrell's recent history on the long legacy of the 'five techniques', involving the combined use of wall-standing, hooding, subjection to noise and deprivation of sleep, food and drink, assessed in *Ireland v. UK*, in its fixation on exceptional suffering, similarly cuts against the linear grain. In the three instances when the claims were brought before adjudicators (in 1976, 1978 and 2018), the European Commission of Human Rights in 1976 qualified these as torture, ECtHR in 1978 downgraded the qualification to inhuman and degrading, and refused to open the case after new evidence in 2018.[126] The exceptionally high threshold of 1978, Farrell finds, remains unduly fixed to this day. A convincing progress is not recorded here – at the very bedrock of

[122] Dembour (2006) 35.
[123] Fitzpatrick (1992) 50–51.
[124] Ibid 40–41.
[125] Dayan (2011) 26.
[126] Farrell (2022).

anti-torture jurisprudence. Deferring to the power of legal precedent, judicial fact-finding and reasoning are easily let off from fully accounting for itself. The difficulties should not be accepted as excusatory. This draws us closer to the discussion on 'exceptionality' in Chapter 4.

The anti-torture field is no exception when it comes to mythologising and marking its foundational moments and its subsequent anniversaries – fixing the gazes of its advocates and adjudicators firmly to the future and away from past and present failings. Conventions are not ahistorically or statically understood – drawing in language around evolution, civilisation and progress (but not regress which is also present in torture's prevalence). To be clear, there is no dispute that torture's practices change over time; it is rather the recognition advocates and adjudicators bring around the identification of their harms that remains vague and definitely less than linear and indubitably progressive. Whilst its natural law logic advances the normative prohibitions of torture as long accepted (i.e., *jus cogens*), they are also time-specific – embodying and responding to contemporary values and issues – living, evolving, changing and progressing. Hope of progress (however incremental) is entrusted to time. Time is embedded in forward-looking impulses and the notion of the 'living instrument'. The *longue durée* comes to aid in overlooking the contestations in the *courte durée* – with seriously questioning the present taken to jeopardise progress in and at hand.

3.5 CONCLUSION

> Chronologies of progress are always unreliable, especially when these narratives are told by the free in the name of the bound.[127]

So, what does all this mean for the anti-torture field? For practice, incrementalism in 'seeking to effect gradual changes [risk] "humanizing" coercive systems and practices [and] stifle a potentially more effective approach to torture prevention that radically interrogates the state's coercive powers and social realities' – although '[p]ragmatically, one may say that this is the best we can hope for'.[128] What does this mean for

[127] Colin Dayan, *The Law Is a White Dog* (Princeton University Press 2011) 26.
[128] Oette (2024) 153.

torture's conceptualisation? In all, differentiating *inherent* from *illegitimate* suffering can be said to be inextricably interlinked to public as political emotions, undergirding or undercutting legal protection. Shared moral feelings as consolidated into common sense thus bring with it emotional associations and engender drives to *punish* as well as to *protect*. When viewed historically, sociologically and anthropologically, the notion of 'progress' has had important ideological implications for how the field has operated – imbuing it with a sense of purpose, functioning as a way-marker towards an endpoint: torture's eradication. Changing understandings of pain and punishment are indeed revealed to be socio-culturally contingent, with legal assessments of torture too beholden to this broader context.

What legal doctrine takes to essentially be unidirectional with social sentiments informing legal enactments is rather circular, interactive and reiterative – with society shaping but also being shaped by a consciousness around punishment. Historical accounts on law's contemporary relationship to torture prove largely unreliable in their linearity under scrutiny. Legal interpretation of torture's prohibition is rather more 'pendulous' than merely progressive in reality and more political and less principled than generally presumed.[129] Whilst torture's interpretation is not ahistoric nor static, there is a lack of clarity as to how sociocultural and political forces have influenced this exercise. This chapter has charted the broader contours of the central factors at play here, namely, shifts in prevailing social and scientific views, values and knowledge – as channelled or challenged through judges and taken to constitute torture's sociality.

Historical differences around significations of pain and punishment (for instance, that the psychological was generally dismissed) serve to reject universality and timelessness of torturous suffering, which demands a holistic analysis which evade a single discipline. Sociopolitical factors, configuring associations, proxies, values and responses around pain, serve to qualify what and whose pain is counted, how and how much – central to how we make sense of suffering. These forces render certain forms of suffering necessary and in turn acceptable, by some measure,

[129] *Myrna Mack Chang v. Guatemala* [2003] IACtHR separate opinion of Trindade [8].

given their instrumentality for a supposed common good, social cohesion or justice.[130] The longitudinal take, through the *longue durée,* too attests to progress. So, there is more at play in this historical-theoretical reading in how *raison d'etat* evades attention in shaping and sustaining sociopolitical sensitivities. This 'more' points to the temporal, to the work the notion of time is entrusted. Expediency turns into exceptionality, that the prohibition concern itself with certain forms of harm and not others. What the progressive push leaves behind is wrapped up in what the state needs, in necessity. Beyond historical and theoretical perspectives, so how is necessity assessed by advocates and adjudicators in legal settings? Chapter 4 offers further clues.

[130] Ivan Illich, *Medical Nemesis* (1976) 133–134.

CHAPTER 4

Exceptionalising Suffering

I WAS LATE TO PRISON ABOLITIONIST SCHOLARSHIP, only having been introduced to it by prison researchers at Dignity (Andrew Jefferson and Tomas Max Martin). This line of thinking had been placed out of my range of possibilities, probably by my legal education. It was violations of existing laws I was to be concerned with. It was not police or prisons as institutions in and of themselves that needed to be questioned but it was excessive uses of pre-trial detention or punitive solitary confinement. The prevalence and longevity of certain means of law enforcement (police and prisons) stood in for their effectiveness, attested to their necessity to state function. The question, therefore, short-sightedly became not of the institution (should police or prisons exist) itself but of implementation (how should it exist). Implicit in the backgrounding or vanishing of the question of abolition here was that these institutions of 'pain delivery' were acceptable and legitimate, and therefore non-justiciable, institutions. Legal advisors swiftly went from labelling an act a 'use of force' when deemed to be legitimate and 'violence' or 'violation' when not. It was a distinction that concealed my own frames of reference. Divorcing practices like solitary confinement from broader systemic questions was common, born out of viewing problems technically not structurally. A legal provision allowing for indefinite solitary confinement was sizeable enough practically speaking for a human rights intervention – but dismantling the carceral logics producing and sustaining the practice was not.

In the minutes before a meeting with fellow legal advisors, talk turned to torture methods that unquestionably (automatically) broke the person; were electrocution and rape to be thought of as torture per se? Need each case not be argued and assessed on an individual basis? As human rights lawyers, we had an interest in finding severe suffering and advancing rules of thumb but could this lead to unintended consequences – in pathologizing victim-survivors as necessarily 'bent' and 'broken'? What about victim-survivors who no longer suffered or felt 'broken' after their torture? Were they to be denied recognition? Had they not suffered long enough? What emerged in this 'small talk' for me was how our imagination of the victim (and the duration of their suffering) served to frame the harms before us. Torture needed a spectacle, an event, and other categories most likely involved prolonged and cumulative suffering. Perhaps some suffering was too short to count at all. And what to say, if anything, of short-cuts?

***

> Jurists have always preferred to define torture narrowly, while activists have favored definitions that are quite broad. The latter can be so inclusive as to make the term useless, while the former can be so narrow as to miss important features of modern torture. Since the nineteenth century, some have come to regard any violation of human dignity as torture. ... Defining torture as any indignity fails to distinguish between cases where the physical pain is incidental and the far graver cases where it is inevitable. ... It would be a mistake, then, to say all punishments are torture (for sometimes there is no direct physical torment) and conversely that all tortures are punishments (for many are not authorized by custom or law).[1]

How violent acts and impacts are named matters – both symbolically and materially.[2] Symbolically, naming matters for the due recognition and representation of lived realities – in 'differentiating the cries we can hear from those we cannot, the sights we can see from those we cannot'.[3] Naming promises a rhetorical power towards stronger recognition.[4] Naming exudes a political signification – motivating individuals or institutions claiming to speak on behalf of victim-survivors to have authorities inscribe practices they aim to change, such as human trafficking, conversion therapy or domestic violence, under the rubric of torture's prohibition. Materially, naming matters for investigators, detention monitors, advocates and adjudicators – in deciding where to look and

1 Rejali (2007) 35–39, 562.

2 Or alternatively 'categorisation' or 'qualification'.

3 Butler (2009) 51.

4 Clare McGlynn, 'Rape as "Torture"? Catharine MacKinnon and Questions of Feminist Strategy' (2008) 16 (1) *Feminist Legal Studies* 71.

what to look for – informing, in turn, access to protection, prevention, rehabilitation and redress. Not just any suffering can be recognised or responded to given limitations on precious energies.

Naming matters to scholars playing into hierarchies, placing torture at the apex of a 'pyramid of pain', or 'aberrational' with inhuman and degrading treatment as a 'fence around that wall', encumbering states 'not just from crossing the torture threshold, but to keep them from even approaching it'.[5] There is a common slippage here. It starts with appreciating that all categories are prohibited (and to recognise that to 'say that something is "not torture" is not to commend or even to tolerate it') only to continue to emphasise the need to nevertheless 'differentiate between "degrading treatment" and "torture", lest one end up trivializing the concept of torture and diminishing the special horror attached to that term'.[6] Through naming practices, whether intentional or intuitive, advocates, academics and adjudicators actively maintain discursive frames of reference and operation, wielding symbolic and material power in what and who matters.

Language, its concepts and categories, matters especially to states, who have endlessly deployed euphemisms in shifting the narrative over harmful practices. States begrudgingly live with and explain away such violations, but not torture. It is torture that draws their precious energies with its orbiting categories following suit. For states, reputation is at stake, in being differentiated between the 'civilised and the uncivilised, the compassionate and the barbarous' – as problematic as those prisms are.[7] It is the denial of torture that is 'initiated, structured and sustained by the massive resources of the modern state [and] built into the ideological façade of the state'.[8] Whilst inhuman and degrading are *equally* prohibited and exude strong significations, it is torture which captures the public and political imagination.

[5] Waldron (2010) 277–278. Waldron, to be fair, goes on to relate that he later rethought his position and came to appreciate the importance of the categories of inhuman and degrading treatment.

[6] Sanford Levinson, 'In Quest of a "Common Conscience": Reflections on the Current Debate About Torture' (2005) 1 *Journal of National Security Law & Policy* 231–252, 242.

[7] Kelly (2012) 6.

[8] Stanley Cohen, *States of Denial: Knowing about Atrocities and Suffering* (Polity 2001) 10.

How does language feature and function in this interpretive exercise? Whilst the first half of the book traced the contours of legal definitions and standards, it has also alluded to the continuous control, configuration and contestation involved in torture's qualification and the sociopolitical utility in state-sponsored suffering. How then is the relation between law and violence, where law legitimates some forms of violence whilst not others, to be understood? I now delve deeper into political considerations in how advocates and adjudicators name torture, inhuman and degrading treatment and what falls outside the prohibition's paradigm altogether. In Section 4.1, I start with how in these naming practices the category of torture has been exceptionalised through its association with a 'special stigma' at the top-end (torture) and excluded through requirements that violence be 'unusual' at the bottom-end (lawful sanctions). In Section 4.2, I examine how exclusions operate through related conceptual devices. In surveying what is included, how that is categorised and what is excluded, I identify that psychologically oriented practices have had difficulty in attaining recognition under the prohibition (in Section 4.3) with a view to solitary confinement (Section 4.3.1). Exceptionality, I argue, runs through the need for physicality in suffering, serving to excuse a distinct degree of psychological suffering on which contemporary modes of state violence rely.

4.1 EXCEPTIONALITY AND EXTREMITY

> Modern sensibilities display a definite selectivity. They are highly attuned to perceive and recoil from certain forms of violence, but at the same time they have particular blind spots, or sympathetic limitations, so that other forms are less clearly registered and experienced. Consequently, routine violence and suffering can be tolerated on condition that it is discreet, disguised, or somehow removed from view.[9]

Exceptionalisation has (re)produced the expectation that torture must somehow 'destroy' its subjects, physically and irremediably. Jean Améry

[9] Garland (1993) 243.

chillingly wrote that '[w]hoever was tortured stays tortured' and that it is 'ineradicably burned into him, even when no clinically objective traces can be detected'.[10] The first UN Special Rapporteur on Torture, Peter Kooijmans, reflected that 'the harm done is mostly irreparable, not so much from a physical as from a psychological point of view [and that] [o]ften the victim's personality is irreparably damaged: he never will be the same person again'.[11] This has informed the imagination around torture, that it ought to be unspeakable and permanent – constituting an unreflected rhetoric enjoying common currency. The unspeakable, as others to be invoked have critiqued, has rendered the category of torture as nearly unattainable. While no international legal framework requires that the harm caused to persist or be permanent, to 'destroy',[12] the moral condemnation associated with findings of torture has perpetuated this high threshold. The point advanced from a critical perspective, therefore, is not to reject that torture destroys but to reject that it must *necessarily* destroy for recognition to follow – the point advanced is rather that survivors can be 'changed but not shattered'.[13]

That torture is exceptional and aberrational has become a central idea in this politics of naming and framing, hindering torture's recognition rather than reflecting its empirical reality.[14] The 'special stigma' indelibly inscribed onto torture's judicial conceptualisation has been a key factor. A fraction of cases in international human rights law assessed under the prohibition of torture, inhuman and degrading treatment have specifically been found to amount to *torture* because the facts

[10] Jean Améry, *At the Mind's Limits: Contemplations by a Survivor on Auschwitz and Its Realities* (Indiana University Press 1980) 34.

[11] Pieter Kooijmans, 'The Ban on Torture: Legal and Socio-Political Problems' in Franz Matscher (ed), *Folterverbot sowie Religions- und Gewissensfreiheit im Rechtsvergleich* (Kehl 1990) 93.

[12] Whilst the *Inter-American Convention to Prevent and Punish Torture* (IACPPT) definition does not require severe pain, its definition still expects torture to 'obliterate the personality'.

[13] Andrew M Jefferson and Sinwa Naw, 'The Consequences of Penal Repression on Political Hope and Action in Myanmar' (2025) *Justice, Power and Resistance* 3.

[14] Some may well say that the right cases are not being brought before relevant international courts and committees but I argue here that the threshold has been fixed so high that it unduly excludes a vast majority of cases striving for the specific recognition as torture.

somehow lacked the 'special stigma'.[15] The ECtHR, for instance, did not find a torture violation in a single case from 1978 to 1996 and only 110 or so times thereafter – with comparable bodies as the UN Committee against Torture as the Inter-American Court of Human Rights too setting such high thresholds for torture.[16]

The concept of 'stigma' is all the more unclear because there has been 'virtually no jurisprudential development of what is meant by stigma or what exactly it is that the Court seeks to stigmatize' – nor more generally in doctrinal 'law and torture' practice or research.[17] Whatever is meant by it, the 'stigma' has served to fix the judicial gaze and search on the victims' bodies for 'marks of suffering', and to entrench the crude question of 'how much do we think these men have suffered'.[18] There has, in the wake of this reasoning, emerged a *weak* association between torture and practices that do not leave lasting physical marks, inflicted and controlled bureaucratically (according to specific regulations) and justified on the victim's profile.[19] With no 'special stigma' ultimately being associated with the psychological suffering in *Ireland v. UK* in 1978, the case in which it was introduced, the torture qualification was denied to psychologically oriented suffering there and thereafter. Recent scholarship has found that the ECtHR conversely 'remove[d] the stigma from the specific acts in question' – namely, the 'five techniques' of wall-standing, hooding, exposure to constant noise, sleep deprivation and deprivation

[15] Primarily at the European Court of Human Rights (ECtHR, the caselaw which this chapter draws upon) but also the Inter-American Court of Human Rights and the UN Committee Against Torture.

[16] Ergün Cakal, 'Recognising psychological suffering in adjudicating torture's prohibition: Between precedent and practice at the European Court of Human Rights, the Inter-American Court of Human Rights and the UN Committee Against Torture', PhD dissertation, University of Copenhagen (2025).

[17] Kathleen Cavanaugh, 'On Torture: The Case of the "Hooded Men"' (2020) 42 (3) *Human Rights Quarterly* 519, 532.

[18] Farrell (2022) 7.

[19] Rodney Morgan and Malcolm Evans, *Combating Torture in Europe: The Work and Standards of the European Committee for the Prevention of Torture* (CoE 2001) 60. This early study into the European Committee for the Prevention of Torture (CPT) found that its members 'reserved' torture for 'what are perhaps best described as specialised, or exotic, forms of violence' and almost exclusively for 'physical ill-treatment employed instrumentally by the police'.

of food and drink – preserving torture's associations with the physical, exceptional and civilisational.[20]

Exceptionality has thus become a mark of modern torture in that it must clearly be an aberration. For this reason, as one scholar has noted, 'we do not associate torture with normal practices – that is, with the legal and constitutional forms that we expect to constrain everyday government conduct'.[21] 'Normal' here can be taken to mean the practices generally taken to be accepted in international police and prison standards – handcuffing, searches and, as we will come to towards the chapter's end, solitary confinement. This association with the aberrational has disserved the recognition of torturous suffering very much present in everyday and prolonged grievances, denying stronger condemnation. It is not that these are never found as violations but they, by not being called out as torture, have been perpetuated as ambiguous, deniable or even acceptable to some degree.

Advocates and adjudicators have thus come to take their role as differentiating the 'usual' suffering from, after the American parlance, the 'unusual' (or in another formulation: 'different from the usual degree of humiliation inherent in arrest or detention').[22] Deviations are considered 'unjustified' or 'unusual',[23] if not rational and purposeful for the preservation of the state, but not suffering 'as such'.[24] In reserving and restricting its recognition to the 'most serious' violations, the law 'operates so as to remove classes of persons from the hearing of the legal system ... excluded by reason of capacity, inarticulacy or ability to convey suffering in a legal language constantly demonstrate the inherent restrictive nature of law'.[25] That is to say, that in 'focusing on the abhorrent

[20] Farrell (2022) 2 and 7.

[21] John T Parry, 'The Shape of Modern Torture: Extraordinary Rendition and Ghost Detainees' (2005) 6 *Melbourne Journal of International Law* 516.

[22] *Öcalan v. Turkey (no 1)* [2005] ECtHR 46221/99 [181].

[23] Tim Owen QC and Alison Macdonald, *Livingstone, Owen and MacDonald on Prison Law* (3rd ed, OUP 2003) [5.74] find that the ECtHR requires 'a fairly significant deviation from what it regards as the normal conditions of imprisonment'.

[24] Linda Ross Meyer, 'Suffering the Loss of Suffering: How Law Shapes and Occludes Pain' in Austin Sarat (ed), *Knowing the Suffering of Others: Legal Perspectives on Pain and its Meanings* (University of Alabama Press 2014) 15.

[25] Williams (2007).

and the seemingly abnormal practice of torture, there is an obvious danger of implicitly legitimizing other forms of violence perpetrated by the state under the cover of law'.[26] In merely acknowledging but not addressing 'lesser' violations, the law has actively tolerated their practice.[27] Associating torture with exceptionalities and extremities, to put this differently, has served to sustain state deniability around practices that are more everyday and mundane.[28] In all, narrowing too much has meant that we fail to recognise forms that have a legitimate claim to our attention, and 'invites states to play games over where the line lies, rather than dealing with the issue of ill-treatment more broadly'.[29]

The baseline is thus fixed with prevalent practices in mind, those rendered inevitable, trivial as necessary and justified. This operates as to expect, for instance, blindfolding as needing to be aggravated.[30] As I discuss later in this chapter, such exceptionalities are clearly at play in how adjudicators have deployed the 'total' and 'partial' distinction in cases on prolonged solitary confinement – downgrading and dismissing lived experiences in deference to the state. This comparative exercise objectifies harm, aiming to draw and situate it in a hierarchy. How life sentences without parole are normalised through a comparison with the death penalty offers another prime example.[31] This is particularly difficult where a practice inflicts serious suffering despite its prevalence. Less unusual is equated with less cruel. That is to say, what is deemed excessive is closely dependent on the commonality of practice – with judges finding it easier to categorically condemn the unusual but not the usual. The more 'commonplace' of a practice the less questioned it becomes. The 'usual' cloaks and conceals the suffering at play. As in *Tyrer* before

[26] Tobias Kelly, 'The Cause of Human Rights: Doubts about Torture, Law, and Ethics at the United Nations' (2011) 17 *Journal of the Royal Anthropological Institute* 728.

[27] Veitch (2007) 77, 83.

[28] Etienne Balibar, *Politics and the Other Scene* (Verso 2002) 138; Denise Ferreira da Silva, *No-bodies: Law, Raciality and Violence* (2009) 213.

[29] Kelly (2012) 17.

[30] *Öcalan* [183]: 'Artificially depriving prisoners of their sight by blindfolding them for lengthy periods spread over several days may, when combined with other ill-treatment, subject them to strong psychological and physical pressure'.

[31] Marion Vannier, 'Normalizing Extreme Imprisonment: The Case of Life without Parole in California (1972–2012)' (2019) 25 (4) *Theoretical Criminology* 519.

the European Commission of Human Rights (ECmHR), the UK government argued that 'corporal punishment existed in many countries at [the] time of the adoption of the Convention'.[32] Accepting this logic, Commissioner Mangan reflected to have:

> in my early life, suffered slaps from the hand of a concerned, though sometimes angry, parent. During my school career, I and my fellow pupils were often slapped on the hand by the teachers ... I am, now, what I am. I do not consider that my parents or teachers subjected me to degrading treatment or punishment. ... As a parent, I sometimes administered slaps to my sons. More recently, I find myself with four grandsons between 4 and 8 years of age who, occasionally, seem to me to merit a slap from the hand of a parent, or grandparent.

Exceptionalisation thus runs parallel to exotification. Exceptionality, it should be pointed out, is not exclusive to anti-torture – readily identifiable through the notion of the spectacle, the representation of the archetypal violation or the 'ideal victim' leading to near unattainability of violations such as 'genocide'.[33] In anti-torture as elsewhere, this logic has based itself on a faulty commonsensical assessment that fails to be receptive to lived experiences of victim-survivors. Understandings of torture as unusual 'perilously politicizes the human experience of torture as an issue isolated to distant lands and cultures beyond the scope of Western legal standards',[34] meaning that widely abandoned practices are more probable to come into law's vision whereas 'modern forms will not'.[35] As parts of the state must harm, the state pressures its observers to stay deaf to harms it perceives as inhering to its existence and

[32] Nigel Rodley, 'Tyrer v. United Kingdom (1978)' in Eirik Bjorge and Cameron Miles (eds), *Landmark Cases in Public International Law* (Hart 2017) 329.

[33] Christine Schwöbel-Patel, 'Spectacle in International Criminal Law: The Fundraising Image of Victimhood' (2016) 4 (2) *London Review of International Law* 247; Randle DeFalco, *Invisible Atrocities: The Aesthetic Biases of International Criminal Justice* (CUP 2022); A. Dirk Moses, *The Problems of Genocide: Permanent Security and the Language of Transgression* (CUP 2021).

[34] Danie Meyer-Parlapanis and Thomas Elbert, 'Torture and Its Consequences, Psychology' in JD Wright (ed), *International Encyclopedia of the Social and Behavioral Sciences* (2nd ed, Elsevier 2013) 22.

[35] Khan (2008) 21.

preservation. I will first turn to devices through which such arguments have been legitimated: inevitability, necessity and triviality.

4.2 INEVITABILITY AND TRIVIALITY

> Violence stands before the law, unruly; it defies the law to protect us from its cruelest consequences. It demands that law respond in kind, and requires law to traffic in its own brand of force and coercion. It is thus that point of departure from which complete departure is impossible. It is the task of law and of much legal theory to insist, nonetheless, on the difference between the force that law uses and the unruly force beyond its borders. Legal theorists name the superiority of the former by calling it legitimate.[36]

> If we were able to suffer the sufferings of everyone, we could not live.[37]

That the law does not concern itself with trifles, *de minimis non curat lex*, operates as to limit recognition at the bottom end of the prohibition of torture, inhuman and degrading treatment. It operates in this terrain to emphasise that suffering needs sorting through and differentiating between, that suffering ordinarily expected in life are tolerated and that those which are aberrational merit redress. As alluded to in Chapter 2, this is hardcoded onto the *UN Convention against Torture and Other Cruel, Inhuman or Degrading Treatment or Punishment* (UNCAT)'s 'lawful sanctions' clause and ECtHR's 'minimum severity' threshold which are analogous devices used to assess whether any alleged conduct falls within the scope of the prohibition against torture, inhuman and degrading treatment.[38]

Whilst lawful sanctions finds little conceptual depth, the 'minimum level' has been described as requiring something other than difficult or 'undoubtedly unpleasant or even irksome' requiring the conduct in question to be 'harrowing' though 'far from ideal',[39] as requiring

36 Sarat and Kearns (1993) 212.

37 Primo Levi, *The Drowned and the Saved* (Simon and Schuster 1989) 56.

38 The 'minimum level of severity to warrant consideration by an international court' operates similarly under other articles: *Korolev v. Russia* [2010] ECtHR 25551/05, p. 4; *Finger v. Bulgaria* [2011] ECtHR 37346/05 [61]. Similar here is the 'significant disadvantage' test: *Obote v. Russia* [2020] ECtHR 58954/09 [25–28, 52].

39 *Limoni v. Sweden* [2007] ECtHR 6576/05 [90].

a special level of humiliation,[40] needing to involve particularly acute hardship,[41] more than 'discreditable and reprehensible',[42] more than 'cramped and insalubrious',[43] 'distressing and humiliating'[44] or a 'lack of respect for the applicant as a person' and 'interfering with human dignity'.[45] That which is unpleasant but therapeutic or necessary is also considered to not meet the minimum.[46] More conceptually, the minimum threshold has been articulated as: high and necessarily so;[47] more than evoking judicial misgivings;[48] as other than the usual;[49] as evolving;[50] irreducible to a numerical calculation;[51] as informed by social consensus;[52] also referred to as minimum level of gravity[53] and 'prohibited severity'.[54] This 'minimum' threshold operates through three distinct devices that serve to neutralise and naturalise state-inflict suffering: inevitability (and necessity) and triviality. These permeate the international caselaw and commentary, particularly the European, and will be unpacked in turn.

4.2.1 INEVITABILITY. The language of inevitability has become a reliable (though again a critically unreflected) corollary to articulate suffering not to reach the threshold, and has been alluded to in various formulations (inevitable, unavoidable, inescapable) whenever advocates and adjudicators have sought to dismiss or detract from a

40 *Öcalan v. Turkey* [2003] ECtHR Chamber 46221/99 [220].

41 *Mouisel v. France* [2003] ECtHR 67263/01 [48].

42 *Ireland v. UK* [1978] ECtHR 5856/72 [181].

43 *Trepashkin v. Russia* [2018] ECtHR 34473/05 [36].

44 *Guzzardi v. Italy* [1980] ECtHR 7367/76 [107].

45 *Raninen v. Finland* [1997] ECtHR 20972/92 [50, 55].

46 *D.D. v. Lithuania* [2012] ECtHR 13469/06 [171].

47 *R.R. v. Poland* [2011] ECtHR 27617/04, dissent of Judge Bratza [5]: (intense anxiety but no violation); *McGlinchey and others v. the UK* [2003] 50390/99, dissent of Judge Bratza; *Ojei v. the Netherlands* [2017] ECtHR 64724/10 [43]; *Budina v. Russia* [2009] ECtHR 64724/10, p. 7.

48 *Costello-Roberts v. the UK* [1993] ECtHR 13134/87 [32].

49 *Salapa v. Poland* [2001] ECtHR 35489/97, p. 1; *L.J. v. Finland* [1995] ECtHR 21221/93, p. 9; *Remer v. Germany* [1995] ECtHR 25096/94, p. 5.

50 *Alekseјeva v. Latvia* [2012] ECtHR 21780/07 [36]; *D.F. v. Latvia* [2014] ECtHR 11160/07 [85].

51 *Mursic v. Croatia* [2016] ECtHR [GC] 7334/13 [123].

52 *V. v. the UK* [1999] ECtHR 24888/94 concurring opinion of Lord Reed, p. 43.

53 *Shamayev and others v. Georgia and Russia* [2005] ECtHR 36378/02 [338].

54 *Gülmez v. Turkey* [2008] ECtHR 16330/02 [21].

given harm.[55] Findings often presume that suffering *must not have been* sufficient to meet the minimum threshold of severity without deeper reasoning. The European framework has used the notion of 'inevitable' from its very first cases. In the *Greek Case*, the ECmHR offered a stark reading of what it deems to be 'inherent' and 'inevitable' expecting that 'a certain roughness of treatment of detainees by both police and military authorities' and that 'such roughness may take the form of slaps or blows of the hand'. The ECmHR, in a logic not since repeated so explicitly, understood that 'the point up to which prisoners and the public may accept physical violence as being neither cruel nor excessive varies between different societies and even between different sections of them'.[56] This has been consistently understood through the logic that 'the suffering and humiliation involved must in any event go beyond that inevitable element of suffering or humiliation connected with a given form of legitimate treatment or punishment' or as involving 'a manner and method of the execution of the measure do not subject [the applicant] to distress or hardship of an intensity exceeding the unavoidable level of suffering inherent in detention'.[57] This rather assumes that punishment is about suffering and humiliation, that suffering is incidental to certain forms of punishment.[58]

Advocates and adjudicators also choose to sift and sort through suffering through the language of 'necessity' (as well as related

[55] *Zakhatrkin v. Russia* [2010] ECtHR 1555/04 [140]: 'the acceptable threshold of suffering'; *Khatsiyeva and others v. Russia* [2008] ECtHR 5108/02 (inevitable lethal force); *Sambor v. Poland* [2011] ECtHR 15579/05 (police shooting man's leg inevitable); *Iustin Robertino Micu v. Romania* [2015] ECtHR 41040/11 (inherent and inevitable suffering); *Taymuskhanovy v. Russia* [2011] ECtHR 11528/07 (inevitable emotional distress).

[56] *The Greek Case* [501].

[57] *Kudla v. Poland* [2000] ECtHR [GC] 30210/96 [92, 94]; *Tyrer v. UK* [30].

[58] Offering rather elaborate reasoning, *Ilascu and others v. Moldova and Russia* [2004] ECtHR 48787/99 [430–431] differentiated between unavoidable and aggravated suffering related to a death sentence. The ECtHR reasoned that 'some element of delay between imposition and execution of the sentence and the experience of severe stress in conditions necessary for strict incarceration are inevitable' but 'a long period of time must be spent on death row in extreme conditions, with the ever present and mounting anguish of awaiting execution of the death penalty' holding the 'anxiety and suffering engendered by … the arbitrary nature of the proceedings which led to it' as aggravated. The suffering needed to be 'unusual' or exceptional – excessive even – to be recognised.

justifications in resilience, dangerousness, risk, mitigating factors and social value).[59] Necessity, that the state authorities had to act as to inflict suffering on an individual, has been used in a number of cases to find no violation including but not limited to where police publicly displayed dead bodies during investigation in fronts of relatives,[60] irreducible life sentences,[61] and, as the case-study to be presented shortly will demonstrate, prolonged solitary confinement. These practices have predominantly involved psychologically oriented suffering despite growing evidence-base of health impacts. With necessity at the fore of judicial assessments, the state's functioning (*raison d'etat*) is poised to prove, and often has, a paramount barrier to the recognition of torturous suffering.[62] This point is picked up on in the discussion on 'Psychological suffering'.

More recently, the notion of *necessity* has become even more interchangeable with *inevitability* in the ECtHR caselaw.[63] The Court's Guide entitled 'Key Theme, Article 3: The minimum level of severity test in

[59] *Rohde v. Denmark* [2005] ECtHR 69332/01 [88]; *Öcalan v. Turkey* [2005] ECtHR 46221/99 [232–233]; *Öcalan v. Turkey (no 2)* [2014] ECtHR 24069/03, 197/04, 6201/06 and 10464/07 [107]; *Ramirez Sanchez v. France* [2006] ECtHR 59450/00 [113].

[60] *Cangöz and others v. Turkey* [2016] ECtHR 7469/06.

[61] Life not justified on 'legitimate penological grounds': *Bancsok and Laszlo Magyar v. Hungary (no.2)* [2022] ECtHR 52374/15 53364/15 [47]; *Vinter* [2013].

[62] *Tyrer v. UK*, p. 63, per Mr Blom-Cooper (arguing for the UK in public hearings of 17 January 1978): 'Some punishments may be degrading in the ordinary sense of that word, but … not degrading within Article 3 because they are effective in preventing serious social harm. They possess what the Commission rightly, in our submission, describes in para 39 of its report as a "redeeming social value"'. The discussion in Tyrer around 'social value' of corporal punishment remains revealing on this point, where it was decided that the 'absence of obvious social value was a factor in determining whether the treatment was contrary to the Convention' (Ibid 58, per Commissioner Kellberg).

[63] To be sure, the two focal points of severity and necessity were long present in the ECtHR caselaw before the Grand Chamber decision in *Bouyid* in 2015, a case arguably more about the psychological suffering inflicted although through the infliction of a slap by a police officer on a minor and a young man. In *Bouyid*, the Court famously adopted the rule that any recourse to (i) physical force not strictly necessary, (ii) in a custodial context, (iii) which diminishes dignity is to be viewed as an Article 3 violation. The Court therefore shifted the focus away from severity to necessity. What can be lost in this discussion is that the easier recognition was limited to the application of physical force not without – conceivably ruling out threats, irreducible life imprisonment, and solitary confinement which lack such force.

light of *Bouyid v. Belgium*' published in 2022,[64] holds this to be a 'bright-line rule', inextricably binding *necessity* with *dignity*. The *Guide* is thin as to how inherent or incidental harm is to be gauged. In navigating this terrain of minimum severity, the notion of operational (policing, penological, military or medical) necessity is emphasised and encouraged.[65] How judges should assess what is necessary for state authorities, however, is neither precisely spelled out beyond the adjectives of indispensable and not excessive – which can similarly prove vague and left to the specific context of a case. Behavioural risk assessments, criminal records and history of violence, though, are accepted as potentially helpful by the *Guide*. This has not meant however that the severity test has disappeared entirely from view. In one case involving metal cages in courtrooms, one judge lamented the majority's insistence on not following the necessity test[66]

> Applying that logic [of *Bouyid*] to the use of metal cages in courtrooms could have liberated the reasoning of the Court from the rather speculative effect of intense suffering of the applicant. Putting a person on trial in a metal cage without any necessity is degrading in its denial of human dignity. It is a pity that the Court did not depart from the threshold of severity test in the present case and that it even chose not to refer at all to the *Bouyid v. Belgium* case.

In dissent in another case, a judge wrote that even though 'social science has shown that harsh penal policies do not have the desired effects … the Court does not have jurisdiction to rule on the rationality of choices made in the field of penal policy'.[67] Questioning necessity, from this perspective, brought judicial assessment disagreeably into the

[64] ECtHR, 'Key Theme, Article 3: The minimum level of severity test in light of Bouyid v. Belgium' (2022).

[65] Particularly regarding practices of handcuffing, similar restraints such as in psychiatric facilities or cages in courtrooms, tasers, pepper-sprays, searches, forced medical interventions (such as psychiatric treatment, feeding, sterilisation and removal of items from the body), isolation and punishment (lengthy or life imprisonment).

[66] *Urazov v. Russia* [2016] ECtHR 42147/05, concurring opinion of Judge Silvis.

[67] *Rezmives and others v. Romania* [2017] ECtHR 61467/12, 39516/13, 48231/13, opinion of Judge Wojtyczek [4].

realm of penal policy and beyond ECtHR's remit despite an established evidence-base. Such a note reverberated in *Bouyid* where three dissenting judges wrote along similar lines that it was 'not for the Court to impose general rules of conduct on law-enforcement officers'.[68] Deference here meant a deferral to official discretion, despite the evidence on offer, to state power. This has also been described as 'the legitimacy loop' – where the Court circularly reasons that suffering is illegitimate if it crosses the minimum threshold yet 'invokes legitimacy as a criterion based on which a punishment may not be inhuman or degrading'.[69] It suffices to say here that these assessments and aspirations do not critically take due account of – in fact often conceal – the broader frameworks in which they operate. The ECtHR's identification with state authorities reveals an operative logic, endangering the absolute nature of the prohibition, and potentially leading to the denial of full recognition as sought by its victims. Far from politically neutral, there is an active decision to defer the decision to state authorities, effectively shielding certain forms of suffering in the service of the state away from scrutiny – as is also the case with the invocation of 'triviality'.

4.2.2 TRIVIALITY. Suffering has also been often discounted through invoking the language of *triviality*: that the nature of injuries sustained were of 'a merely trivial nature',[70] 'comparatively trivial beatings',[71] and that though suffering might be 'far from ideal'[72] or 'while regrettable' were no violations.[73] States have also used such language distinctly in cases involving domestic violence.[74] Triviality is thus used to equate

68 *Bouyid* [GC] dissenting opinion of De Gaetano, Lemmens and Mahoney [6].

69 Mavronicola (2021) 114.

70 *Beganovic v. Croatia* [2009] ECtHR 46423/06 [68].

71 *Ireland v. UK* [1978] [115].

72 *Magomedov v. Russia* [2017] ECtHR 20933/08 [54].

73 *Kuparadze v. Georgia* [2017] ECtHR 30743/09 [63].

74 *Tunikova and ors v. Russia* [2021] ECtHR 55974/16: 'the Russian authorities' stereotypical attitude to domestic violence as a "private and trivial matter"'; *Valiuliene v. Lithuania* [2013] ECtHR 33234/07 [55]; *Opuz v. Turkey* [2009] ECtHR 33401/02 [46]. This is particularly interesting material because such detailed reasoning around suffering is not usually present, as in the case of 'special stigma'. To be sure, certain harms are often found not to meet the threshold without offering due reasoning:

suffering with 'discomfort' rather than 'degradation'. 'Discomfort' is an adjacent notion here that is evoked by states and is accepted by adjudicators to stand for trivial suffering.[75] Academics have also, in a similar vein, urged the need to differentiate between 'psychological fears of pain and pain itself' so as to avoid torture becoming a slippery word of which 'analytic discussion becomes meaningless'.[76] This argument has been formulated in different ways, that torture could easily become 'a moral-sentimental term designating the infliction of suffering, however defined'[77] and in terms of a need to avoid 'a level of frequency and banality that will be met with sheer indifference by the governments concerned'.[78] Putting all this together, the maintenance of a high threshold for the prohibition (for the categories of torture, inhuman and degrading treatment collectively and respectively) is ruled by a fear of dilution, devaluation of the deterrent and rhetorical effect of torture's prohibition – a fear of making the prohibition commonplace and endangering its normative force.[79]

see *ZHU v. the UK* [2000] ECtHR 36790/97 (difficult and undesirable but not minimum); *Anatoliy Kuzmin v. Russia* [2015] ECtHR 28917/05 (far from adequate but not minimum); *Makuc and others v. Slovenia* [2007] ECtHR 26828/06 (although anguish-insecurity but not minimum); *Gatt v. Malta* [2010] ECtHR 28221/08 (anxiety but not minimum); *D.G. v. Ireland* [2002] ECtHR 39474/98 (depression, frustration and anger not minimum); *Fetisov and others v. Russia* [2012] ECtHR 43710/07, 6023/08, 11248/08, 27668/08, 31242/08 and 52133/08 (conditions far from adequate but not minimum).

[75] *Ilias and Ahmed v. Hungary* [2017] ECtHR Chamber 47287/15 [81]: Hungary 'argued that any discomfort allegedly suffered by the applicants at the transit zone did not attain the minimum level of severity'; *H.G. v. Switzerland* [2001] ECtHR 36833/97, p. 8, 'possibly uncomfortable'; *Shanidze v. Georgia* [2017] ECtHR 60867/08 [46]; *Wiktoriko v. Poland* [2009] ECtHR 14612/02 [55]: 'must have caused her great distress and physical discomfort'; *Ireland* [1978] separate opinion of Fitzmaurice, he finds one instance of the 'five techniques' to be 'mere aches, pains, strains, stresses and discomforts'.

[76] Rejali (2007) 382; Kelly (2012) 9.

[77] Peters (1996) 2.

[78] Marc Bossuyt, 'Belgium Condemned for Inhuman or Degrading Treatment Due to Violations by Greece of EU Asylum Law, M.S.S. v. Belgium and Greece, Grand Chamber, 'European Court of Human Rights' (2011) *European Human Rights Law Review* 581–596.

[79] This was an argument made by the state respondent and rejected in CAT-C-55-D-575-201 [5.18]: on Article 16, 'the argument that all detainees are subjected to the same conditions of detention does not make the situation with regard to the complainant acceptable and in no way relieves the State of its responsibilities in this regard'.

The language of triviality has also long featured in the reasoning of dissenting judges – of which Judge Fitzmaurice represents a prime example in the early caselaw. In *Ireland*, in dissent, Fitzmaurice found one instance of the use of 'five techniques' to be 'mere aches, pains, strains, stresses and discomforts', and as the 'common lot of mankind'.[80] In *Tyrer*, he saw that 'all punishment is degrading, at least if it involves imprisonment and the (mostly unpleasant and often humiliating) incidents of prisons life and discipline' and he required 'a degree of degradation recognisably greater than that inherently bound-up with any normal punishment that takes the form of coercion or deprivation of liberty'.[81] He also added that the 'fact that a certain practice is felt to be distasteful, undesirable, or morally wrong and such as ought not to be allowed to continue, is not a sufficient ground in itself for holding it to be contrary' to torture's prohibition.[82]

Cautionary remarks around not 'cheapening' torture or avoiding the 'drift into the trivialisation of Article 3 rights'[83] through overuse, as alluded to, are not uncommon in dissents.[84] This is also invoked as the 'flood-gates' problem.[85] Other dissenters have also argued 'to avoid trivialising the term [torture] should be reserved for the most serious violations',[86] have 'oppose[d] an *inflation* of the category' of torture,[87] identified 'dangers in weakening the protection [offered by article 3]',[88] urged 'to stop the trivialisation of Article 3 rights [and]

[80] *Ireland v. UK* [1978] dissent of Fitzmaurice [28]: 'Feelings of "fear, anguish and inferiority" are the common lot of mankind constantly experienced by everyone in the course of ordinary everyday life: this is "la condition humaine"'.

[81] *Tyrer*, separate opinion of Judge Fitzmaurice [6].

[82] Ibid 14.

[83] *Tanase* [65] separate opinion saw setting the threshold as double-edged: '[e]very stick has two ends' [81] that the 'alleged trivialisation of Article 3 may be the lesser possible evil'.

[84] *McGlinchey and ors v. UK* [2003] ECtHR 50390/99 concurring opinion of Judge Costa [2]; *Bouyid v. Belgium* [2015] part dissent of Gaetano et al [7].

[85] Corina Heri, *Responsive Human Rights: Vulnerability, Ill-Treatment and the ECtHR* (Hart 2021); Cohen (2001).

[86] *Nikiforov v. Russia* [2010] ECtHR 42837/04 opinion of Judges Malinverni, Rozakis, Jebens [2–11]; *Tomasi v. France* [1990] ECmHR 12850/87 [32–33].

[87] *Korobov v. Ukraine* [2011] ECtHR 39598/03, concurring opinion [6], original emphasis.

[88] *Warwick v. UK* [1986] ECmHR 9471/81 [21] opinion of Judges Schermers et al.

to avoid the trivialisation of Article 3 and the application of its procedural limb in such a manner as to impose unreasonable demands on investigative authorities and divert resources from investigating grave human rights violations'.[89] Dissenting opinions also provide a site for the opposite, where judges have argued that the threshold is too high;[90] they reveal a strong contestation to lowering, or rather expanding, thresholds of recognition. Beyond the notes of discord, regret and caution, such dissents also mark that the narrative of recognition has never simply been linear but reflective of the plurality of opinions in broader society whether conservative or progressive.[91]

Again, as with the invocation of necessity, what is common to these cases is that they predominantly identify psychologically oriented suffering (e.g., distress, insecurity, anguish, depression, frustration and anger) to not surpass the prohibition's threshold. Moreover, when determining degrading acts, that which just pass the 'minimum' threshold, the ECtHR has looked for treatment which 'grossly humiliates [the victim] before others or drives to act against his will or conscience'[92] or 'showing a lack of respect for or diminishing his or her human dignity, or arouses feelings of fear, anguish or inferiority capable of breaking an individual's moral and physical resistance'.[93] There is a connection made here between the psychological on both sides of the minimum recognition on offer, that is, degradation or discomfort, the latter which is steeped in the language of triviality and inevitability. I will now focus squarely on how psychologically oriented suffering has had difficulties in these naming practices.

[89] *Kraulaidis v. Lithuania* [2017] ECtHR 76805/11, concurring opinion of Judges Sajo et al [7–9]; *Nicolae Virgiliu Tanase v. Romania* [2019] ECtHR 41720/13 [82] dissent of Judge Kuris.

[90] *Penaranda Soto v. Malta* [2018] ECtHR 16680/14, dissenting opinion of Judges Pinto de Albuquerque, Ranzoni and Bosnjak [8]. Regarding the geographical: 'the Convention has a minimum core … regardless of where in Europe this standard is applied. To pretend otherwise would mean that human dignity has a different value according to the area of Europe in which Article 3 is applied. This is, again, unacceptable'.

[91] Ram Prakash Anand, 'The Role of Individual and Dissenting Opinions in International Adjudication' (1965) 14 *International and Comparative Law Quarterly* 788, 805.

[92] *The Greek Case* [1969] [186].

[93] *Strelets v. Russia* [2013] ECtHR 28018/05 [54].

4.3 PSYCHOLOGICAL SUFFERING

> Punishment, whether in seventeenth- or twenty-first century America, turns on whether it is the body or the mind that receives the hard knock of the law.[94]

> In the present-day world there can be little doubt that torture may be inflicted in the mental sphere.[95]

Histories of pain, punishment and torture record broad shifts in state violence toward being 'directed at the mind' and having 'replaced a cluster of punishments – whipping, branding, the stocks, and public hanging'.[96] Anti-torture organisations have documented the increased prevalence in the exposure of victims to practices inflicting psychological suffering,[97] whilst others have argued that it is the *recognition* of psychological suffering, rather than harmful state practices which produce such suffering, which is changing.[98] Whether due to the increased prevalence or recognition, there has emerged an increased conceptualisation aiming to more precisely draw attention to harming individuals without leaving overt physical marks. Countless overlapping and adjacent concepts have been proffered by advocates, academics and adjudicators alike.[99]

[94] Colin Dayan, 'Legal Terrors' (2005) 92 (1) *Representations* 42.

[95] *Ireland v. UK* [1978] separate opinion of Judge Evrigenis.

[96] Ignatieff (1978) xii.

[97] See Crew Against Torture (Russia), 'Prohibited methods of psychological influence: analysis of Russian and international law', Public Committee Against Torture in Israel (PCATI), 'Torture in Israel 2019: Situation Report'.

[98] I accept the question as worthy of attention but I will leave others to debate its validity. Fassin and Rechtman (2009) 160 argue that the 'reality of this suffering [trauma] is of course not new, but the recognition of it certainly is. And does recognition not make it a little more real?'.

[99] E.g., 'non-physical torture', 'clean torture', 'mental torture', 'stealth torture'. Another concept that is increasingly studied has been that of 'moral injury'. It has been understood by legal philosophers as being excluded 'from equal moral consideration', recognition as human per Jessica Wolfendale, 'Prison as a torturous institution', 303; Matthew Talbert and Jessica Wolfendale, 'Moral injury, Moral Suffering, and Moral Health' in Justin McDaniel et al (eds), *Preventing and Treating the Invisible Wounds of War: Combat Trauma, Moral Injury, and Psychological Health* (OUP 2023) or as 'damage done to one's conscience or moral compass when that person perpetrates, witnesses, or fails to prevent acts that transgress one's own moral beliefs, values, or ethical codes of conduct' per Syracuse Moral Injury Project, https://moralinjuryproject.syr.edu/about-moral-injury/.

Distinctions have abounded between, for instance, 'scarring' and 'clean' techniques.[100] Following the *Ireland v. UK* case in 1978 where psychological harm was downgraded to inhuman and degrading, it was in findings of torture against Turkey between 1996 and 2000 where the ECtHR resumed earnestly emphasising notions of 'mental anguish',[101] 'mental violence'[102] and 'psychological pressure'.[103]

Although it has become legally acceptable to split suffering into the physical and psychological (as is found in the torture's definition in the UNCAT), this distinction fails on medical,[104] philosophical and anthropological grounds.[105] Pain exists rather between the mind and the body.[106] Whilst there may indeed be pedagogical reasons to work with the split, it can feed a false hierarchical thinking that the physical is more real than the psychological – that sees 'when not accompanied by recognizable external physical signs, pain ... easily disregarded as existing only "in the mind" of the sufferer'.[107]

Whatever may be the case, the conceptualisation of psychological suffering has seen strong contestation from states interested in preserving their coercive powers meriting specific attention in and of itself. States have variably labelled psychologically oriented practices and experiences as 'enhanced interrogation', as 'permitted procedural side-effects', as 'certain verbal and non-physical techniques', 'non-violent psychological pressure through a vigorous and extensive interrogation', and 'merely'

[100] Rejali (2007) 7.

[101] *Aydin v. Turkey* [1997] ECtHR 57/1996/676/866 [84].

[102] Ibid 86.

[103] *Akkoc v. Turkey* [2000] ECtHR 22947/93 and 22948/93 [116].

[104] Metin Başoğlu et al, 'Torture vs Other Cruel, Inhuman, and Degrading Treatment: Is the Distinction Real or Apparent?' (2007) 64 *Archives of General Psychiatry* 277.

[105] Nimisha Patel, 'Psychological Torture' (2020) 29 *Torture* 79; Nora Sveaass, 'Destroying Minds: Psychological Pain and the Crime of Torture' (2008) 11 *New York City Law Review* 303, 315; Boddice (2017) 77: 'distinct notions of emotional and physical pain perpetuates the dualism that denies [their] interrelation and interdependence'; DelVecchio Good (1994) 11: 'The dichotomy between mind and body upheld by both medical and psychological research is invalid and unavailing'; Boddice (2017) 2; Michael Davis, 'Torture and the Inhumane' (2007) *Criminal Justice Ethics*.

[106] Mark D. Sullivan, 'Finding Pain Between Minds and Bodies' (2001) 17 (2) *The Clinical Journal of Pain* 146–156.

[107] Käll, 'Intercorporeality and the sharability of pain' in Käll (2013) 29.

as 'long established police practices'.[108] To be sure, there is no *formal* requirement that psychological suffering be necessarily coupled with physically overt suffering in international human rights law.[109] Yet, it has been physical suffering which has been emphasised in adjudication as in codification.[110] Given the premium placed on visible marks, states have also increasingly resorted to practices that are psychologically oriented (as opposed to those leaving overt physical marks), in order to avoid accountability.[111]

Since its increased sociopolitical recognition, the figure of psychological suffering has represented a distinct contest in international courts and committees.[112] Whilst psychological suffering has been formally recognised as equally harmful as physical suffering,[113] no case to date has specifically found a torture violation where psychological suffering, for instance with respect to threats, sleep deprivation or solitary confinement, essentially stood on its own. Language here has also dominated how psychological suffering has been conceptualised and contested, recognised or not. Beyond the euphemisms, the devices outlined so far ('special stigma', inevitability, necessity and triviality) have worked hard to legitimate psychological suffering as 'lawful sanctions' or falling below a 'minimum severity'.

Why is physical suffering more readily recognised than the psychological? As outdated as this problematique may read at first glance, this effectively remains the case – politically as well as legally. Whilst it can be answered politically as we have just read, others have proffered a

[108] Ergun Cakal, 'At the Threshold of Justiciable Violence: Configuring and Contesting Torture's Production' (2024) 20 (2) *Law, Culture and the Humanities* 355.

[109] *Gäfgen v. Germany* [2010] ECtHR 22978/05 [108].

[110] See Cakal, PhD dissertation (2025); *Myumyun v. Bulgaria* [2015] ECtHR 67258/13 [74]: 'the offence of bodily harm ... does not appear sufficiently to take into account psychological suffering'; Antonio Marchesi, 'Implementing the UN Convention Definition of Torture in National Law' (2008) 6 *Journal of International Criminal Justice* 208 on the difficulties of its Italian codification.

[111] UN SRT, Report (2010) A/56/156 [55]; UN SRT, Report (2020) A/HRC/43/49.

[112] Physical practices are often understood to include direct physical impact on the body: electricity, used of chemicals, beatings, asphyxiation, cuts. Psychological practices are often understood to include: threats, isolation, sensory deprivation, witnessing of torture, deprivation of food and water, sleep deprivation, mock executions, humiliations.

[113] *Aydin v. Turkey* [86]; *Akkoc v. Turkey* [117].

sociocultural account, pointing to sketchy views that emotional reactions can be controlled: 'we are the keepers of our own minds, and the law should reflect a morality where individuals cannot be compensated for harms over which they have relatively more control',[114] '[e]motional distress is not simply an uncontrolled or uncontrollable reflex, as is the bodily response to a blow or a toxin'[115] and that '[w]e can teach ourselves to toughen up and not be so sensitive, and we can steel ourselves against even exceedingly unpleasant experiences'.[116] Some scholars have argued that the undervaluation at this juncture is a gendered one – since these 'injuries are seen to afflict women'.[117] And again, another account emphasises the public's role not political values embedded in the law in writing:

> There is no doubt that the public draws a distinction between the neurotic and the cripple, between the man who loses his concentration and the man who loses his leg. It is widely felt that being frightened is less than being struck, that trauma to the mind is less than lesion to the body. ... The law has reflected this distinction as one would expect, not only by refusing damages for grief altogether, but by granting discovery for other psychiatric harm only late and grudgingly, and then only in very clear cases.[118]

Prominent scholars such as Scarry, Rejali and Spierenburg too have all insisted on the physicality of torture: that it consists of 'a primary physical act, the infliction of pain, and a primary verbal act, the interrogation'; that it is the 'systematic infliction of physical torment on detained helpless individuals by state officials for police purposes: that is, for

114 Erica Goldberg, 'Emotional Duties' (2015) 47 *Connecticut Law Review* 809, 814–815.

115 John Goldberg and Benjamin Zipursky, 'Unrealized Torts' (2002) 88 *Vanderbilt Law Review* 1625, 1681.

116 Gregory Keating, 'When is Emotional Distress Harm?' in Stephen Pitel et al (eds), *Tort Law: Challenging Orthodoxy* (Hart 2013) 300.

117 Prue Vines et al, 'Is "nervous shock" Still a Feminist Issue? The Duty of Care and Psychiatric Injury in Australia' [2010] *University of New South Wales Faculty of Law Research Series* 45.

118 Tony Weir, *Casebook on Tort* (7th ed, Witherby and Company, 1988) 88.

confession, information, or intimidation';[119] and, accordingly, needs to be distanced from 'structural and psychological violence, which appear to me excuses for an ideological argumentation rather than scholarly concepts'.[120] This has certainly resonated in the adjudication of solitary confinement cases which represent one prevalent and politically guarded practice in this domain. In the following, with a view to a systematic examination of the European caselaw, I explore its contestation despite its well-established psychological impacts.

4.3.1 PRACTICE IN POINT: SOLITARY CONFINEMENT. Whilst not all potentially torturous practices (e.g., threats and restraints) come with explicit bright-lines, solitary confinement is one of the rare few which now does. In 2015, informed by legal and health experts,[121] the UN formulated and adopted a legal framework on the use of solitary confinement in the *Nelson Mandela Rules* (more fully: the UN *Standard Minimum Rules for the Treatment of Prisoners*, hereafter 'NMR'). This marked a shift, compared to what had come before in its 1955 iteration, in several important ways: (i) solitary confinement was defined for the first time as 'the confinement of prisoners for 22 hours or more a day without meaningful human contact' (rule 44) and (ii) its indefinite, prolonged (longer than 15 days) and particular uses (on children, pregnant and breastfeeding women and mentally ill if likely to exacerbate the condition) were considered torturous and, as such, prohibited.[122]

There have also been shifts in the Council of Europe's own standards. The European Committee for the Prevention of Torture (CPT) has come

[119] Elaine Scarry, The Body in Pain: The Making and Unmaking of the World (OUP 1985) 28; Darius Rejali, 'Torture and Democracy: What Now?' in Shampa Biswas and Zahi Zalloua (eds), *Torture: Power, Democracy and the Human Body* (University of Washington Press 2011) 26. See also Richard Posner in Levinson (2004) who distinguishes between psychological and physical torture arguing that we should 'respect the line that separates psychological from physical coercion, and permit it to be crossed only in extremis' holding that the latter is worse than the former.

[120] Pieter Spierenburg, *Violence and Punishment: Civilizing the Body through Time* (2013) 2.

[121] Jennifer Peirce, 'Making the Mandela Rules: Evidence, Expertise, and Politics in the Development of Soft Law International Prison Standards' (2018) 43 (2) *Queen's Law Journal* 263; see also UN SRT, Report (2016) A/66/268.

[122] UN *Nelson Mandela Rules* (2015), rules 43 and 45.

to promote a 14-day limitation and similar prohibitions to that of the NMR.[123] Whilst the *European Prison Rules* (*EPR*), revised and finalised in 2020 by the Council of Europe, notably adopt the definition of solitary confinement as found at the UN level,[124] the question of upper time limits is explicitly deferred to national systems.[125] Yet, only a single case handed down by the ECtHR has referred to UN and CPT standards on solitary confinement[126] – opening it up to critique. The otherwise extensive caselaw on solitary confinement has remained undisturbed – despite significant shifts. The prevalence of prolonged solitary confinement, particularly in Europe, thus begs the question: in light of the well-established evidentiary and normative bases of the suffering it inflicts, why has the practice been largely *legitimated*?[127] Despite the more recent standards, thresholds have historically been set particularly and unduly high for prolonged solitary confinement – with no case ever been deemed sufficiently total nor exceptional to amount to torture. To be sure, the ECtHR caselaw is replete with cases on solitary confinement which are found to amount to inhuman and degrading treatment, many of which could have amounted to torture (and with numerous instances surprisingly not amounting to any violation).

An early case to set the tone with psychological suffering was the 1978 case of *Ensslin, Baader and Raspe v. Germany*,[128] which concerned

[123] Council of Europe, Committee for the Prevention of Torture, 'Solitary confinement of prisoners', CPT/Inf(2011)28-part2.

[124] *European Prison Rules* (2020) 60.6.a: 'the confinement of a prisoner for more than 22 hours a day without meaningful human contact, shall never be imposed on children, pregnant women, breastfeeding mothers or parents with infants in prison'.

[125] *European Prison Rules* (2020) 60.6.d: 'maximum period for which solitary confinement may be imposed shall be set in national law'.

[126] *Schmidt and Smigol v. Estonia* [2023] ECtHR 3501/20, 45907/20, 43128/21 [134].

[127] As mentioned, all violations of all categories are equally significant but, as states notably exert energies in avoiding the torture qualification than orbiting categories, I proceed on the basis of torture's symbolic significance. See *Renolde v. France*, [2008] ECtHR 5608/05 (history of mental illness, 45 day's detention in a punishment cell); *GB v. Bulgaria* [2004] ECtHR 42346/98, (regime very restrictive with very little human contact for more than eight years, alone in cell almost 23 hours per day); *A.L. (X.W.) v. Russia* [2015] ECtHR 44095/14 [75] (detained in solitary confinement in immigration detention for four and a half months – with no contact with other inmates, and restricted visits from his wife, and no access to reading materials, etc.). See further *X v. Turkey* [2012] ECtHR 24626/09 and *AB v. Russia* [2010] ECtHR 1439/06 near total social isolation for over three years.

[128] *Ensslin, Baader and Raspe v. Germany* [1978] ECmHR 7572/76.

the simultaneous use of sensory isolation and complete social isolation on Red Army Faction members. The three applicants were subjected to a strict regime and were ultimately found dead in their cells (officially recorded as suicides). The ECmHR, in this case, found that the 'segregation of a prisoner from the prison community does not in itself constitute a form of inhuman treatment' yet 'complete sensory isolation coupled with complete social isolation can no doubt ultimately destroy the personality' and would conceivably be a violation. The ECmHR's assessment entailed regard to 'the particular conditions, the stringency of the measure, its duration, the objective pursued and its effects on the person concerned' – and in so doing recognised the need for 'stringent security arrangements ... for dangerous prisoners'.[129] Given that the sensory and social isolation was 'partial', as access to books and news and contact with each other, families and lawyers were allowed, the ECmHR found there to have been no violation of Article 3. This approach, especially the distinction between 'total' and 'partial', a device of the ECmHR's own invention, has been instrumental in the subsequent case law on solitary confinement – setting a particularly high threshold to reach the specific finding of torture. *Ensslin* looks to be disfavoured, with some cases avoiding its citation, but its logics flow freely in the cases to have followed.

A more contemporary and consistently cited case is *Rohde v. Denmark*.[130] There, the applicant was held in pre-trial solitary confinement for eleven and a half months, and was excluded from activities with other prisoners. Reasoning that the applicant had access to television and newspapers, language lessons and visits from the prison chaplain, his lawyer and members of his family, the ECtHR did not find a violation of Article 3. The Court, like the Commission in *Ensslin*, viewed such factors as pulling the applicant's isolation away from the total (and intolerable) towards the partial (and tolerable). Underscoring the lengthier durations in similar cases, the Court in *Rohde* found that 'lasting less than a year', though 'such a length may give rise to concern because of the risk of harmful effects upon mental health', did not violate Article 3. Durational

129 Ibid 111.

130 *Rohde v. Denmark* [2005] ECtHR 69332/01.

comparisons have proven fertile grounds for contest in numerous cases. In *Valasinas v. Lithuania*, a period of solitary confinement of 15 days was not found to have attained the minimum level of severity.[131] In *Csüllog v. Hungary*, we also find the archetypal comparison with *Rohde*[132] and to *Ramirez Sanchez*:[133] 'the number of contacts granted to the applicant was lower than that in *Rohde*' and he was not 'in complete sensory isolation and that his isolation was partial and relative'.[134] The logic is one of, yes it was an unfair punishment, but you are resilient, seven days are acceptable, just look at how bad others have had it.

In *Öcalan v. Turkey (no 1)*, the ECtHR considered a similar case of another high-profile prisoner isolated (then) for five years. Accepting that the 'detention posed exceptional difficulties for the Turkish authorities', and despite 'CPT's recommendations that the applicant's relative social isolation should not be allowed to continue for too long', the ECtHR Grand Chamber did not find a violation of Article 3 on the account of his prolonged solitary confinement.[135] The dissents there were less progressive; a separate opinion of six judges[136] reasoned that '[i]mposing standards that are too high does not appear to us to be the best way of encouraging such cooperation or of expressing satisfaction to the States that provide it' – thereby pointing to the need to maintain an exceptionally high threshold. When brought back before the Court in *Öcalan (no 2)* nearly 10 years later, the Grand Chamber was more receptive and found a violation.[137] Another dissenting opinion there strikingly dismissed that there was any violation of Article 3 reasoning that his isolation was necessary.[138] It is also noteworthy that torture was not even considered in the Court's reasoning in either case, with the starting question being whether the acts amounted to inhuman treatment.

131 *Valasinas v. Lithuania* [2001] ECtHR 44558/98 [112].
132 *Csüllog v. Hungary* [2011] ECtHR 30042/08 [33].
133 Ibid 36.
134 Ibid.
135 *Öcalan v. Turkey (no 1)* [2005] ECtHR 46221/99 [192–196].
136 Dissent of judges Wildhaber, Costa, Caflisch, Turmen, Garlicki and Borrego.
137 *Öcalan v. Turkey (no 2)* [2014] ECtHR 24069/03 [138].
138 Ibid, separate opinion.

In the Chamber ruling in *Ramirez Sanchez*, to return to the point on duration, the Court had noted that the applicant was isolated for eight years and two months. It reviewed durations in other solitary cases in normalising the eight years.[139] Dissenting judges there foregrounded the duration in arguing against such a comparative normalisation and how this could not be considered the use of solitary confinement 'as a last resort' as dictated by the Court's own jurisprudence. Their dissent noted that a 'period of more than eight years cannot stand up to any objective examination'.[140] The Grand Chamber also failed to find a violation of Article 3 in its review of *Ramirez Sanchez*[141] – although a dissenting opinion there considered the treatment inhuman.[142] In prefacing their reasoning with an acknowledgement of the pressures faced by the French authorities, as in *Öcalan*, the dissenters recognised 'that the danger posed by someone of the applicant's character can give rise to complicated problems for the prison authorities'.[143] The dissenters were thereafter scathing in their view of the majority reasoning – characterising the majority as being 'comforted in its view by the fact that the applicant cannot be considered to have been in complete sensory isolation or total social isolation'.[144] The dissenters argued that no reliable scale existed between 'partial' and 'total'.[145] It is remarkable that so many judges called out the artificiality of the central device established by their own institution.

That an instance of solitary confinement had not amounted to complete sensory or total isolation has presented the Court with a convenient way to avoid finding a violation of on multiple occasions.[146] The device

[139] Approximately three years in *Ensslin* and approximately ten and a half years in *Kröcher-Möller v. Switzerland*.

[140] *Ramirez Sanchez v. France* [2005] ECtHR Chamber 59450/00 [separate opinion 5].

[141] *Ramirez Sanchez v. France* [2006] ECtHR GC 59450/00.

[142] Dissent of judges Casadevall, Rozakis, Tsatsa-Nikolovska, Fura-Sandström and Popović.

[143] Ibid [separate opinion].

[144] Ibid [separate opinion].

[145] Ibid [separate opinion 4].

[146] *Ulemek v. Croatia* [2019] ECtHR 21613/16; *Hansen v. Norway* [2018] ECtHR 48852/17; *Fenech v. Malta* [2022] ECtHR 19090/20 [34, 74]: Malta argued that 34 days of solitary was not 'complete sensory deprivation nor total isolation' and the Court followed this reasoning in not finding a violation of Article 3.

has been criticised outside of the Court as 'a fairly easy way out' and as 'fallacious' in its abstraction as the 'total' is an illusory and extreme instance, expecting a 'kind of tomb', with the late Antonio Cassese forcefully arguing that

> It is no coincidence that so far the Commission has never come across any cases of this kind; without going to the lengths of saying that such treatment can only exist as a figment of the imagination, it is at least probable that it is not ever carried out – at any rate not among [CoE] Members. Indeed, this isolation, as envisaged by the Commission, would presuppose a combination of a medieval dungeon, where the prisoner would not even be able to speak to the jailer and where food and water would be passed through a small slot, and a highly sophisticated modern cell, equipped with soundproofing and permanent electrical lighting. Having ruled out the compatibility of this extreme sort of isolation with Article 3, the Commission has opted for the admissibility – in principle, and subject to the circumstances of each case – of what we may call 'ordinary' solitary confinement. It then has hastened to add a caveat: 'it is undesirable'. Now, it is precisely this latter category of isolation that constitutes the typical deprivation of social intercourse in prisons – witness the fact that it is with precisely this issue that the Commission has had to deal any time it has been presented with the question of solitary confinement. On this typical form of isolation, the Commission has uttered pronouncements that often appear questionable.[147]

These, for him, were dubious grounds on which psychological suffering has been overlooked by adjudicators – erecting a strawman not grounded in scientific knowledge and perpetuating the expectation that torture need 'destroy one's personality' so as to downgrade and dismiss suffering where that is not found.[148] It has, to put it pithily,

[147] Antonio Cassese, 'Prohibition of Torture and Inhuman or Degrading Treatment or Punishment' in Paola Gaeta and Salvatore Zappalà (eds), *The Human Dimension of International Law* (OUP 2008) 308.

[148] In *Onofriou v. Cyprus* [2010] ECtHR 24407/10, Cyprus argued that there 'was no sensory isolation brought about by a substantial reduction in stimulation of the sensory organs' [57] and argued that the applicant did not have medical evidence to show he 'suffered mental or physical deterioration as a result of his confinement or that the

served to render torture as 'unique, unrivalled, or incomparable' and, unnecessarily unattainable.[149]

In all, these cases mark an exceptionally high threshold of recognition, continuing to exude a permissibility absent on the face of the relevant conventions. They have come to serve as grounds for governments to argue the legitimacy of their restrictive solitary confinement regimes.[150] Notions of 'exceptionality', 'totality' and 'necessity' (as adjacent concepts) have worked hard to invisibilise psychological suffering inflicted by practices as solitary confinement, deferring to state arguments that their violence is inherent, inevitable,[151] incidental or unavoidable.[152] Notably, these impulses are not exclusive to the ECtHR and also exist in comparable jurisdictions.[153] These legal fictions have denied claims involving psychological suffering – as undesirable though ultimately inescapable, as overridable unless exceptional, and as legitimated when purported to be rational, proportionate thus necessary and indispensable. These have thereby sustained understandings of torture as *physical, exceptional, direct* and *visible* as opposed to *psychological, routine, indirect* and *invisible.*

physical conditions entailed distress and hardship beyond that which was necessarily incidental to such confinement'.

[149] Kelly (2014) 158.

[150] *Karpenko v. Ukraine* [2021] ECtHR 45397/13 [46]; *Geanopol v. Romania* [2013] ECtHR 1777/06 [56].

[151] *Kafkaris v. Cyprus* [2008] ECtHR [GC] 21906/04 [96].

[152] *Kudla v. Poland* [2000] ECtHR [GC] 30210/96 [94].

[153] The UN Human Rights Committee, in *Brough v. Australia,* for instance, ruled the punitive solitary confinement of a child for 72 and 48 hours, as a violation of Article 10 (the right to be treated with humanity and with respect for the inherent dignity) not 7 (the prohibition of torture, inhuman and degrading treatment). The CAT consistently rules solitary confinement to be an Article 16 violation (cruel, inhuman and degrading) and never torture (CAT-C-68-D-817-2017 [8.5]; CAT/C/49/D/412/2010 [7.4]; CAT-C-52-D-478-2011 [11.2]; CAT-C-62-D-672-2015: where 21 days solitary were argued by the (mentally ill) victim and accepted by the CAT as Article 16 with the use of the UN Nelson Mandela Rules and the use of a report from an UN SRT; CAT-C-62-D-672-2015 [7.3]). *Aarrass v. Morocco* [2019] CAT-C-68-D-817-2017 [8.5] presents a distinctly interesting case. The case concerned a man who has been held in pre-trial detention for over nine years – recent years being in solitary confinement. In its reasoning, the CAT recalled the definition and prohibitions as found in the NMR yet held the treatment to amount not to torture but to another form of ill-treatment.

4.4 CONCLUSION

> Human rights law … constitutes a language of governance rather than an authentic response to human suffering.[154]

> [T]he differentiation between forms of pain and suffering in stories that are told, and between those that are told and those that are not told, is a crucial mechanism for the distribution of power.[155]

Whilst categorisation and conceptualisation remain essential, usefully guiding human imagination and action, their routine and repeated use, without scrutiny however, renders them as not simply essential but as natural and neutral, where in fact they are configured through contestation.[156] Accepting or presuming them as natural, the user of a category or a concept risks uncritically equating it as simply capturing a universal reality without any exclusions, silences or grievances. This is all to point out that, in pursuing clarity, a definition or a category can become harmfully narrow or fixed – and therefore invisibilising 'a political or ideological action rather than the neutral delineation of a theoretical terrain'.[157] The difficulties outlined merit a radical shift of attention to a more critical rendering of the law's relationship to the state – characterising it as one of taming, containment and control, with violence standing 'as the limit of law, as a reminder of both law's continuing necessity and its ever-present failing'.[158]

This chapter has argued for a number of interlocking premises, that torture exists in continuity with inhuman and degrading treatment, but that torture has emerged as a distinctly politically guarded category in this scheme. The prevalent assumption in the field is that law is antithetical to violence, that torture is an aberration in law enforcement practice, not born from the same production line of violence that inextricably serve the liberal state. The more critical position would be to characterise

[154] Oette (2024) 3.

[155] Ahmed (2014) 32.

[156] GC Bowker and Susan Leigh Star, *Sorting Things Out: Classification and Its Consequences* (MIT Press 1999).

[157] Margaret Davies, 'Exclusion and the Identity of Law' (2005) 5 *Macquarie Law Journal* 5.

[158] Sarat and Kearns (1993) 2.

torture, inhuman and degrading treatment as an expected manifestation of state function, given that it 'belongs on a continuum with other coercive practices [which are] a routine aspect of our personal, social, and political arrangements'.[159] Legal actors time and again have failed to challenge notions in their reasoning which vanish violence that law views as indispensable, rarely asking: what is necessary for the state?

There are thus significant assumptions and interests embedded in these interpretive exercises. Legal interpretations, as authoritative as they are, do not simply reflect the reality of state violence but are busy backgrounding or foregrounding, sorting, differentiating, prioritising or naturalising the suffering which is deemed to merit attention and that which does not. Although the prohibition is absolute in nature (accepting no exceptions or derogation), its interpretation reveals it to be an exercise that balances the interests of victim-survivors (who demand recognition and redress occasionally of emergent harmful practices) against states (who resist stricter demands on their use of coercive powers).

Law's protection comes prescribed and pre-packaged, its expansion selective and reticent. Judicial reasoning (particularly based on a deference to 'necessity' and deference to prison authorities) in solitary confinement cases is a productive prism to view such dynamics. Whilst the claim that 'no one shall be subjected to torture or to inhuman or degrading treatment or punishment' is readily defended in principle, thresholds shapeshift depending on the nature of the violation and victim in question.

Why doesn't the law talk about the body with more complexity? What are the attributes of a tortured body? These beg a fundamental question: 'what can be seen and said, and what has to be ignored, when we understand suffering and cruelty through the legal category of torture'?[160] The ambiguity of who is excluded from the prohibition's protection reveals law's fixity on particular values, victims as well as the possibility (inability and unwillingness) of law's incomprehension of unfamiliar lived experiences.

[159] Parry, 'Just for fun' (2005) 275–276. This is conceivably a charge that can be directed at any legal category (process, element and consideration), reducing questions to what is 'commensurable and therefore resolvable'.

[160] Kelly (2011) 328.

The discussion has shown that prevalent state practices are closely associated with or characterised by quantifiable (measured, calculated) and qualifiable (purposeful) suffering. Necessity, together with concepts such as 'lawful sanctions', 'minimum severity', 'inherent or incidental', 'discomfort', 'special stigma', 'triviality', have emerged and been deployed out of political incentives to exceptionalise as to invisibilise and render deniable certain forms of state violence. These devices have worked hard to characterise torture as aberrational. Practices that inflict psychological suffering have often had a difficulty here – with many *physical* forms of violence coming to be viewed as primitive and redundant whilst protecting the less physical replacements as permissible and beyond contest. Practices as prolonged solitary confinement and irreducible life imprisonment which serve state-centric purposes, for instance, have been bracketed off as legal, inevitable or non-justiciable.

Readers might also warn of dilution. I certainly would not intend to 'widen the apertures' to a point where notions of torture and law's violence are all encompassing to a point of meaninglessness. I agree that not all fits, nor should be made to fit. That said, the scholarship has been poorer for acting on this fear of diluting the ethical charge of 'torture' or reigniting the 'lawful sanctions' debate. That is to say, questionably, very little has been found to fit the definition of torture specifically.

Also emerging here is a dialectic interplay between the ideational and evidential, the symbolic and material, the principle and processual, about what we think torture is and how we look for it. That is to say, exceptionality seems to undergird an undue need for evidentiary certainty (particularly of the causality, intentionality and measurability of suffering), informing the practices around how torture is *evidenced.* Moreover, exceptionality results in a demand for normative and evidentiary certainty (or caution). Adjudicators generally want to be certain before they move to pin a practice with the torture label, and are therefore more readily poised to identify the 'extreme borders of cruelty',[161] particularly elsewhere and when it comes to 'states of exception' such as Guantanamo. Common torture documentation practices, including those based on the *Istanbul Protocol,* have also been charged with

[161] Balibar (2002) 138.

under-perceiving the extent of torture and thus feeding an exceptional construction of torture. The practices, it has been argued, lead to reinforcing the understanding that in 'the public and political imagination, and particularly at the international human rights level, torture is an extreme and singularly horrific event'.[162] A question remains of the connection between imagining torture as an exceptional spectacle and evidentiary certainty – between imagining and evidencing. Is recognition simply a question of knowing, of epistemology, not ontology? Can the lack of recognition of some suffering be explained by difficulties in its substantiation, as it is suppressed? These connections are followed in Chapter 5.

[162] Steffen Jensen et al, 'Torture and Ill-Treatment Under Perceived: Human Rights Documentation and the Poor' (2017) 39 *Human Rights Quarterly* 393, 402–403.

CHAPTER 5

Substantiating Suffering

'IS THE SQUEEZE WORTH THE JUICE?' asked a UN treaty body (UNTB) member of participants at an academic symposium on evidence in international adjudication. This was a rhetorical retort to persistent calls for the UNTBs to adopt more rigorous evidentiary practices despite their limitations. It revealed an operative but concealed logic in practice, gesturing to what I've come to think of as 'evidentiary expedience', namely that evidence is often evaluated in a manner convenient and not necessarily most comprehensive by human rights adjudicators. Could common-sense, experience- or context-based reasoning convincingly speak for what happened in an individual case without a full-blown fact-finding expedition? My broader research at the time centred on the practice of convincing decision-makers to better appreciate and address psychological suffering in torture-related cases, finding its genesis in Dignity's project to improve medico-legal documentation of practices which do not leave physical marks (think threats, sleep deprivation and solitary confinement). Advocates were finding these practices difficult to litigate and expressed a need to develop new tools that could substantiate the suffering in question. Whilst many precious hours have been poured into producing and sharpening documentation protocols, the uptake and impact (it has to be said) has been negligible. The optimist would cut in with 'well, so far …' but I've come to realise that stronger forces are at play that mean that it is not simply a question of 'producing more convincing evidence'. It was, and remains, predominantly a question of how what is viewed is valued – which moves us beyond 'what does the psychologist say' instead to 'do we even need a psychologist for this' or even 'what can psychology tell us anyway'.

> [E]vidence is key to how the law apprehends the world.[1]

> There is … an evidence-shaped hole at the centre of our notion of torture.[2]

In the first ever international case on torture, the *Greek Case*, the European Commission of Human Rights heard testimony (after testimony) of political prisoners systematically tortured at the hands of the Greek Junta. Amnesty International generated these testimonies in effectively mobilising Denmark, Norway and Sweden to institute the case before the Commission.[3] Being the first case, the Commission was called onto formulate a definition of torture (with Article 3 of the *European Convention on Human Rights* merely offering a *prohibition*) notably addressing its psychological aspects, a definition that was a direct antecedent to that which is now found in Article 1 of the UN *Convention against Torture*. Yet, the case was ground-breaking in another important aspect: evidentiary practices around torture. The Commission ruled that torture cases needed to be proven 'beyond reasonable doubt', which was taken to mean 'not a doubt based on a merely theoretical possibility or raised in order to avoid a disagreeable conclusion'. The Commission also importantly recognised evidentiary difficulties in understanding the following: (a) that 'a victim or a witness able to corroborate his story might hesitate to describe or reveal all that has happened to him for fear of reprisals upon himself or his family'; (b) that 'acts of torture or ill-treatment by agents of the police or armed services would be carried out as far as possible without witnesses and perhaps without the knowledge of higher authority'; and (c) that 'physical traces of torture or ill-treatment may with lapse of time become unrecognisable, even by medical experts, particularly where the form of torture itself leaves little external marks'.[4] These have become foundational principles and are often repeated in standards, reports and cases.

[1] Law and the Senses, The Westminster Law & Theory Centre Westminster Law School London, Conference booklet (18–19 April 2013).

[2] Kelly (2014) 158.

[3] See Kostis Kornetis et al (eds), *The 1969 'Greek Case' in the Council of Europe: A Game Changer for Human Rights* (Bloomsbury 2024) for contextualised readings of the case.

[4] *The Greek Case*, p. 197 [31].

The *Greek Case* also represented a watershed moment for prominent human rights organisations, such as Amnesty International and Human Rights Watch, especially in how the production of reliable evidence, namely documentation, became central to their work more broadly. Documentation, as in the *Greek Case* and since, has shaped historical accounts, primarily through collecting, triangulating, reporting and preserving first-hand accounts. Documentation has become 'the eyes and ears of the human rights movement'[5] – integral in clarifying what was done, who did it, why it was done, where it was done towards activating reform, redress as well as research.[6] These practices have actively determined the 'parameters for how human rights organizations and practitioners perceive and act in the world' – informing the legibility of types of harms, victims and perpetrators.[7] This has been as true with report writing, standard setting as with litigation. Evidence, as produced through documentation efforts, whether from human rights organisations or more broadly, has been an indispensable means for legal actors, often geographically removed, to reach into the contexts in which violence is inflicted – with increased sensitivity to empirically and scientifically grounded understandings of the conditions under which violence is produced and experienced. Advocates have relentlessly set about producing and presenting evidence for the public, policymakers and adjudicators alike, to attain an end that serves them (and their clients: victim-survivors), viewing evidence as an obvious means of amplifying their demands and substantiating their cause (most commonly in the form of a legal case).

None of this is different in the anti-torture field. Accepting the promise of evidence, prominent 'law and torture' commentators have called

[5] Jensen et al (2017) 394.

[6] Although legal processes of attributing culpability for torture, whether criminal, civil or human rights-based, dominate the imagination, there are other contexts to situate the discussion on torture and evidence. Beyond attribution, evidence may be crucial in assessing loss and quantifying compensation or other forms of redress (especially in civil and human rights processes). Evidence of torture may be instrumental in excluding confessions or other information in criminal trials. In asylum claims, evidence establishing that applicant was tortured or risks being tortured if returned to a country of origin may be crucial in establishing the applicant's credibility.

[7] Jensen et al (2017) 394.

for closer collaboration between the law and medicine towards producing evidence as a key means towards recognition and eradication. Whilst evidence, especially that which is viewed as scientifically rigorous, has become central in substantiating torture in legal settings, deep-seated (epistemological) tensions between the law and science (particularly in how they approach evidentiary certainty) occasionally complicate and frustrate the pursuit of legal redress. Legal actors, for one, have preferred manageability and simplicity in the face of evidentiary difficulties and complexities – holding onto a 'correctness' that what the law says goes. Pulling these threads together, this chapter will first identify the *principles* of evidence in international law before exploring the *problems* to have arisen in how evidence is used in practice.

5.1 EVIDENTIARY PRINCIPLES

> Evidence is not a discrete entity, nor is its production a straightforward practice.[8]

Since the *Greek Case*, there has emerged a general acceptance that evidencing torture is difficult; that it is unusual to have anything other than the testimony of the victim, as 'gathering evidence from witnesses and other sources can be difficult or impossible'.[9] Not counting official and expert evidence, 'the only evidence [a torture victim] can produce is his own testimony [and that an] independent expert or other evidence may not be available to confirm such testimony and the respondent Government may invoke such lack of substantiation'.[10] Expert evidence also relies

[8] Morten Koch Andersen, 'Filtering Information: Human Rights Documentation in Bangladesh' (2019) 11 (1) *Journal of Human Rights Practice* 73–95, 77.

[9] Redress, 'Istanbul Protocol Medico-Legal Reports: Practice Note 3' (2021) 8; Ingelse (2001) 190. Courts or committees have limited powers in fact-finding and documentation. The *Greek Case* itself depended significantly on the Commission's on fact-finding in Greece. The abolition of the Commission has almost entirely, though not completely, seen the European system's fact-finding capacity disappear. The ECtHR has conducted the odd trip, for example, visiting Ukraine to assess the prison regime, but has largely depended on CPT reports in lieu of such fact-finding.

[10] Loukis Loucaides, *Essays on the Developing Law of Human Rights* (Nijhoff 1995) 160 as quoted in Ugur Erdal, 'Burden and Standard of Proof in Proceedings Under the European Convention' (2001) *European Law Review Human Rights Survey* 26/1.

heavily on the words of the victim-survivor, who may be 'too traumatized or scared to give the detailed or consistent accounts of their experiences, which documentation can demand'.[11] Victim-survivors may also fail to recognise their experience as something of a violation – especially if it is to do with mental health or related to a sexual taboo. Access to professional services to reliably document may be limited. And in cases of access, professionals may be ill-equipped to ask the right questions and ask for expertise themselves. Whilst evidence is key, it is thus also plagued by difficulties related to *availability* (from survivors as from the state), questionable *flexibility* (afforded to survivors from human rights adjudicators) and limitations on *technology* (access to and application of expertise-based documentation practices). I will elaborate on what I mean.

5.1.1 AVAILABILITY.

> [Torture] is practiced in secret, often by experienced interrogators who are skilled at ensuring that it leaves no visible signs on the victim. All too frequently, those who are charged with ensuring that torture does not occur – courts, prosecutors and medical personnel – are complicit in its concealment.[12]

Availability of evidence of torture is commonly approached as a question of state denial – with states seasoned in suppressing, concealing, rationalising and justifying their uses of violence.[13] Denial, as discussed in Chapter 4, has been a key central state strategy in responding to claims under torture's prohibition. The difficulty in compelling a state to investigate and address a particular human rights violation, and the resulting concerns of impunity, are front and centre here. States may simply not initiate investigations, in discretely covering-up wrong-doing by inaction. The survivor, as mentioned, might have difficulty accurately recalling their experience,[14] or might have not been forthcoming about their

[11] Jensen et al (2017) 394.

[12] *Othman (Abu Qatada) v. UK* [2012] ECtHR 8139/09 [276].

[13] Penny Green and Tony Ward, 'Understanding State Crime' in Alison Leibling et al (eds), *The Oxford Handbook of Criminology* (OUP 2017).

[14] *AMD et al v. Denmark*, CAT/C/60/D/653/2015 [9.7]: 'complete accuracy is seldom to be expected by victims of torture'.

experience fearing reprisals[15] or upon a broader backdrop of impunity. The survivor might not be granted access to police or prison records, might not effectively summon complicit officials to bear witness even if not directly involved or might be denied impartial forensic investigation or documentation if sought, and local adjudicators before whom these complaints are brought might not push so hard in the interest of covering for the system. Documentation, even where accessible, might not even be an ethically sound course of action.[16]

When there is access to documenting doctors and psychologists, cases rarely prove to be 'straightforward' as the evidence produced is at best 'partial or incomplete ... only provid[ing] a restricted amount of information to help corroborate a claim'.[17] Upon this background, advocates and adjudicators are routinely called onto operate on inferences and to reduce the interpretation of evidence 'to making a series of more or less educated guesses'.[18] Documenting and deciding these cases, in other words, involve piecing together 'disparate bits of information, filter[ing]

[15] *Labita v. Italy* [2000] ECtHR 26772/95, partly dissenting opinion of judges Pastor Ridruejo et al [1]: 'While we agree with the majority that the material produced by the applicant constitutes only prima facie evidence, we are nonetheless mindful of the difficulties which a prisoner who has suffered ill-treatment on the part of those responsible for guarding him may experience, and the risks he may run, if he denounces such treatment'.

[16] This also means that, even when access to legal aid is established, caution must be exercised in presuming the wishes of a victim-survivor: is it recognition, rehabilitation or redress of another form that is most suitable (e.g., compensation)? From a survivor-centric point of view, documentation (usually an interview-based assessment or examination) might be best avoided for a specific individual if doing so might risk re-traumatisation and incurring various costs particularly given the uncertainty of a favourable outcome. Whilst the simple act of speaking about an experience may itself have a rehabilitative impact under certain circumstances, this is not always the case or it need not mean that the experience must be legally verified or oriented at whatever the cost. In fact, these wishes must be express and, even when expressed by the survivor, genuinely scrutinised by the supporting professionals. This has happened before and gives rise to an ethical question: to what extent must professional 'do no harm' in potentially preventing future harms? From systemic and societal points of view, which is what most strategic litigation, advocacy and reform is essentially geared towards, the individual's wishes could but should not be balanced out and overridden by considerations to prevent and punish perpetrators as deterrence.

[17] Anthony Good, *Anthropology and Expertise in the Asylum Courts* (Routledge 2007) 133.

[18] Ibid.

statements that could lead in the wrong direction, and finally try[ing] to work out what is wrong' all from[19]

> traces of the past that can be vague, indirect, or apparently contradictory. Bodies on their own do not speak, but wounds must be interpreted alongside verbal accounts and then filtered through clinical expertise and experience. … far from being definitive and absolute, clinical evidence about torture is necessarily indirect and often hesitant. Clinicians are faced with a legal system of proof that all too often appears to be demanding a level of certainty that cannot be given.

Furthermore, where cases are documented and brought before decision-makers, despite these difficulties, responding states have demonstrated vested interests in resisting interpretations that their coercive practices were unduly harmful or that they even took place. Here, the sociology of denial, as developed by Stanley Cohen, offers a basic understanding of strategies to include: *outright* or *literal* denial (direct factual rejection of allegations as 'it didn't happen'); *interpretive* denial (renaming as 'yes, something did happen, but it was not torture' through reliance on euphemism and legalism, soft language to recast the situation in a milder light); and *implicatory* denial (bad apples metaphors).[20] States have long argued, for instance, that injuries alleged existed before state actions (e.g., detention) were unintentional,[21] accidental[22] or provoked.[23] This

[19] Kelly (2012) 85.

[20] Cohen (2001).

[21] *Wainwright v. UK* [2006] ECtHR 12350/04 [36]: 'there was no intention to humiliate; that the search was carried out in good faith for the legitimate object of searching for drugs in a prison with a serious drugs problem; that it was relatively brief; and that the applicants were given the choice to leave without being searched and at no point voiced any complaint or objection. If the first applicant had felt strongly about the blinds not being drawn, she could have asked for them to be closed'.

[22] *Makaratzis v. Greece* [2004] ECtHR [GC] 50385/99 [82]: 'The Government maintained that the applicant's injuries were accidental and regrettable consequences of a lawful arrest'; *Ahmet Özkan and others v. Turkey* [2004] ECtHR 21689/93 [333]; *Krastanov v. Bulgaria* [2004] ECtHR 50222/99 [49] 'police officers had explained that there had been a mistake and had apologised'.

[23] *Jevtovic v. Serbia* [2009] ECtHR 29896/14 [73]: 'the applicant who had provoked the use of force on the part of the authorities'. There are additional common state strategies focusing on procedural issues such as non-exhaustion of domestic remedies (by far the most commonplace argument at least at the European Court of Human Rights).

is not meant to read conspiratorial but rather critical of the public 'scripts' as presented by states – compelling arguments 'designed to be impressive, to affirm and naturalize the power of dominant elites, and to conceal or euphemize the dirty linen of their rule [but which] to have any rhetorical force ... necessarily involves some concessions to their presumed interests'.[24]

An evidentiary asymmetry, in all, between states and victims expectedly permeates principle and practice around the documentation and adjudication of torture – perpetuating the vulnerability of the torture victim beyond the initial instance of suffering in itself to the subsequent pursuit of justice. So how have authorities, as in the *Greek Case*, responded beyond recognising such difficulties?

5.1.2 FLEXIBILITY.

> [T]he ECtHR ranges between tradition and progress, between protection and the development of human rights, between flexibility and legal certainty.[25]

In view of such difficulties, international human rights courts and committees have afforded themselves a wide flexibility since their inceptions. In *Ireland* (1978), the ECtHR famously saw itself as 'entitled to rely on evidence of every kind, including, insofar as it deems them relevant, documents or statements emanating from governments, be they respondent or applicant, or from their institutions or officials'. It led to the formulation of the oft-cited position that 'being master of its own procedure and of its own rules ... [the ECtHR] has complete freedom in assessing not only the admissibility and the relevance but also the probative value of each item of evidence before it'.[26] Formulations of so-called free assessment are also found in the work of the UN CAT, UN HRC and IACtHR.

Difficulties (and the ensuing need for flexibility) have also informed the wide admissibility of forms of indirect (or circumstantial) evidence: medico-legal reports; X-rays and similar medical records; testimonies

[24] James C. Scott, *Seeing Like a State: How Certain Schemes to Improve the Human Condition Have Failed* (Yale 1988) 18.
[25] Tulkens (2022) 293.
[26] *Ireland* [1978] [209–210].

of witnesses and family; administrative information from records and other documents in the place of detention; photos or videos, including from social media; weapons and other physical evidence; as well as NGO or similar reports, as from the CPT. There is also strong reliance on international standards where state-sanctioned suffering is systemic and systematic but difficult to prove in a specific instance. That is to say, a general prevalence and pattern of violations has also been grounds for finding a violation in a specific case where direct corroboration was not available.[27]

In countering evidentiary complexity, asymmetry, evasiveness and absence, another discussion has centred on adjusting (shifting or sharing) standards and burdens of proof. Rules of proof and evidence, therefore, have needed to necessarily flex with the generally established complexities of torture. Given respondent states have *peculiar knowledge* of what is alleged to have occurred, the evidentiary burden has come to be viewed as shared in torture-related cases. That victim-survivors only need to establish a prima facie case puts the primary onus on the state, which represents such a position. This has operated to the advantage of victims where authorities could not reasonably account for injuries inflicted in the course of arrest,[28] deaths in custody[29] where the authorities were altogether silent or inactive in investigating,[30] or where the difficulty of proving suffering, as in the case of psychologically oriented practices, mandated 'exhaustive' investigations.[31]

[27] See *Velazquez* [175]; *Fernandez Ortega et al v. Mexico* [116]; *Onofriou v. Cyprus* [2010] ECtHR 24407/04.

[28] *Juan Carlos Abella v. Argentina*, Case 11.137, Report N° 55/97, IACmHR, OEA/Ser.L/V/II.95 Doc. 7 rev. at 271 (1997).

[29] *Juan Humberto Sánchez v. Honduras* [2003] IACtHR; *Salman v. Turkey* [2000] ECtHR 21986/93 [100]; see also *Iskandarov v. Russia* [2010] ECtHR 17185/05 [108].

[30] *Velasquez Rodriguez v. Honduras* [1988] IACtHR [135–138]: 'the silence of the accused or elusive or ambiguous answers on its part may be interpreted as an acknowledgment of the truth of the allegations'; *Case of the White Van (Paniagua-Morales et al.) v. Guatemala* [1998] IACtHR; *Maritza Urrutia v. Guatemala* [2003] IACtHR; *Timurtas v. Turkey* [2000] ECtHR 23531/94 [66]; *Selmouni* [76].

[31] *Puertas v. Spain*, UN HRC, CCPR/C/107/D/1945/2010 [8.6]: 'all physical or psychological damage inflicted on a person in detention – and particularly under the incommunicado regime – gives rise to an important presumption of fact, since the burden of proof must not rest on the presumed victim'.

This wide discretion (or 'free assessment') has, as will be shortly discussed in the problems arising from these principles, however, led to an unpredictability in evidentiary practices. Such flexibility, that is to say, ultimately has remained subject to judicial discretion – which can either be used in a 'virtuous' or 'disingenuous' manner.[32] The discretion in what evidence is used and how much weight it is attributed, often left implicit in legal decisions, is rendered paramount. That testimony is normally valued less, proving 'subjective' (and potentially self-serving) and requiring to be checked against the 'objective' (or other testimonies), arises out of such discretion. Adjudicators have occasionally announced that evidence is not necessary, as 'it may well suffice that the victim is humiliated in his own eyes, even if not in the eyes of others'.[33] Yet, what operates here is not a simple acceptance of the victim's words but one which is checked against established presumptions that certain acts have certain impacts. The position that 'actual personal experiences cannot be determinative in the application of the legal standards' emerges not out of a legal diktat but discretion.[34] The question of testimony will be returned to in Chapter 6 and the question of discretion returned to in 'Evidentiary problems'.

5.1.3 TECHNOLOGY.

> Torture is 'the kind of problem that recommends [and lends] itself for genuinely interdisciplinary inquiry and translation ... dialogue and knowledge production'.[35]

> The increasingly central role of the suffering body in humanitarian and human rights activism has given the medical profession a privileged role in addressing various social problems and crises, including torture.[36]

[32] Marie-Bénédicte Dembour, 'Beyond Reasonable Doubt at its Worst – But Also at its Potential Best: Dissecting Ireland v the United Kingdom's No-Torture Finding' (2023) 4 *European Convention on Human Rights Law Review* 375, 380.

[33] *Bouyid* [89].

[34] Webster (2018) 71.

[35] Nick Cheesman, 'Police Torture: A Case for Interdisciplinarity' in Shauhin Talesh et al (eds), *Research Handbook on Modern Legal Realism* (Elgar 2020).

[36] Başak Can, 'Human Rights, Humanitarianism, and State Violence: Medical Documentation of Torture in Turkey: Human Rights, Humanitarianism, and State Violence' (2016) 30 *Medical Anthropology Quarterly* 342, 343.

Torture documentation has built an evidence base around certain torture methods over the years: that falanga is likely to impair the ability to walk; or, that telephono is likely to cause hearing loss and tinnitus. These are then drawn upon in their reform and regulation. Solitary confinement, as already discussed in Chapter 4, is an example *par excellence*.[37] The evidence has informed the prohibition of certain uses under international law, including indefinite and prolonged uses and uses against children, pregnant and breastfeeding women and persons with disabilities where the condition might be exacerbated. In so doing, sustained documentation has helped formulate useful presumptions as to what acts are likely to lead to torturous suffering. These presumptions must be, are not always, however, qualified in important ways: that both physical and psychological consequences should be expected from any torturous suffering; that methods are often combined; that consequences cannot be predicted with precision; that no two individuals react to the same treatment identically; that there are no physical signs does not mean that no torture took place.[38]

In the flexibility afforded to victim-survivors, *Istanbul Protocol*-compliant reports have emerged as being most desirable, together with the rise of medical doctors in documentation.[39] Their probative power has been explicitly mentioned in numerous international cases.[40] Whilst no scan, electrode or X-ray exists to directly answer the

[37] See Lobel and Scharff Smith (2020) for a useful collection on this topic.

[38] To understand the documentation of torture, one must understand the common consequences of torturous violence. This is as complex as the nature of suffering itself but is conventionally viewed in terms of the immediate impact as well as the after-effects (sequelae) on the mind and body. Consequences of torturous violence are best understood as a continuum: from none to death. There is also increasing attention on the impact on family and friends of the victim-survivor. The impact is known to be wide-ranging from depression and anxiety, to intrusive thoughts, avoidance, emotional numbing, hyper-arousal, sleep problems and PTSD. The social consequences of torture can be stigma, shame and guilt leading to isolation, reduced ability to function in the family, the workplace or other social settings.

[39] Rejali (2007) 16: 'because they had a specialized set of skills to diagnose the use of some clean techniques'.

[40] *Savin v. Ukraine* [2012] ECtHR 34725/08 [61]: 'the Court attaches weight to the forensic medical experts' findings according to which the applicant's disability was a direct result of the ill-treatment in question'; *Lyapin v. Russia* [2014] ECtHR 46956/09 [116]: 'There is medical evidence of the applicant's injuries following his release from police custody

'what', 'where' and 'who' and even the 'how much' did the person suffer, the *Istanbul Protocol* consolidates available diagnostic, linguistic and interpersonal knowledge into a 'tool to objectively determine whether a person's claim that he or she has been tortured can be medically verified'.[41] Put differently, the *Protocol* is a technology in the most elemental sense of the word – a tool to translate medical causation to legal causation, understood to bring a certain level of objectivity and reliability to legal processes that have historically operated in its absence and processes which have viewed the survivor's claims as self-serving and with scepticism. A key framework for translating causality is in how it provides for five levels of consistency: 'not consistent', 'consistent', 'highly consistent', 'typical' and 'diagnostic'.[42] This spectrum, as does medicine, operates on the notion of probability not certainty or binary causality.

As with any such tool, it must be borne in mind that the *Protocol* is a product of its history.[43] It finds its origins in the Turkish anti-torture movement, duly sceptical of state forensic institutions. The *Protocol*'s first international iteration in 1999 has been broadly represented as an arduous process of formulating scientific consensus, as 'the result of three years of analysis, research and drafting, undertaken by more than 75 experts in law, health and human rights, representing 40 organizations

including reports by forensic medical experts, which corroborates his account'; S. L. Lustig et al, 'Asylum Grant Rates following Medical Evaluations of Maltreatment among Political Asylum Applicants in the United States' (2008) 10 (1) *Journal of Immigrant and Minority Health* 7–15; R. J Haar et al, 'The Istanbul Protocol: A Global Stakeholder Survey on Past Experiences, Current Practices and Additional Norm Setting' (2019) 29 (1) *Torture* 70–84.

41 IRCT, *Shedding Light on a Dark Practice* (2009) 8.

42 UN *Istanbul Protocol* (2022) 380: 'Not consistent' means that the 'finding could not have been caused by the alleged torture or ill-treatment'. 'Consistent' means that the 'finding could have been caused by the alleged torture or ill-treatment, but it is non-specific and there are many other possible'. 'Highly consistent' means that the 'finding could have been caused by the alleged torture or ill-treatment and there are few other possible causes'. 'Typical of' means that 'the finding is usually observed with this type of alleged torture or ill-treatment, but there are other possible causes'. 'Diagnostic' is 'the finding could not have been caused in any way other than that described'. Diagnostic is characterised as being rare occurrence.

43 Jensen et al (2017) 399.

or institutions from 15 countries'.[44] Aiming to enhance this potential and build on the evidence base, practitioners have sought to supplement the *Protocol* producing other protocols such as the protocols on methods of psychological torture,[45] 'Torturing Environment Scale',[46] and on self-documentation.[47]

A rare anthropological examination of the Turkish origins points to the culmination of the political, professional and personal motives of the Human Rights Foundation of Turkey (HRFT) in producing an 'objectivist' methodology in the face of state denial and distortion of documentation.[48] This was not straightforward, according to this study, given the constant negotiation required: 'the high moral, legal, and political stakes involved in official medical documentation, the scientific authority of physicians is thus also continuously under the risk of being seen as compromised'.[49] In all, the *Protocol* can be described as an 'ethically motivated objectivist inquiry' as shaped by its political and professional history.[50]

[44] Vincent Iacopino, 'The Istanbul Protocol: Development, Practical Applications, and Future Directions' in Jason Payne-James et al (eds), *Monitoring Detention, Custody, Torture, and Ill-Treatment: A Practical Approach to Prevention and Documentation* (CRC Press 2018) 254. The most recent revision of the Protocol was also led by an international civil society coalition including: HRFT, International Rehabilitation Council for Torture Victims (IRCT), Physicians for Human Rights, DIGNITY, REDRESS, and the International Forensic Expert Group. Its 2022 update too frames the practices and consequences to be taken as prevalent, and the professionals taken as central to their documentation.

[45] Elna Søndergaard et al (eds), *Three Protocols for the Medico-Legal Documentation of Psychological Torture* (Dignity 2024); Elna Søndergaard et al, 'Development of Interdisciplinary Protocols on Medico-legal Documentation of Torture: Sleep Deprivation' (2019) 29 (2) *Torture* 23: 'advanced documentation instruments, using medical evidence in non-torture contexts and legal research, should be developed to effectively identify and record other psychological torture methods'; see also Pérez-Sales (2016) 308.

[46] Pérez-Sales (2016) 360.

[47] IRCT and Independent Forensic Expert Group, 'Justice starts with Truth: A Form for You to Document and Report Torture and Other Human Rights Violations during Protest' (2021).

[48] Can (2016) 346.

[49] Ibid 348.

[50] Ibid 346; although a non-binding soft-law, its proponents often argue that the Protocol draws on binding legal power from serving Article 12 of the UNCAT (obliges states to ensure accountability, prevention and redress). In short, it has come to represent the international standards for documentation, assessment, reporting and investigation of torture.

As no scientific method is value-free neither is the *Istanbul Protocol* – which too is built on the personal and professional values of its authors and users. Documentation, whether grounded in the *Protocol* or not, is a 'situated endeavour [which is] formed and informed by contextual conditions and situated practices, and aims to facilitate political and societal change'.[51] Evidence, as the experience in anti-torture litigation as elsewhere has shown, is 'produced, circumscribed and categorized by expert knowledge and vocabularies amid a complex and multifaceted political process of power contestations [with] notions of victimhood and suffering [being] the result of technical exercises (often of enumeration)'.[52] For these reasons, documentation practices can never be objective tools that reveal an objective reality.

But who should use it? The *Protocol* formulates standards for three disciplines: medicine, psychology and law. It sets out the standards concerning how to best understand, examine, document (interview and write-up) and evaluate torture (its consequences and veracity). The *Protocol* does not fix a minimum length of a report or minimum specialisation – but it is clear that lawyers are privileged in dominating the language of torture, doctors in understanding of the tortured body and psychologists in the tortured mind. Often being the first to see a victim-survivor after their experience, doctors are viewed as well-situated to initiate documentation (noting the visible marks and taking the survivor's account). Lawyers too are, in many settings, the key interlocutors for survivors of torture seeking justice. Like doctors, lawyers may also be the first to be contacted by a detainee, either directly or through their family – the first person from outside to hear the story of abuse. Whether at local or international levels, lawyers are encouraged to document so as to prompt authorities to investigate, present evidence and assist decision-makers in investigations, prosecutions or compensation claims.[53] For all professionals, the *Protocol* facilitates obtaining and preserving reliable statements from victims and witnesses, and enables a proper assessment and determination of the facts of the case.

[51] Andersen (2019) 73–74.

[52] Ibid 75.

[53] The *Protocol* also emphasises that prosecutors and adjudicators also have a role in ensuring that investigations and assessments are in conformity with international standards.

Researchers, however, have scrutinised the *Protocol* and have questioned its operative assumptions, particularly (i) its use without taking account of the context and (ii) its conceptualisation of torture. Speaking to the first question, researchers have argued that:

> Much human rights documentation implicitly assumes that more knowledge is of value. If we can produce rigorous evidence about particular incidents of torture, we will be in a better place to hold perpetrators to account. As such, the underlying assumption behind the IP is that production of detailed, objective and reliable legal evidence is central to the fight against torture. This is certainly true. Yet, at the same time, knowledge should always be thought of as a means to an end, rather than an end in itself; it is important because it helps human rights practitioners realise other more substantive goals, such as the eradication of torture. We therefore need to understand the role of particular forms of knowledge in working towards context specific goals. This means asking why civil society organizations use human rights instruments, what they want to achieve, and the issues they face when doing so.[54]

In terms of the second question, the same researchers found that documentation practices (i) characterise torture as an extraordinary act, effectively excluding its everyday occurrence, (ii) treat torture as predominantly custodial excluding its extra-custodial aspects and (iii) 'implicitly prioritize forms of torture that can be documented to the required level of legal proof'.[55] So there is a risk identified here between standardisation becoming too broad and inflexible to be meaningful when applied in a particular context. The point here is that how torture is understood (what it is, how it is inflicted and where it is inflicted) frames its documentation. Understanding it to be an extraordinary and secret practice might be rhetorically powerful, but it can also serve to exclude its everyday and accreted infliction. These findings then invoked a strong response from the medical doctors who produced and have since championed the *Protocol*, who instead argued that it represented *minimum*

[54] Tobias Kelly et al, 'A Comparative Study of the Use of the Istanbul Protocol Amongst Civil Society Organizations in Low-Income Countries' (2016) 26 (3) *Torture* 62.

[55] Jensen et al (2017) 410.

standards and emphasised that it was capable of being contextualised in application – countering that:[56]

> Most clinicians who use the Istanbul Protocol understand that brief medical evaluations can be conducted in accordance with the Istanbul Protocol principles for many different purposes, for example, in human rights investigations, human rights monitoring, prevention, and advocacy activities, as well as clinical encounters with alleged victims that are not intended to be comprehensive forensic evaluations. The presumption that the Istanbul Protocol requires comprehensive forensic evaluations in all circumstances is, unfortunately, not consistent with the content of the Istanbul Protocol or actual practices.

This tension is representative of that which operates more broadly between those more critically oriented and others wanting to preserve dominant approaches in the anti-torture field. How the principles, as established in the *Greek Case* and since, have been followed (or not) points to problems in practice – often not admitted by the doctrinally committed. I continue to explore these 'problems', or alternatively 'difficulties' in interpretation, in what follows. I preface that discussion with two lesser-known cases, decided a decade apart, which bring the state of evidentiary problems into stark relief. These point to problems seemingly impervious to extra training, gesturing to (a) demands on evidence for undue certainty especially between claimed acts and impacts (that it prove facts beyond reasonable doubt despite difficulties) and (b) the implications choices made by decision-makers have to believe or disbelieve evidence from different sources, namely the authorities, the victims and their experts.

5.2 EVIDENTIARY PROBLEMS

> The crucial issue for the vast majority of people claiming protection as torture survivors is not law but evidence. Put simply, they are not believed. Far from being treated as passive and fragile victims, those claiming protection are seen as active agents who are always capable of manipulation.[57]

[56] Rusudan Beriashvili and Vincent Iacopino 'Comment I: Istanbul Protocol in Low-income Countries – a Reply' (2016) 26 (3) *Torture* 74–76.

[57] Kelly (2014) 145.

Case 1. *Veznedaroglu v. Turkey*. The Turkish state, before the ECtHR, was accused of arresting an applicant on suspicion of being a PKK member, who was blindfolded, interrogated, forced nude, hung by the arms, electric shocked, threatened and deprived of food for four days until a forced confession was induced. The applicant was released and acquitted, went on sick leave for 20 days with a medical certificate. Emblematic of the denial which inspired the *Istanbul Protocol*, state forensic authorities only reported minor bruising after some days. The applicant also arranged a medical certificate from a university hospital attesting to the torture. The Turkish authorities argued that this medical certificate was falsified and referred to its own doctors' reports. The majority of judges was not persuaded that the hearing of witnesses by the Court would either clarify the facts of the case or make it possible to conclude beyond reasonable doubt.[58] The judges refused, therefore, to find a substantive violation (that the torture happened) but instead found a procedural violation against Turkey (for not properly investigating the applicant's allegations). In a scathing dissent, Judge Bonello disagreed with how the majority used its discretion in assessing the evidence. He argued that the Court indeed had enough evidence to decide on a substantive violation. He underscored the spirit of the passages of the *Greek Case*, namely that we know that marks disappear over time, in holding that the burden should have been shifted to the Turkish state. He argued that the standard should never effectively be 'beyond reasonable doubt', holding this out this as realistically unachievable and unfair. He also made the point that the context of the violation should be looked at – to the Turkish security forces' track record and the official apparatus' routine denial of similar accusations.

Case 2. *Sonko v. Spain*. On a late September night in 2007, Lauding Sonko drowned trying to cross from Morocco to the Spanish enclave of Ceuta. Before the CAT, his brother blamed his death on the Spanish Coast Guard, alleging that they had punctured his dinghy and thrown him into the sea despite his pleas for help and screams that he could not swim. This, his brother claimed, amounted to torture or alternately

[58] *Veznedaroglu v. Turkey* [2000] ECtHR 32357/96 [30].

inhuman or degrading treatment. Spain disputed these allegations. The majority of CAT members found that it could not be sure about the puncture (and in turn the intent element required by the torture definition) in finding a violation of Article 16 (which doesn't need intent). In not being drawn in on the dispute of intent, a majority of members did not see the CAT's 'task to weigh the evidence or to reassess the statements made regarding the facts or the credibility of the relevant national authorities'.[59] A single member, Felicia Gaer, dissented, called this out to be a 'shocking pronouncement' given that the CAT was entitled to a 'free assessment'. Although she didn't disagree with finding a violation of Article 16, and couldn't simply accept that this was just an 'unfortunate accident', it was the lack of a principled assessment in the majority's reasoning that she couldn't abide by. What explained the CAT's reticence in this case to engage on the evidentiary dispute? Could it not have drawn on the well-established patterns in Spain's brutal pushback operations to infer that this is also what happened in this particular case? How did it expect the applicant to prove intent with certainty given the expected state denial?

Both cases illustrate that the recognition of suffering has been contingent not only on the availability of evidence but how what is available is interpreted. In other words, there are as many issues when the documentation so painstakingly produced and put together finally does make it before an adjudicator. Where principles (particularly as to availability and flexibility) are overlooked, judicial expectations and preferences are warped and recognition is likely rendered unattainable, much to the disadvantage of victims. Evidence thus becomes grounds on which state denial is enacted and numerous states, as Turkey, have been creative thinkers on this front. On this backdrop, I discuss two couplets in turn: firstly, certainty and causality, and secondly, discretion and deference. I argue that, as with the factors discussed above impede the documentation of torture, these represent the key factors in shaping the interpretation of available documentation by adjudicators.

[59] *Sonko v. Spain* [2011] CAT/C/47/D/368/2008.

5.2.1 CERTAINTY AND CAUSALITY.

> While we may want to rely on scientific evidence to verify (and be able to ease) the pain of another person, we nevertheless know from our own first-person experience of pain that all we can rely on is her own testimony. … Only the person in pain can give testimony of her own experience, and doubting this testimony will likely magnify her suffering.[60]

> None of these questions are adequately answered by philosophy, psychology, or science. Yet law must judge these matters anyway if it seeks to provide protection against and redress for pain.[61]

Despite the flexibility prescribed, legal processes assessing torture-related cases are often challenged by the lack of evidentiary certainty. Adjudicators have nevertheless remained in pursuit of precision, looking to scientific evidence for objectification as 'the surest indication' of truthfulness of suffering[62] – and in their absence falter on the promises of flexibility. *Sonko* as *Veznedaroglu*, as numerous other cases, evoke the problem of causal certainty. Decision-makers simply want to be certain before making strong rulings. Those in *Sonko* considered a finding of intention as being vague and those in *Veznedaroglu* resorted to a procedural instead of a substantive violation in not wanting to decide on the veracity of the competing evidence.

Persisting in demands for 'corporeal proof', for instance, have generally overlooked the potency and probity of the victim's words – with the expert being called in to 'vouch for' or 'authenticate' thus 'involuntarily confirming the devaluation' of strong testimony.[63] Legal processes have come to demand that victim-survivors transform their language to a scientific one to attain recognition.[64] A parallel concern here is how advocates themselves have accepted and played into these evidentiary thresholds. With certainty in demand, in the name of pragmatism, only

60 Käll (2013) 28.

61 Meyer (2014) 14.

62 Didier Fassin and Estelle D'Halluin, 'The Truth from the Body: Medical Certificates as Ultimate Evidence for Asylum Seekers' (2005) 107 *American Anthropologist* 597.

63 Fassin and Rechtman (2009) 246.

64 Veena Das, 'Sufferings, Theodicies, Disciplinary Practices, Appropriations' (2010) 49 *International Social Science Journal* 563.

the most convincing cases end up being argued.[65] States too squarely and strategically play into these ambiguities – with a state in one instance arguing (though unsuccessfully) that the suffering there was 'beyond the evaluation and could not be objectively measured, as it related to psychological aspects, such as the emotions and personalities of the individuals concerned'.[66] A judge not mindful of the difficulties as articulated in the *Greek Case* and since might simply accept such arguments.

When put together, this has led, whether intentionally or not, to raise the evidentiary demands made of victim-survivors. Growing reliance on medico-legal documentation by adjudicators, that is to say, have unduly heightened demands of proof in legal proceedings. Given that such documentation may not be available to a victim (for instance, due to issues of access), an adjudicator's insistence on such evidence may lead to de facto denial of recognition and redress. This was, in fact, the experience of the UK-based anti-torture organisation Freedom from Torture, whose doctors provide medico-legal reports for asylum processes. Over a period of time, doctors there found that the demands made by asylum officials increased, for longer reports which take more time, more certainty in their conclusions and more challenges.[67]

Whilst medical evidence is strongly corroborative of allegations of torture, its absence has indeed become problematic. This risk has been identified by the ECtHR itself:

> that although medical evidence plays a decisive role in establishing the facts for the purpose of the Convention proceedings, the absence of such evidence cannot immediately lead to the conclusion that the allegations of ill-treatment are false or cannot be proven. Were it otherwise, the authorities would be able to avoid responsibility for ill-treatment by not conducting medical examinations and not recording the use of physical force or special means.[68]

[65] Cakal PhD dissertation (2025). I also thank Grant Shubin for making this point in the context of gendered dimensions of torture cases in international criminal law.

[66] *Akhiyadova v. Russia* [2008] ECtHR 32059/02 [82].

[67] Freedom from Torture, '"Proving" Torture: An ever-rising bar for medical evidence?' Conference, October 2015.

[68] *Artyomov v. Russia* [2010] ECtHR 14146/02 [153].

Expectations from legal processes, overlooking these difficulties, leads to 'pressurise experts to *greater* certainty than they really feel' and being 'forced to submit to the hegemony of the judiciary'.[69] Upon this schema, advocates and adjudicators are propelled to transform uncertainty into certainty – as they are often dependent on 'incomplete, incoherent, and suspected evidence, designed to bring into view past acts of violence and cruelty'.[70] In engaging with judicial expectations, that is, experts may ultimately be co-opted – to play into the narrow demands of the law, namely its concern 'with stripping away all possible causes, only to leave the legally relevant'.[71] Judicial impulses for certainty and correctness thus readily render medicolegal reports a 'technology of causal attribution' and a 'technology of visibility' – not of *probability* as they purport to be.[72] The tension between the certainty expected by legal actors and uncertainty are very much present here, with:[73]

> the gap between provisional clinical claims about the causes of pain and suffering, and the legal demand for specific causal certainty creates the space for doubt to grow ... Although the Istanbul Protocol was designed to give stability to the often-ambiguous process of linking scars to claims of torture, given how it is being used in the legal processes it can also add another layer of uncertainty and obfuscation. ... The legal recognition of torture is not about sharing intimate experiences, making deep claims about the nature of being or acknowledging the other with all their differences and similarities. Legal recognition is instead instrumental, concerned with the distribution of rights and the acceptance of obligations, and the meeting of the conditions necessary to make those decisions ... When the law defines torture, it picks out suffering and its specific causes as important, but then complains that clinical evidence on those issues is too vague. Legal processes demand that people speak the language of law, but then claim that what is being said is not clear.

[69] Good (2007) 130, 209.

[70] Kelly 'Recognising Torture' (2014) 178.

[71] Kelly (2012) 74.

[72] Tobias Kelly, 'The Causes of Torture: Law, Medicine and The Assessment of Suffering in British Asylum Claims' in Ian Harper et al (eds), *The Clinic and the Court: Law, Medicine and Anthropology* (CUP 2015) 73–74.

[73] Kelly (2012) 74–91.

Undue degrees of scientific certainty and objectivity required by adjudicators can foster a 'scientism', a positivistic distortion and reduction that expects scientific expertise to speak clearly and conclusively when it cannot. This stems from radical differences in training between lawyers and non-lawyers and, in turn, misapprehension as to scientific 'objectivity'. Scientific objectivity instead operates, amongst other qualities, through caution, probability and contingency. One prominent documentation expert has rejected legal notions of causality in favour of probability, pointing out that it is a fallacy to expect science to establish 'an unequivocal causal relationship between certain practices and their consequences in order to determine the limits of torture' and that:

> When medicine in general and specifically psychiatry face the issue of defining torture, they can establish practices with a high risk ratio [relative risk] of causing damage, and that this damage is of sufficient magnitude to be banned internationally. ... They can also establish operational (reviewable) criteria that allow a combined group of techniques to qualify as 'torture' based on the relative likelihood that these combined practices will cause physical or psychological harm.[74]

Science, in short, does not provide the certainty that adjudicators seek. Torture may indeed be a dark practice, and its survivors might not reappear with scientifically grounded verification. Failing to realise this reality has entrenched an undue evidentiary certainty not only in litigation but in standard-setting or reform processes that unreasonable demands for evidence are made to effectively act as barriers to justice, delaying and frustrating processes. The terrain this depicts is unquestionably tricky requiring a cautious use of deference and discretion, in how to *value* the evidence that is before *view*, whether framed in legal or non-legal language, whether submitted by the state or the victim.

5.2.2 DEFERENCE AND DISCRETION.

> [A] legal understanding of torture provides protection from torture to the extent that it comes closer to its psychological formulation [based on]

[74] Pérez-Sales (2016) 274–275.

> scientific formulations of traumatic stress and empirical evidence rather than on vague distinctions … that are open to endless and inconclusive debate.[75]

> There are some things which just *are* acts of torture.[76]

Despite promises with respect to multi-disciplinary medico-legal documentation, its effective use has proven problematic in practice for other reasons – primarily because it is contingent on competence and capacity by all sides, namely the non-legal expert preparing the report, the advocate litigating based on the report and the adjudicator assessing and accepting the report. Acceptance means deference. Deference to the others' authority. Advocates and adjudicators might generally lack the technical competence to adequately assess what is brought before them. Essential knowledge, necessary to establish and evaluate certain facts central to a case, is often found outside of legal settings and, where available, resource-intensive to draw upon. Despite increased legal receptivity to non-legal expertise in the twentieth century more generally, torture-related cases have demonstrated that adjudicators continue to 'enjoy an unrivalled position as diviners of the facts'.[77]

Wait you may say: an adjudicator might simply not ('feel' the) need to, nor have the time to, require scientific expertise to assess the gravity of every fact in question – and instead reach for presumptions born out of notions of vulnerability, precedent, 'rules of logic and based on experience', or appeals to intuition or empathy. At times the suffering is thought to be so obvious that rhetoric like 'outrage' or 'moral shock' is used, with adjudicators reasoning that the victim 'must have felt' or 'could only have been tortured'.

Discretion in evidentiary evaluations is indispensable in breaking through any contingency of evidence, allowing for adjudicators to definitively determine a case, 'to justify conclusions reached on more intuitive, less formally logical, grounds'.[78] Discretion, as in the weighing of evidence, in its veracity or probity, works through an 'appeal to common

[75] Başoğlu (2017) 397.
[76] Evans (2023) 22.
[77] Jones (1994) 18.
[78] Good (2007) 239.

experience' and the 'application to common sense'.[79] Perceptions and presumptions of suffering are always at play. We always use shortcuts in our cognition. When adjudicators find presumption in precedent, they are happy to use it. So what is the problem? The problem is where decisionmakers 'substitute their own opinion for that of the clinician on the cause of injuries', partly based on common-sense reasoning – especially where they are rejecting cases. Yet discretion has allowed adjudicators to override and evade difficulties posed by expertise.[80] Reflecting on the possibility of explaining the process, one scholar lends some support:[81]

> There is no way for outsiders to know how decisions were in fact reached, and even decision makers themselves may not be fully able to reconstruct that process, because it is not necessarily (or even usually) a matter of the kinds of *conscious* manipulation ... these aspects of judicial decision making are almost impossible to verbalise. My attempts to get adjudicators to describe how they reach decisions yielded little of substance. This does not impugn the honesty of their response, but simply reflects the ineffability of the processes of cognition whereby experienced practitioners assimilate and evaluate complex information.

That adjudicators rarely consult 'theoretical texts not explicitly oriented towards the law' in resorting to internal references, the same scholar finds, 'is yet another sign of law's modernist, non-reflexive nature'.[82] Extensive documentation efforts, 'the prolonged examination process and the thousands of working hours and documents', are observed to be dismissed with 'seeming effortlessness' by another observer,[83] who painfully admits that, following repeated judicial denials of recognition, her organisation found

> itself at a professional crossroads. On one side is the IP, a tool we believe in and struggle to introduce into Israel. On the other is a legal system that

[79] Ibid 211 (references omitted).

[80] Ibid 237.

[81] Ibid 240.

[82] Ibid 262.

[83] Efrat Shir, 'How Do You Say Istanbul Protocol in Hebrew? The Curious Case of Mr Firas Tbeish' (2019) 29 (2) *Torture* 92.

> discredits the IP's potential while digging deeper into its own conception of torture. In the current context, should we continue advocating for the IP and its medico-legal reports, even though a legal brick wall awaits us?[84]

Discretion to defer to medical or related scientific evidence by decision-makers has proven problematic in both national and international processes. This has all too often led human rights bodies to, for instance, uncritically 'rationalize older people's deprivation of liberty for care on the basis that they purportedly *deserve* or *need* such treatment because of their characteristics'.[85] Such unquestioned recognition of 'medical necessity', that 'a measure which is of therapeutic necessity from the point of view of established principles of medicine cannot in principle be regarded as inhuman and degrading',[86] has ended in the faulty logic that 'it is for the medical authorities to decide, on the basis of the recognised rules of medical science, on the therapeutic methods to be used, if necessary by force, to preserve the physical and mental health of patients who are entirely incapable of deciding for themselves and for whom they are therefore responsible'.[87] This is reminiscent of the dissent cited earlier where another judge chose to disregard social scientific evidence 'that harsh penal policies do not have the desired effects' as that was more a policy-related question.[88] As much as this raises questions of competence, there is also caution detected in such positions.

Decisionmakers in asylum processes in the UK and the Netherlands, research has revealed, have similarly challenged and dismissed medical reports without substantial reasons based on statements including 'that scar could not have occurred in the way described', 'could have occurred

[84] This reflection resonates with the UK-based Freedom From Torture, see Strength and Solidarity Podcast, with Sonya Sceats, '33. Strategy: The pain of charting a new course– and the gain', 20 April 2023, https://strengthandsolidarity.org/podcast/33-strategy-the-pain-of-charting-a-new-course-and-the-gain/ (accessed at 18 March 2025).

[85] Maeve O'Rourke, *Human Rights and the Care of Older People: Dignity, Vulnerability, and the Anti-Torture Norm* (OUP 2024) 217.

[86] *VC v. Slovakia* [2011] ECtHR 18968/07 [103].

[87] *Herczegfalvy v. Austria* [1992] ECtHR 10533/83 [82–83].

[88] *Rezmives and others v. Romania* [2017] ECtHR 61467/12, 39516/13, 48231/13, opinion of Judge Wojtyczek [4].

in some other way' and 'such torture must have left scars'.[89] Again – it may well be good for judges to act on physical marks, prolonged or permanent damage but what happens where that doesn't exist – does it mean in the absence that it wasn't serious enough. These devices also serve the ECtHR's 'avoidance of analyzing psychological suffering or in general of providing more elaborate analyses but it has also served the applicants who do not submit evidence of psychological harm'.[90] Critical psychologists, writing for experts operating in the same space, have also urged other psychologists and adjudicators involved in medico-legal documentation to resist a biomedical 'box-ticking' approach (if symptom then diagnosis, if not nothing to do). Failure to do so, for them, can mean reductivity reigns and visibility remains unduly central.[91]

The dominant position in anti-torture practice advances multidisciplinary (between legal, medical and psychological expertise) as crucial to properly assessing and appreciating suffering. In the spirit of the *Istanbul Protocol*, prominent commentators look upon the 'close collaboration between both professions in the investigation and documentation of torture allegations' as indispensable.[92] Working with and across disciplines is oft-espoused but rarely recognised as problematic. Why may this be? Addressing difficulties at this juncture, a DIGNITY documentation manual takes a rare reflexive stance:[93]

> From very early on in the training, professionals are socialized into a specific profession – often to a degree that they do not even realize

[89] David Rhys Jones and Sally Verity Smith, 'Medical Evidence in Asylum and Human Rights Appeals' (2004) 16 *International Journal of Refugee Law* 381, 396, 392; Marcelle Reneman, 'Forensic Medical Reports in Asylum Cases: The View of the European Court of Human Rights and the Committee against Torture' (2020) 38 *Netherlands Quarterly of Human Rights* 206.

[90] Liana Morica Muntean, 'Determining Torture in Interrogation Cases: Comparative Analysis of the Case Law of the European Court of Human Rights, the UN Bodies and the US Courts', Doctor of Juridical Science Thesis, Central European University, Budapest (2017) 144.

[91] Nimisha Patel and David Pilgrim, 'Psychologists and Torture: Critical Realism as a Resource for Analysis and Training' (2018) 17 (2) *Journal of Critical Realism* 176–191.

[92] IRCT (2009) 10.

[93] Dignity (Marie Brasholt and Elna Søndergaard), 'Collaboration between medical doctors and lawyers when documenting torture in North Africa' (2021) 11.

themselves. They learn to see the world as it is seen by their profession, to pay attention to some things and to ignore others, i.e., a narrative specific for their profession is developed.

The authors continue to identify four points of disciplinary difference resulting in difficulty: focus, language, methodology and ethics. These relate to how the respective professionals (doctors or lawyers) view the tasks before them: what is it that is important, how is it to be best understood, how is it best undertaken. The authors urge for a self-awareness amongst professionals of their own 'strengths and limitations', increased awareness of 'each other's language, ethics, techniques' and for improved 'communication, understanding, openness and respect from both sides'.[94]

For more critical scholars, as Sheila Jasanoff, tensions between legal and non-legal expertise arise because 'what counts as true for the law need not count as true for science, and in exceptional cases even scientific truths may not be accepted as valid for legal purposes'.[95] Evidence, when all this is put together, invokes an age-old contest between adjudicators and experts as to what counts as reliable. The degree to which judges have heeded medical insights or the age-old imperative to have law 'marching with medicine'[96] so as to objectively 'distinguish the genuine from the spurious' stands to be questioned here (as it has in the broader scholarship on evidence).[97]

Despite the acknowledged difficulty in producing evidence in torture-related cases, advocates and adjudicators continue to privilege objectifiable, verifiable and manageable evidence.[98] Many scholars have concluded that 'from an evidentiary perspective it is much easier to give legal significance to physical injuries than to psychological

94 Ibid 12.

95 Sheila Jasanoff, 'Just Evidence: The Limits of Science in the Legal Process' (2006) 34 *Journal of Law, Medicine & Ethics* 328.

96 *Mount Isa Mines v. Pusey* [1970] HCA 60; (1970) 125 CLR 383 [395].

97 *Tame v. New South Wales; Annetts v Australian Stations Pty Ltd* [2002] HCA 35 [183]. Danuta Mendelson, *The History of the Liability for Negligently Caused Psychiatric Injury (Nervous Shock): A Study in the Interfaces of Medicine and Law* (Ashgate 1998) 5.

98 Nimisha Patel, 'The Psychologization of Torture' in Mark Rapley et al (eds), *De-Medicalizing Misery* (Palgrave 2011) 428.

experiences',[99] and that 'actual bodily injury' still seems to hold the most valuable evidentiary currency.[100] A search for visible injuries has become a feature of the practice in the field, amounting to 'a "we know it when we see it" approach'.[101] This mode of reasoning is vague and varied, unpredictable beyond certain patterns and practices. There is a speculation here that does not always lead to the most progressive receptivity to new claims and new evidence – privileging established or common understandings of what severe suffering, or credibility, looks like or should look like.

5.3 CONCLUSION

> [L]aw is awash in epistemological and ethical problems associated with knowing and imagining suffering. In each of these domains we might ask: How well do legal actors know and imagine suffering in these various domains of legal life? What problems of representation and interpretation plague efforts to know the suffering of others?[102]

This chapter has canvassed the principles and problems pertaining to the substantiation of torture-related cases. Legal recognition is indeed a question of evidence – its production and, as importantly, its interpretation. Principles, I have argued, formulated in and since the *Greek Case* depict a survivor-centric appreciation of the difficulties in producing evidence and, in turn, a prescription that adjudicators act accordingly in determining evidentiary demands. Evidence, sadly, has not settled the question of recognition. The assumption that it does, in all likelihood, has drawn and drained the field's energies towards the production of evidence over and above its reception by decision-makers.

Evidence, even at its strongest, does not speak for itself – it requires interpretation. That evidence of torture needs to be interpreted means that it opens it up to how torture is imagined and, more pointedly, to political factors such as state deference. The interpretation, therefore, is as

[99] Muntean (2017) 147–148.
[100] Mavronicola (2021) 96.
[101] Muntean (2017) 89.
[102] Sarat, 'Knowing the Suffering of Others' (2014) 4.

good as its users – their competence, need for certainty and convenience. Evidence feeds a field of institutional and ideological factors which determine the demands made of evidence (often referred to as standards and burdens of proof). Evidentiary practices, to put this slightly differently, inform and are informed by imaginational, ideological as institutional capacities – what torture and its victim looks like, where torture should be looked for and how that can be recognised and reported. In all, that documentation leads to recognition is not as simple as presumed.

Ready to push aside broader debate for the sake of disposing a case, actors are busy invisibilising the human hands at work in downplaying the practice of interpretation afoot, abstracting facts from their sociocultural-political contexts. They are busy masking the complexities and ambiguities through a language of objectification not leaving reasoning to chance but closely constructing and controlling what evidence is made to support. In the name of pragmatism, ambiguities are transformed either into absolute certainties or obfuscated altogether. Whilst evidence stands to serve the law, the legal impulse remains to avoid deferring judgment to the word of the victim or speculating dangerously – preserving the discretion of what suffering counts as ultimately legal.[103] Evidentiary practices in legal processes have been characterised as being informal and variable, common and quotidian, as 'plural', 'primitive' and 'presumptive',[104] exuding a 'pragmatist habitus', serving to conceal and silence, casting an objectivist cloak over judicial reasoning.[105] So how can the legal and non-legal expertise be reconciled? Should it simply prevail in cases of disagreement?

As emerging from the opening vignette's quip ('is the squeeze worth the juice?') and further discussed under matters of convenience, there are also impulses to short-circuit an extensive examination of evidence in favour of commonsensical assessments – to instead draw on image-, value- and emotion-based presumptions. So what informs these

[103] In *Coker v. Georgia* (USSC (1977) 433 USSC 584, p. 598), where the death penalty was argued to constitute a cruel and unusual punishment, the USSC openly ruled that 'in the end our own judgement will be brought to bear on the question'.

[104] Sarat et al (2007) 1–2.

[105] Mariana Valverde, 'Theoretical and Methodological Issues in the Study of Legal Knowledge Practices' in Sarat et al (2007) 89–90.

impulses? How does emotionality, visibility, textuality and temporality of torture come to bear? This draws in, what I have called, sense-centric reasoning (through common-sense, common knowledge, empathy, presumptions, intuition and impression) that serves to undercut the weight of scientific expertise. This is what I turn to explicate and explore in Chapter 6.

CHAPTER 6

Sensing Suffering

I CAST MY MIND BACK TO YET ANOTHER FORMATIVE EXPERIENCE – this time in overlooking my own emotive reactions in being moulded into an anti-torture lawyer. As initiation to new staff at Dignity, I was informed that Dr. Jens Modvig's was offering his 'horror show'. What could be better than to learn from a world-renowned anti-torture physician? Graphic images of bruises and burns, painstakingly collected over his countless years of experience, were beamed onto the wall. Having had little previous exposure, I found it upsetting and sickening. Perhaps this was a steeling and strong introduction to the field, for lawyer and non-lawyer alike. When the discussion turned to the universal definition and to its element of severity, I asked Jens how one exactly went about assessing severity: could we have recourse to electrodes or other technological means of measurement? He pushed back, explaining that the term was a legal one and that I ought to busy myself with getting to grips with its complexity.

I soon thereafter started on a project, which ultimately led to my PhD research, on improving the medico-legal documentation of psychological torture, where the question provoked me even more pointedly. As ignorant as I was then, than now hopefully, I missed that there was something key coded into my visceral reaction to the images: that others, in even more powerful positions to decide the question of severity, too relied on such reactions in constructing an idea of severe suffering. It is medico-legal evidence, not emotions, that remain privileged in principle – all else was dismissed as poor practice. It was only when, some years later, I fortuitously happened on work which connected law, emotions and violence, that I came to dignify the visceral reaction I had and started to see it feature and function in the jurisprudence. Emotional responses were all over: in rhetorical moral flourishes harkening to the 'shocked conscience' or thin reasoning that certain acts 'must have' had a certain impact. It is this literature, missed by 'law and torture', that I dived into and with which I hope to establish connections in this chapter.

> The experience of pain is itself a complex, interconnected, and interactive system involving the physical, emotional, perceptual, spiritual, and cognitive. There may be no way to evaluate suffering pre-interpretively, nor is it clear that what we would find would necessarily matter to us, even if there were such a way.[1]

> To have sympathy or compassion for someone's plight, again, you have to believe something about the seriousness of what that person has suffered.[2]

How do we make sense (access and assess) another's suffering? Is it possible through mere words, concepts and images? In this chapter, I argue that this is more difficult than doctrinally admitted but not impossible as some critical scholars have advanced. Sensing suffering is complex and contingent on a range of influences – visceral, sensorial and relational.[3] Whether admitted or not, so are all determinations of suffering guised as technical doctrinal readings of precedent. Legal characterisations of torture as 'shocking the conscience' or as causing 'moral outrage' are but two rhetorical gestures to these broader social-cultural-political impulses and influences.[4] The stakes of recognition are high – emotionally, medically, socially, politically and legally.[5] Those legally trained struggle with individuation, intersubjectivity and 'shareability' – aspects beyond text-based law. For them, as others, the boundaries of 'what [kinds of] suffering is recognised is clearly still to be fully developed' and perennially presents 'irresolvable challenges for text-based law'.[6] Invocations of dignity, vulnerability, empathy, relationality and embodiment, increasingly brought into interpretations, have *aided* but have not

[1] Sarat, 'Knowing the Suffering of Others' (2014) 37.

[2] Martha Nussbaum, 'Emotion in the Language of Judging' (1996) 70 *St John's Law Review* 23, 25.

[3] Butler (2009) 51 finds that this language of recognition can be equally sensorial as metaphorical: 'differentiating the cries we can hear from those we cannot, the sights we can see from those we cannot'.

[4] Judith Shklar, *Justice and Equality Here and Now* (Cornell University Press 1986): 'the present function of rights is the expression of personal outrage at injustice and cruelty'.

[5] Laura Kolbe, 'Where Does It Hurt?' (23 June 2022) *New York Review of Books*.

[6] Dermot Feenan, 'Law and Compassion' (2017) 13 *International Journal of Law in Context* 121, 122.

ended questions of what the nature of suffering is precisely. Definitions remain disembodied and distant, 'pain and fear are remote, unreal and largely unshared',[7] 'how the punishment hurt, how it feels, the suffering and the sorrow, these are elements most often completely lacking in the texts'.[8] Definitions, categories, concepts or standards have not solved these fundamental issues.

Suffering of another, whatever the means, is not directly accessible. Even where there is ample evidence of suffering, that evidence does not speak for itself. It must, as argued in Chapter 5, be interpreted. Interpretation reaches beyond technical knowledge and engages the senses – seeing, feeling, hearing, imagining. Senses filter, sort and prioritise through the instances of suffering which merit attention and those which do not.[9] We might not, for instance, 'reward people for allowing themselves to be provoked by trivial slights', or we might 'withhold compassion from people if we think that they are just "spoiled", moaning and groaning over something that is not really so bad'.[10] Senses (as 'passions' we read in Chapter 4) fuel social, political and judicial drives to punish – evident in invocations of anger, fear, disgust, retribution and pleasure.[11] Conversely, Amnesty International's campaign against torture in the 1970's, culminating in the adoption of the *UN Convention against Torture and Other Cruel, Inhuman or Degrading Treatment or Punishment,* was itself grounded on emotional appeals, 'compassion for the victims of torment, indignation against the perpetrators and disgust'.[12] Senses pervade all facets of 'law and torture'.

7 Robert M Cover, 'Violence and the Word' (1986) 95 *Yale Law Journal* 1601; Robert Cover, *Justice Accused: Antislavery and the Judicial Process* (Yale 1975) 210.

8 Christie (1981) 15.

9 Martha Nussbaum, *Hiding from Humanity: Disgust, Shame, and the Law* (Princeton 2004) 50 we 'withhold compassion from people if we think that they are just "spoiled", moaning and groaning over something that is not really so bad'.

10 Ibid 40.

11 Nussbaum (2004); Magnus Hörnqvist, *The Pleasure of Punishment* (Routledge 2021); Henrique Carvalho and Anastasia Chamberlen, 'Why Punishment Pleases: Punitive Feelings in a World of Hostile Solidarity' (2018) 20 (2) *Punishment & Society* 217–234.

12 Sylvia Kesper-Biermann, 'Security, Transnational Law and Emotions: The History of the Transnational Anti-Torture Regime from the Enlightenment to the 1984 United Nations Convention Against Torture' (Max Planck Institute for European Legal History Research Paper Series No 2018-01).

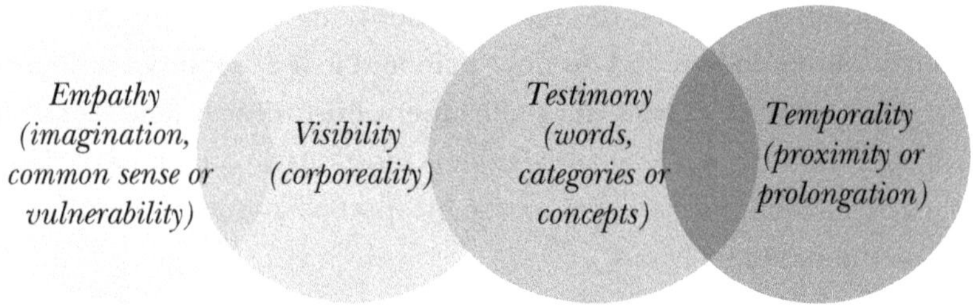

Figure 6.1 Registers of sense-centric reasoning.

As true and intuitive as these assertions seem, doctrinal scholarship normally forecloses such entry-points as missing the mark, as suspicious, ambiguous, unpredictable and as extra-legal. Whatever the emotion, or any concept that stands adjacent and aligned, it is viewed 'as a synonym for prejudice, irrelevance, or lack of intellectual rigor'[13] or as the 'antithesis of the detached scientific mind and its quest for "objectivity", "truth" and "wisdom"'.[14] With a view not only to adjudication but to anti-torture practice more broadly, I disagree.

Drawing on 'law and emotions' and adjacent scholarship, I split this chapter into four inter-locking discussions (Figure 6.1): (i) 'empathy: imagining suffering' (how empathy has been selectively deployed to aid the recognition of suffering as well as cognitive shortcuts and presumptions, for example, common sense, aiding to imbue suffering); (ii) 'visibility: seeing suffering' (how visibility of marks through the gaze or photographic evidence has dominated imaginations of what torture looks like); (iii) 'testimony: saying suffering' (the difficulties with the production and receipt of testimonial evidence); and (iv) 'temporality: timing suffering' (how concepts related to time such as proximity and prolongation are used in assessing the veracity and gravity of suffering). Before all that, I will sound two notes of caution, firstly on conceptual conflation and secondly on the interplay between the individual and social (under 'Caution before conflation').

[13] Susan A Bandes et al (eds), *Research Handbook on Law and Emotion* (Elgar 2021) 1–4.

[14] Simon J Williams and Gillian Bendelow (eds), *Emotions in Social Life: Critical Themes and Contemporary Issues* (Routledge 1998) xvi; Anne Saab, 'Engaging with Emotions in International Law' in Simon Koschut and Andrew A. G. Ross (eds), *The Oxford Handbook of Emotions in International Relations* (2025).

6.1 CAUTION BEFORE CONFLATION

> That word, feel, remains operative because it encapsulates not only sensation but also emotion, cognition, and, importantly, communication. How a sufferer feels at any point in time is directly related to the degree to which she is able to tell someone how she feels, and the extent to which she is confident that anybody is listening. We imbue the damage, especially the sight of the damage, with all of its potential harmful implications.[15]

Whilst I urge the reader to move towards recognising that their understanding of suffering engages their senses (emotion, cognition and imagination), I hesitate to map this ephemeral terrain with precision. I admit to a conceptual difficulty in writing about such visceral registers, alternating between senses, emotions, affect and all adjacent. I have no desire to draw rigid distinctions given the trickiness of the terrain.[16] Emotions, as is suffering, are difficult to define, yet emotions constitute suffering. In a non-committal manner, I understand sensing as 'the capacity to register or to be affected' and sensemaking as 'the capacity for such sensing to become knowledge of some kind'.[17] Beyond this, I hesitate because of the inextricable interplay between the various sensorial dimensions. Empathy, for instance, is closely linked with visibility[18] and

[15] Boddice (2017) 102, 79.

[16] Sharyn Roach Anleu and Kathy Mack, *Judging and Emotion: A Socio-Legal Analysis* (Routledge 2022) 5 who attribute this 'to the increasing dominance of the natural science paradigm, instead of metaphysics or philosophy, to explain emotion'. The word 'emotion' has not always been dominant, having gradually come to displace 'feeling, passion, fervour, affect, sensibility, sentiment, appetite, changes of temper, and its inclination'. Nor is there consensus on defining what an emotion or an adjacent concept is taken to mean. A composite approach characterises emotion as 'interactive, interdependent and context specific as well as subjective, internal and personal … psychobiological (recognising instinct or impulse) and individual [and as] social practice performed in, emergent from and embedded in social settings and situations'. Peggy A Thoits, 'The Sociology of Emotions' (1989) 15 *Annual Review of Sociology* 317, 318: Sociologists of emotions accept that emotions can come in various forms: '(a) appraisals of a situational stimulus or context, (b) changes in physiological or bodily sensations, (c) the free or inhibited display of expressive gestures, and (d) a cultural label applied to specific constellations of one or more of the first three components'. This is also a wide take.

[17] Matthew Fuller and Eyal Weizman, *Investigative Aesthetics: Conflicts and Commons in the Politics of Truth* (Verso 2021) 33.

[18] Wilson and Brown (2009) 3.

'the way we see things is affected by what we know or what we believe'.[19] The relationship between seeing, hearing and saying is dialectic, not settled or static.

Seeing no reason to follow common distinctions, I also do not differentiate between 'thinking (cognition) and feeling (emotion); between mind (cognition) and heart (emotion)'.[20] I take empathy, visibility, testimony and temporality simply as sense-centric means and modes of reasoning *towards* as *against* recognition – as powerful yet fallible visceral registers. Instead, I look upon such conflations as somewhat productive, cutting against the opposite (namely, fragmentation) exuded by the dominant medico-legal paradigm which has

> Perception, experience, and coping run into each other and are lived as a unified experience. When reconstituted as a medical problem, however, that experience is fragmented into a series of dichotomies that represent the deep cultural logic of biomedicine. Both [medical and psychological] traditions tend to ignore how a person's immediate experience of pain unites its bodily, psychological, and social origins.[21]

What then can concretely be said about the senses? I have alluded, as in Chapter 3, to their 'shifting and elusive qualities, constantly reshuffled by socio-cultural and technological changes',[22] and found them 'likely to shift as society's norms undergo change', coming to reflect 'common shared values within a political community'.[23] Senses, to articulate one

[19] John Berger, *Ways of Seeing* (Penguin 2008) pp. 7–8.

[20] Andrea Bianchi and Anne Saab, 'Fear and International Law-Making: An Exploratory Inquiry' (2019) 32 *Leiden Journal of International Law* 351, 354.

[21] DelVecchio Good (1994) 8–10.

[22] Nussbaum (2004) 47; Law and the senses (2013): 'The norms and thresholds ... have varied significantly in history and across cultures. Through studying select instances of this variation the contributors to this project will bring to light the sensory codes embedded in legal practice and their relationship to the encompassing sensory models of society'.

[23] Emily Kidd White, 'Images of Reach, Range, and Recognition: Thinking about Emotions in the Study of International Law' in Bandes et al (2021) 227; Nussbaum (2004) 5–6: Without a shared conception or imagination to 'what violations are outrageous, what losses give rise to a profound grief, what vulnerable human beings have reason to fear', Nussbaum observes, 'it is very hard to understand why we devote the attention we do, in law, to certain types of harm and damage'. Nussbaum thus comes to identify emotions as essential, holding that law 'without appeals to emotion is virtually unthinkable'.

unquestionable connection, link the 'micro and macro levels of social reality',[24] themselves being 'the result of a complex interplay among cultural, social structural, cognitive, and neurological forces',[25] and 'guide decisions, both consciously and unconsciously'.[26]

This brings me to my second note of caution on the interplay between the individual and social. Individuals are always channelling the social in viscerally reacting to suffering. It cannot be otherwise. And senses are registers that help capture such social conditioning – as often explained through 'feeling rules', 'emotional regimes' or 'emotion cultures'.[27] This means, as earlier asserted, that 'pain is only pain where it accords with tacit rules for the acceptable expression or the experience of pain'.[28] Whilst the 'seeable, sayable, and sensible' for the individual is shaped socially,[29] caution is also urged not to take social emotions as the direct aggregation of individual emotions (to avoid overdetermination).[30] Neither do I make claims to have settled this interplay with precision.

6.2 EMPATHY: IMAGINING SUFFERING

> Degradation reflects a 'shared sense among us of how one person responds as a human to another human, a shared sense of what humans should be expected to endure, a shared sense of what it is to respond appropriately to the elementary exigencies of human life'.[31]

> The juridical conscience [is] the source of all law.[32]

[24] Jonathan H. Turner and Jan E. Stets, *The Sociology of Emotions* (CUP 2005) 1.

[25] Ibid 9.

[26] Ibid 22.

[27] Thoits (1989) 323.

[28] Boddice (2014) 5, 14.

[29] Michael Richardson, *Gestures of Testimony: Torture, Trauma, and Affect in Literature* (Bloomsbury 2016) 77.

[30] J. M Barbalet, *Emotion, Social Theory, and Social Structure: A Macrosociological Approach* (CUP 2001) 65; David Howes, *Sensorial Investigations: A History of the Senses in Anthropology, Psychology, and Law* (Penn State University Press 2023) 17: perhaps because even the irregular or 'uncommon senses' also play a role in informing collective understandings.

[31] Jeremy Waldron, 'Inhuman and Degrading Treatment: The Words Themselves' (2010) *Canadian Journal of Law and Jurisprudence*, 23(2): 269–286, 284.

[32] *Ituango Massacres v. Colombia* [2006] IACtHR, separate opinion of Judge Trindade [49].

The problem of recognising suffering is a problem of access – one cannot directly access (or readily know) another's suffering. The simplest and, I find, truest response is that, as suffering is invisible, inference through imaginative, instinctive and inductive reasoning becomes essential.[33] Suffering is inferred 'indirectly, from observation (e.g., a broken leg) or through communication from the sufferer – pain behavior'.[34] Can it be anything but inferential? It depends on what we mean by 'access'. This is a rather theoretical question but it emerges in central assumptions of the incommunicability of pain and how testimonial and scientific evidence might be approached. Drawing this closer to torturous suffering, the scientific consensus also errs on the side of inferential reasoning that 'the causal link between particular forms of torture and subsequent sequelae cannot be directly observed, and must be inferred'.[35] In the following, I explore several interrelated concepts in this terrain including empathy, common sense and vulnerability.

6.2.1 EMPATHY. Scholarship, particularly phenomenology, has long concerned itself with the question of access (more specifically, 'other people's minds').[36] Scholars here too take the information about another's mind as a matter of reading and perceiving their body, as inferred and imagined. Since we associate being scalded by hot water as painful, seeing others being scalded by water readily leads to our inference that they are in pain.[37] These scholars argue that we unduly

[33] DelVecchio Good (1994) 139.

[34] Ibid.

[35] Kelly (2012) 756–757. He adds: 'What is more, the patterns that people show after torture are far from determinant, and vary from person to person. Causal links must therefore be forged rather than found from among often incomplete observations'.

[36] Shaun Gallagher and Dan Zahavi, *The Phenomenological Mind* (Routledge 2012).

[37] Ibid 201. Divergent positions speak to inferring and attributing another's mental state, between accounts preferring theoretical-mediation ('common-sense explanation of why people do what they do') and the emotional-engagement (drawing on self-simulation or projection where 'our own mind [is used] as a model of what the other's mind must be like'). Both positions respectively opt for imaginatively and deliberatively hypothesising or deducing another's experiences from theoretical or self- understanding. The meaningfulness of this exercise also turns on what we take to be 'access' – and how exact or exhaustive it must be. Inferential and simulative approaches, as the phenomenological argument goes, narrowly psychologically characterise the source of true experience as located in the mind and away from a more embodied understanding. Rejecting the

underplay the possibility of access. Emphasising the view that emotions are embodied and communicable, they urge a move away from a psychological paradigm of the concealed mind towards foregrounding bodily expressions and impressions as presenting our access to another. The concept of 'empathy' is advanced at this point as a mode of consciousness that helps to render another's bodily expressions as indicative of their mental state. Empathy is, on one socio-legal account, taken to mean as follows

> (1) feeling the emotion of another; (2) understanding the experience or situation of another, both affectively and cognitively, often achieved by imagining oneself to be in the position of the other; and (3) action brought about by experiencing the distress of another (hence the confusion of empathy with sympathy and compassion). The first two forms are ways of knowing, the third form a catalyst for action.[38]

Empathy, to continue this account, is 'a form of understanding, a phenomenon that encompasses affect as well as cognition in determining meanings; [as] a rich source of knowledge and approaches to legal problems – which are, ultimately, human problems'.[39] Accordingly, empathy facilitates our *experience* of 'another's subjectivity, and not merely imagining it, simulating it, or theorizing about it'.[40] This is not taken to proceed, by any means, to a full (*equal, exact* or *exhaustive*) understanding of another's experience. The asymmetry is unquestionable but phenomenological approaches advance that the embodied and empathetic is merely a relatively *fuller* account compared to inferential and simulative approaches centring the other's mind and, in turn, as invisible, intrinsic and impossible. There still remains, after all, the possibility of misunderstanding due to the distance between another's lived experience and our inferred experience.[41]

notion of absolute inaccessibility, they characterise 'the mind as something visible to only one person and invisible to everyone else [is] something cut off from the body and the surrounding world as if psychological phenomena would remain exactly the same, even without gestures, bodily expressions' (207).

[38] Lynne Hendersen, 'Legality and Empathy' (1987) 85 *Michigan Law Review* 1579.

[39] Ibid 1576.

[40] Gallagher and Zahavi (2012) 204.

[41] Maurice Merleau-Ponty, *Phenomenology of Perception* (The Humanities Press 1962) 356.

At the same time, empathy, as any emotion, does not feature and function in isolation but on the background of how suffering is imagined. Empathy works to inform the imagination, and vice versa.[42] Imagination is imbued with the potential to draw us closer to another's experience as it

> serves to see, and not just to dream. Imagination can help think the unthought, shift perspective, and combine things no one would think or dare putting together. A certain 'playfulness of mind', the use of metaphors and analogies are indispensable tools of a creative intellect and a substantial aid to uncovering the hidden structures of knowledge production.[43]

This is no different for law, and its actors, which is 'part of a distinctive manner of imagining the real'.[44] The legal imagination works both implicitly and explicitly, occasionally through notions such as 'vulnerability', 'presumptions' and 'common sense'. These are devices through which legal actors have increasingly reached out to the lifeworld in which suffering is inflicted and signified. Empathy in torture practice is more often characterised as sensitising medico-legal actors to the survivor's experience of torture towards expanding (than endangering) recognition and response.[45] Empathy is argued, for instance, to 'contribute to dismantling, to some extent, the feelings of vulnerability and powerlessness' facing torture victims[46] as well as anticipated to improve documentation. The *Istanbul Protocol*, in fact, explicitly directs interviewing professionals to 'attempt to relate to mental suffering in the context of the individual's beliefs and cultural norms [as] a sensitive empathic attitude may offer the victim some relief from the experience of alienation'.[47] The assumption here holds empathy as advancing and expanding recognition.

[42] Maksymilian Del Mar, 'Imagining by Feeling: A Case for Compassion in Legal Reasoning' (2017) 13 *International Journal of Law in Context* 143, 143; Kidd White (2014) 233.

[43] Andrea Bianchi, 'Knowledge Production in International Law: Forces and Processes' in Bianchi and Hirsch (2021) 178.

[44] Clifford Geertz, *Local Knowledge: Further Essays in Interpretive Anthropology* (Basic Books 1983) 173.

[45] Yildiz (PhD thesis) 219 also attributes the expansion in the scope of article 3 to 'empathizing with the suffering of the victims when identifying violations'.

[46] Heri (2021) 199.

[47] UN *Istanbul Protocol* (2022) 240.

Yet, as with all devices to be invoked, empathy is selective, susceptible to 'bias and stereotype'.[48] Despite its progressive potential, torture's inherent complexity leaves empathetic assessments open to be self-serving, exposed to ends-based reasoning.[49] Appeals to empathy are also contested between majorities and dissenting judges.[50] These concepts, in short, not only pack a potential for creativity and expansiveness but also rigidity and narrowness when used unreflectingly.

6.2.2 COMMON SENSE. As with empathy, professionals also channel their values through common-sensical reasoning, building upon and reflecting 'their ethical, cultural and political values to some degree'.[51] This has been characterised as inescapable for medico-legal professionals alike who

> rely upon retroduction and judgmental rationalism; and, regardless of their different decision-making logic, they both apply common sense reasoning, of some sort. This then is common sense inflected by professional power and expertise, situated in a particular time and place. Professional rationales build upon the common stock of knowledge extant in a contemporary shared world.[52]

Common-sensical reasoning appears in many forms, including through 'the rules of logic and based on experience',[53] through presumptions of vulnerability and through inferential reasoning that is coded into

[48] Kidd White (2014) 105.

[49] Loran F Nordgren et al, 'What Constitutes Torture?: Psychological Impediments to an Objective Evaluation of Enhanced Interrogation Tactics' (2011) 22 *Psychological Science* 689.

[50] *Khan v. Germany* [2015] ECtHR 38030/12, separate opinion of Zupancic: 'A finding of a possible violation in this case if the applicant were to be expelled would have prevented the tragedy. Empathy would require no less'; *S.J. v. Belgium* [2015] ECtHR 70055/10, dissent of Pinto de Albuquerque [10]: 'by introducing considerations of "compassion" or "sympathy" in place of rights-based arguments, the Court leaves unfettered discretion to Governments to do as they please with costly and undesirable sick people'.

[51] Patel and Pilgrim (2018) 182.

[52] Ibid.

[53] *Cantoral Benavides v. Peru* [2000] IACtHR [48] emphasising the importance of reasoning based on 'the rules of logic and based on experience'.

the phrase 'must have felt'.[54] This assumes, though never so explicitly explained, that a victim must have felt a certain degree of suffering given a set of established facts especially where there are evidentiary difficulties. Such 'cognitive short-cuts' are unavoidable by some accounts – as they serve to 'organize our experience' helping 'make sense of current circumstances',[55] especially 'to reduce complex situations to simpler and manageable ones'.[56] These shortcuts become unreflectingly embedded through 'repetition, anchoring, and time' – leading to 'common assumptions' shaping pre-selectivity.[57] Such reasoning involves the 'rapid, effortless, and unintentional processes of information, essentially activating some well-learned set of associations or responses that have developed through the repeated activation of memory'.[58]

That common sense is ubiquitous and useful in practice is abundantly clear.[59] Those working in anti-torture prevention as detention monitors have been upfront about their use of this mode of thinking. Antonio Cassese, on one occasion, wrote that the 'truth of the matter is that in many cases a treatment or punishment is *objectively* inhuman, regardless of the intention of the relevant authorities to cause serious harm'.[60] On another occasion he wrote that common sense was central to fact-finding, 'inspectors would have to work out their own rules of navigation, guided by their expertise, common sense and experience'.[61] Malcolm Evans has similarly positioned himself in writing:[62]

> when we say that we just 'know', intuitively, that something amounts to torture, there is probably something of a conflation of two different things

[54] Heri (2021) 199, citing *El-Masri v. Macedonia* [2012] ECtHR 39630/09 [202]: '[applicant's] apprehension as to what would happen to him next and must have caused him emotional and psychological distress'.

[55] Matthias Wählisch, 'Cognitive Frames of Interpretation in International Law' in Andrea Bianchi et al (eds), *Interpretation in International Law* (2015) 334.

[56] Ibid.

[57] Ibid 335.

[58] Bianchi and Hirsch, 'Introduction' (2021) 20.

[59] Terry A Maroney, 'Lay Conceptions in Emotions of Law' in Bandes et al (2021) 15.

[60] Cassese (2008) 317.

[61] Antonio Cassese, *Inhuman States: Imprisonment, Detention and Torture in Europe Today* (Polity Press 1996) 45.

[62] Evans (2023) 22.

> taking place: it is not that the existence of pain is necessarily irrelevant, but we can confidently assume that pain of a requisite intensity has been inflicted simply because of the nature of the act – it *has* to have been; how could it not? But I am equally sure that if, for some extraordinary reason, the victim did not actually feel any physical pain, it would not have mattered in the slightest. ... There are some things which just *are* acts of torture.

In criticising the field's 'almost voyeuristic' fixation on the pain threshold, Evans explains how in detention monitoring work he avoided the question 'because we just assumed that its effect on the victim was sufficiently painful' and because it was 'obvious':[63]

> because we considered it to be completely unnecessary: the very doing of such things to a person meant that they were acts of torture – how could they not? And precisely *how* painful they were for the victim was just not important at all. These are all things which we simply *knew* should not be done and that, in consequence, the victims were being subjected to torture.

Common-sensical reasoning, according to such accounts, clearly aids in calling certain experiences as torture or not. This has led to repeated beatings at the hands of police,[64] electrocution[65] or rape[66] to be essentialised

[63] Ibid 22.

[64] *Selmouni v. France* [1999] ECtHR 25803/94 [102]: '[w]hatever a person's state of health, it can be presumed that such intensity of blows will cause substantial pain'.

[65] *Polonskiy v. Russia* [2009] ECtHR 30033/05 [124]: 'a particularly serious form of ill-treatment capable of provoking severe pain and cruel suffering and therefore falling to be treated as torture, even if it does not result in any long-term health damage'.

[66] *Aydin v. Turkey* [1997] ECtHR 57/1996/676/866 [83]: unequivocally 'leav[ing] deep psychological scars on the victim which do not respond to the passage of time as quickly as other forms of physical and mental violence'; *Miguel Castro Prison v. Peru* [2006] IACtHR [311]: 'an extremely traumatic experience that may have serious consequences and it causes great physical and psychological damage that leaves the victim "physically and emotionally humiliated", situation difficult to overcome with time, contrary to what happens with other traumatic experiences'; *Rosendo Cantú v. Mexico* [2010] IACtHR [114]: 'the after-effects of rape will not always be physical injuries or disease. Women victims of rape also experience complex consequences of a psychological and social nature'; *Fernández Ortega v. Mexico* [2011] IACtHR [124]; *Río Negro Massacres v. Guatemala,* [2012] IACtHR [134]: 'rape [for a Mayan woman] means dishonor, stigmatization, blame, and the disgrace it somehow causes within the family, [and ...] the neighborhood'.

as torture. This mode of objectification of suffering is also evident where adjudicators characterise harms as not 'appropriate for any person',[67] as 'undeniable suffering',[68] as 'inherently debasing'[69] or as 'objectively degrading'.[70] This has found support in some doctrinal scholarship.[71] The danger is rather for this to lead to 'the all-too-common mistake of consulting the contents of [one's] consciousness to define torture'[72] and 'to accept evidence when it conforms to … commitments and to challenge it when it does not'.[73]

Common sense is, as with empathy, unstable and unpredictable.[74] Shortcuts, after all, provide 'quick guidelines but may lead to systemic errors'.[75] These bring with it a lack of self-reflexivity, meaning the potential failure to 'notice the extent to which their assessments embody contestable value judgments and overlook diverse perspectives'.[76] Indeed, advocates and adjudicators are 'constantly engaged in numbing the senses into commonsense; manipulating, channelling and controlling the sensible; inserting properties and forbidding contacts; dissimulating violence, regulating sounds and defining taste'.[77] That these incentivise ends-driven reasoning is a real risk.

As discussed in Chapter 4, to say unreflectingly that torture carries 'special stigma' is really saying that it *should* carry a 'special stigma' and that it be physical, exceptional and a spectacle. The unquestioned acceptance

[67] *Kaganovskyy v. Ukraine* [2022] ECtHR 2809/18 [125].

[68] *Georgia v. Russia (II)* [2023] ECtHR 38263/08 [250].

[69] *Skorupa v. Poland* [2022] ECtHR 44153/15 [261]: 'Some discomfort for the handcuffed person is inherent in handcuffing'.

[70] *Korban v. Ukraine* [2019] ECtHR 26744/16 [134] 'holding a person in a metal cage during a trial – having regard to its objectively degrading nature, which is incompatible with the standards of civilised behaviour that are the hallmark of a democratic society – constitutes in itself an affront to human dignity'.

[71] Cassese (2008) 317: 'in many cases a treatment or punishment is *objectively* inhuman, regardless of the intention of the relevant authorities to cause serious harm'.

[72] To borrow a phrase from O'Mara (2015) 11.

[73] Maroney (2021) 20.

[74] See Sara Ahmed's literature review (on black common sense, native common sense, colonial and settler colonial common sense, cisgender common sense, queer and queering common sense) <www.saranahmed.com/commonsense>.

[75] Bianchi and Hirsch (2021)18.

[76] Maroney (2021) 23–24.

[77] Law and the senses (2013).

that certain forms of suffering are inevitable, that arrest or pre-trial detention would unavoidably cause anxiety, is also apparent at the bottom end of the spectrum. Such associations have gone 'barely noticed' given how 'intuitive' they seem.[78] Evidentiary practices that operate on stereotypical preconceptions,[79] as overriding evidence through applying presumptions,[80] draw on 'folk wisdom'[81] or the 'invocation of emotional common sense [which] silently privilege their views'[82] can also be characterised as common-sensical thinking. So common sense too can cut both ways – *towards* as *against* recognition.

6.2.3 VULNERABILITY. The concept of vulnerability is another prevalent means through which empathy and common sense features in torture's adjudication – understood to potentially extend legal recognition. As with other concepts, vulnerability is a 'heuristic device, forcing [its user] to examine hidden assumptions and biases folded into legal, social, and cultural practices'.[83] It explicates, for instance, the degree of dependency between the prisoner to prison authorities.[84] Presumptions like vulnerability, that certain groups and situations automatically associated as vulnerable, have also drawn dissent when too broadly used. In one distinct debate on immigration detention, a majority of judges generally presumed certain conditions together with

[78] Farrell (2022) 5–6.

[79] Jeremy Pilcher, 'Listening for Silence' (2021) 33 *Law & Literature* 461; Paul Roberts, 'Why International Criminal Evidence?' in Paul Roberts and M Redmayne (eds), *Innovations in Evidence and Proof: Integrating Theory, Research and Teaching* (Hart 2007) 371.

[80] Mavronicola (2021) 96.

[81] Maroney (2021) 15.

[82] Ibid 20; Reneman (2020); Freedom from Torture, 'Proving Torture, Demanding the Impossible: Home Office Mistreatment of Expert Medical Evidence' (2016) 14: which documents that in the UK '74% of cases in the research involve the asylum caseworker substituting their own opinion for that of the clinician on the cause of injuries' partly based on common-sense reasoning.

[83] Martha Fineman and Anna Grear (eds), *Vulnerability: Reflections on a New Ethical Foundation for Law and Politics* (Routledge 2013) 20.

[84] *Kurt v. Turkey* [1998] ECtHR 15/1997/799/1002 [201]; *Gómez Paquiyauri Brothers v. Peru* [2004] IACtHR [119]: Those detained unlawfully are 'in a situation of heightened vulnerability in which there is a high risk of his or her rights being violated, such as the right to physical integrity and to be treated with dignity'.

the victims' vulnerabilities (being children) to violate the prohibition. In a separate though concurring opinion, a single judge called out the lack of 'specific information concerning the applicants' traumatic experiences as alleged'.[85] This mirrors the divergences of positions, as noted above, between judges on the use of empathy.

Whilst reasoning based on vulnerability is identifiable in the expanding recognition of the suffering of families of victims, there are also stark delimitations that that suffering have a 'dimension and character distinct from the emotional distress inevitably stemming' from the situation.[86] The selectivity with which 'vulnerability' is used, for specific groups such as children and women, can also be invoked here.[87] That judges look not at inherent vulnerability of any given human in a situation but at 'specific' or 'heightened' vulnerability of some creates hierarchies naturalising the suffering of some and emphasising the suffering of others – that it 'suggests that some of us are not vulnerable'.[88] The research on torture-related caselaw supports this in finding that, for the most part, 'vulnerability and judicial empathy thus seem reserved to exceptional cases or at least to less-than-universal application'.[89] One's own pain experience thus may not ultimately be helpful in accessing another's. Objectification can 'expose practices of control and to make the suffering and disadvantages of vulnerable groups visible to dominant ones' but also the opposite (namely, to reify preconceptions).[90]

Whilst a victim's criminal profile and conduct is purportedly irrelevant given the absolute nature of the prohibition,[91] judicial reasoning has often revealed an emphasis on danger and risk in rejecting a

[85] *Elmi and Abubakar v. Malta* [2017] ECtHR 25794/13 28151/13, concurring opinion of Judge Sajo; see also *Mahamud v. Malta* [2016] ECtHR 56796/13, dissent of Judge Sajo.

[86] *Akkum and ors v. Turkey* [2005] ECtHR 21894/93 [258–259]; *Orhan v. Turkey* [2002] ECtHR 25656/94 [358]; *Çakıcı v. Turkey* [1999] ECtHR 23657/94 [98].

[87] Fineman and Grear (2013) 164.

[88] Ibid 16.

[89] Heri (2021) 199.

[90] Sally Engle Merry and Susan Bibler Coutin, 'Technologies of Truth in the Anthropology of Conflict: AES/APLA Presidential Address, 2013' (2014) 41 (1) *American Ethnologist* 1–16, 8.

[91] See *Ahmed v Austria* [1997] ECtHR 71/1995/577/663: 'the activities of the individual in question, however undesirable or dangerous, cannot be a material consideration'.

prisoner's vulnerability – in one case pointing out that 'the applicant could hardly be considered a genuinely vulnerable type of prisoner'.[92] In another case, where a prisoner complained about denial of contact, the ECtHR deemed him a 'danger to society' in finding no violation as it did not exceed the unavoidable level of suffering inherent in detention.[93] Concerns with mafia-affiliated prisoners[94] and other indications of dangerousness persist in countering a reading of vulnerability.[95] While accepting that an

> objective risk of abuse in prison should – and, in the Court's case law, usually does – entitle an individual to the protection associated with this vulnerability, independently of the person's likability, innocence, or responsibility for creating the risk of abuse[96]

the ECtHR's identification with prison authorities reveals an operative logic. This is problematic and endangers the absolute nature of the prohibition. In all, these three concepts (empathy, common sense and vulnerability) are busy presuming that certain acts have certain impacts. They also risk, as discussed, reifying such understandings to the exclusion of lived experiences – affording some suffering with easy access and others with difficulty.[97]

Despite positivistic impulses to foreclose such discussions, sense-centric reasoning (through what one sees, hears, reads) has long been a rich strand of scholarly inquiry. Even Aristotle pondered: 'Why is it that when we see anyone cut or burned or tortured or undergoing any other painful suffering, we share mentally in his pain? Is it because nature is common to us all, and it is this which shares in the sufferer's pain, when we see any of these things happening to him, through kinship with him?'[98] In what follows, I explore what scholars have written since on how visibility of suffering impacts its recognition.

92 *Kardišauskas v Lithuania* [2015] ECtHR 62304/12, concurring opinion of para 3.

93 *Enea v. Italy* [2009] ECtHR 74912/01 [65].

94 *Messina v. Italy (no. 2)* [1999] ECtHR 25498/94.

95 *Horych v. Poland* [2012] ECtHR 13621/08.

96 Heri (2021) 75.

97 See Redress, 'Redress for Rape: Using International Jurisprudence on Rape as a Form of Torture or Other Ill-Treatment' (2013) 51–52.

98 Aristotle as quoted by Kidd White (2014).

6.3 VISIBILITY: SEEING SUFFERING

> How likely is it that we will get outraged about violence like this, that may or may not leave traces, violence that we can hardly be sure took place at all?[99]

> The wince of pain or the scream of agony announce the fact of violence and render it visible, whereas the mental anguish and gradual deterioration of an inmate is much more difficult to observe and much easier to overlook.[100]

Visibility is another sense-centric register of recognition shaping the observer's responses and aiding in what is to be included or excluded. In the opening passages above, visibility explains social responses to state violence – the different reactions particular to those which are physically overt and those which are not. This also feeds the everyday expectation that 'we know torture when we see it'. Images from Abu Ghraib are example *par excellence* of how suffering can be recognised and public sentiment can change through 'sensation, a visceral churning of the gut that calls for metaphors of bodily degradation – sickening and shocking'.[101] To already sound a comparable caution as that which came with empathy-based reasoning, as much as visibility is an aid, its absence can prove problematic.

The pre-histories as introduced in Chapter 3 also speak to how entrenched such reactions have been. Judges in early modern France looked for verbal and bodily responses, 'tremblings, tears, and sighs, their pallors and faintnesses',[102] taken to be 'the silent self-betrayals of the accused, the voiceless accusations of the dead, the mute language of bruises and bleeding interpreted by the experts'.[103] These judges studied and read the accused's 'comportment and gesture, whether intentional or unintentional, planned or spontaneous, produced by both the living and the dead'.[104] In ancient Greece and Rome too, it was thought that

99 Rejali (2007) 2.
100 Garland (1993) 243.
101 Richardson (2016) 81.
102 Silverman (2001) 60.
103 Ibid 62.
104 duBois (1991/2018) 163, 102.

the 'sounds of the slave on the rack must by definition contain truth' and the slave's body as a 'site of truth'; a physician was expected to 'know past, present, and future' and 'also be an interpreter of the inner meaning of the outward sign, of the body's truth that is written on the faces, on the external aspect of his patient ... an interpreter of signs, one who uses the outside of the body to know its inside'.[105] The disconnections 'between the body and language, and between truth and pain' are what is said to be at the core of the abolition.[106] The physical body, as tested by pain, was no longer the source of truth in the embrace of greater complexity in evidentiary practices.

The gaze remains, as 'through traditional law or modern torture, the body has always been a privileged site on which to demonstrate the evidence of power'.[107] This has served to shape its preconceptions of suffering as visible against all principles. Principles which argue: that 'the absence of such physical evidence should not be construed to suggest that torture did not occur, since such acts of violence against persons frequently leave no marks or permanent scars';[108] that it need not be physically visible on the body[109] nor medically certifiable;[110] or that it 'may not be immediately apparent but become so subsequently'.[111] Even a psychological assessment goes beyond taking self-descriptions of pain as[112]

[105] Ibid 35, 89–90, 105.
[106] Ibid 67.
[107] Fassin and D'Halluin (2005) 597; Didier Fassin, *Humanitarian Reason: A Moral History of the Present* (University of California Press 2011) 106.
[108] *Istanbul Protocol* (2022) 393.
[109] *Prosecutor v. Brdjanin* [2004] ICTY IT-99-36-T [484]: 'evidence of the suffering need not even be visible after the commission of the crime'.
[110] *Dikme v. Turkey* [2000] ECtHR 20869/92 [80].
[111] Other notable remarks by the dissenters in *Ramirez Sanchez* (Chamber ruling) include: 'Such a period is not, as the majority note, merely "regrettable", it is also liable to produce harmful effects [- it] substantially exceeds the inevitable level of suffering inherent in detention', and rejected the distinction between 'partial' or 'total' isolation (that the partial 'cannot lead to the conclusion that the regime to which he was subject was not genuine isolation, but akin to an ordinary, even commonplace, measure', 'Prolonging solitary confinement in this way for a period so long as to be virtually permanent ... bringing the measure into the domain of unacceptable suffering').
[112] Kelly (2015) 89.

it involves an assessment of the client's appearance, behaviour, speech and subjective mood. The reading of such signs can be difficult for clinicians, aware as they are of cultural differences in physical and emotional presentations. However, in this process neither bodies nor words are taken at face value but are weighed against one another. Language is interwoven with the corporeal and the visual.

Such 'ocularcentrism', the privileging of the visual, in legal processes have been partly sourced from social-cultural prioritisation 'that sight is more reliable than other senses' and as compounded by 'emergence of photography, film and video and their use as modes of legal detection and proof'.[113] It is rather inherent in orienting in legal processes as in the world more generally. Visible marks are, after all, what anti-torture actors first attend to in the course of an investigation, the first clue for a detention monitor, advocate or adjudicator in needing to act *ex officio* (on their own initiative) in asking what happened. From a social scientific perspective, visibility is 'an aspect of social life that enables us to introduce thresholds of relevance and selective attention', 'a property of subjects, sites, events', and, 'employed as a means of sorting, classifying and ranking'.[114] The value placed on the visibility of suffering is conditioned not predetermined however intuitive the connection might seem.

Others refer to the privileging of the visible as a 'materialist bias',[115] as 'objectivist',[116] as the 'techno-logic of the visual',[117] as the 'visual-evidentiary paradigm' and the 'representational economy of torture.[118]

[113] Lionel Bentley and Leo Flynn, *Law and the Senses: Sensational Jurisprudence* (Pluto Press 1996) 7–8. That the law, psychology and anthropology privilege words has also led to one scholar charging them with 'verbocentrism'. David Howes, *Sensorial Investigations A History of the Senses in Anthropology, Psychology, and Law* (Penn State 2023) 17.

[114] Andrea Brighenti, *Visibility in Social Theory and Social Research* (Palgrave 2010) 44; Jon Simons and JL Lucaites (eds), *In/visible War: The Culture of War in Twenty-first-century America* (Rutgers University Press 2017) 4.

[115] David Luban and Henry Shue, 'Mental Torture: A Critique of Erasures in US Law' (2012) 100 *Georgetown Law Journal* 823, 823.

[116] Yarwood (2008) 336: 'reliance on a solely objective analysis of suffering, due to the difficulties in measuring intangible psychological injuries'.

[117] Elizabeth Dauphinée, 'The Politics of the Body in Pain: Reading the Ethics of Imagery' (2007) 38 *Security Dialogue* 139, 140.

[118] Hedi Viterbo, 'Seeing Torture Anew: A Transnational Reconceptualization of State Torture and Visual Evidence' (2014) 50 *Stanford Journal of International Law* 298, 316.

I myself have referred to the privileging of image-based sense-making as 'corpo-reality'.[119] The common point made by the scholarship is how suffering is reduced to an image, which 'works to contain and delimit the experience of pain by locating it so firmly in the distant and disconnected bodies of others that our ability to engage is relegated to that of observation'.[120] Violence in the eyes of law is thus reduced, with physical forms entrenched as fundamental and archetypal – 'that the physical is more real than the mental'.[121] Given that suffering ultimately 'defies attempts at visual representation', any probative value associated with visibility stands to be scrutinised.[122]

Ephemeral (contextual, environmental and psychological as affective) dimensions thus challenge positivist, materialist or corpo-realist interpretations. The latter 'tend to associate violence with visibility and with actions that can be attributed to an individual subject' and 'restrict violence to the intentional, direct, immediate, and visible infliction of physical harm, the assault or encroachment on the physical integrity of another human being or his or her property'.[123] Physical (or visible) violence thus stands 'fetishised' as the true form of violence and anything else (psychological, cultural, structural, or symbolic) are vanished. The question is not that they are so invisible that they are undetectable; it is that '[s]ociety sees and knows these conditions and the harm they cause and yet does not see them, does not recognize them for what they are'.[124] It might be because these prove too complex to capture and comprehend. This might be because visible marks can readily overcome the 'insurmountable barrier between victims and those with whom

[119] Ergün Cakal, 'Cruelty and Corpo-reality: Connecting Technologies and Practices Integral to the Infliction and Investigation of Torture' (2022) 14 (3) *Journal of Human Rights Practice*.

[120] Dauphinée (2007) 140.

[121] Luban and Shue (2012) 823.

[122] Elizabeth Dauphinée, 'The Politics of the Body in Pain: Reading the Ethics of Imagery' (2007) 38 *Security Dialogue* 139, 139: meaning that 'an image can never unproblematically represent the complexity of a lived reality, the visceral experience of pain, [confounding] attempts to "make sense" of pain within the logic of a culture and a politics that rely for their ethical bearings on the verifiability associated with the visible'.

[123] Yves Winter, 'Violence and Visibility' (2012) 34 *New Political Science* 195, 196.

[124] Ibid 198.

they wish to communicate'.[125] In interviews with psychologists treating victim-survivors, one scholar has noted that the significance of physical marks has become 'engrained in the consciousness of survivors'.[126] And that without 'clear, visible marks of torture, citizens can be uncertain whether pain was in fact experienced'.[127] Doubts are readily confirmed by the victim-survivor's family and community. The privileging of physical marks for both judges as victims can be sourced from 'the difficulties in measuring intangible psychological injuries'.[128] In one ECtHR case, an applicant 'pointed out that he was not complaining about the use of handcuffs and chains during his transfer to hospital – that being a routine if abnormal and degrading practice – since he had simply suffered embarrassment and only mental rather than actual torture'.[129]

As adjudicators demand visible verification and objectification, victim testimony has been directly rendered less significant (as alluded to in Chapter 5).[130] There has been a growing impulse to quantify suffering together with greater recognition of psychological suffering.[131] This is certainly identifiable in how adjudicators demand that subjective (testimonial) be checked against the objective (the 'reasonable'[132]).

125 Darius Rejali, 'Modern Torture as a Civic Marker: Solving a Global Anxiety with a New Political Technology' (2003) 2 (2) *Journal of Human Rights* 153–171, 157.

126 Canning (2023) 49, a practitioner who is interviewed by Canning relates, 50, '"Look what they did to me" – they would lift up their shirts – and sometimes, "Okay, this is not necessary. I totally trust what you're saying". But somehow they believe that if they can't show what they have been through, then people wouldn't believe them'.

127 Rejali (2003) 157.

128 Yarwood (2008) 336.

129 *Henaf v. Turkey* [2004] ECtHR 65436/01 [43]; *Alhowais v. Hungary* [2023] ECtHR 59435/17 [149] the applicant 'did not complain about the adverse psychological effects of the police operation'.

130 Kelly (2012) 14.

131 Boddice (2017) 39: impulses to quantify pain entered pain discourse in the 1970s together with emotional and social components. 105. 'Objective measurements, biological universals, and timeless standards: all attempts to find the key to how pain works have failed to describe how pain feels, precisely because pain experience is in the world and made by minds'.

132 Elaine Webster, 'Degradation: A Human Rights Law Perspective' in Paulus Kaufmann et al (eds), *Humiliation, Degradation, Dehumanization* (Springer 2011) 76: 'the Court's evaluation of whether the applicant had ... "sound reasons" for feeling humiliated or degraded ... i.e., whether the applicant was in social fact placed in a state of humiliation or degradation'.

This engenders a 'recurring tension' between 'contemporary sensibilities on the one hand, and objective judgements about dignity on the other'.[133] Research has also found that bodies 'are placed above words that are spoken' and 'that physical representations of suffering, in the shape of wounded bodies, have a transparent immediacy'.[134] The long-ingrained expectation of visibility has without question disserved the invisible[135] – that to expect photographic evidence to corroborate a victim-survivor's claims have reflected poorly on those who only have their words.[136] Torture, urges this logic, *should have* visual corroboration. The research relates the domination of the materialist bias to the visual-evidentiary paradigm, which treats 'verbal torture testimonies as inferior to photographic or video evidence'.[137] As courts have demanded and privileged voluminous forensic and photographic forms of evidence, standards have been heightened to a *no photo = it didn't happen* logic against deserving victims.[138] Given the suspicion of bogus claims, testimonial evidence, from those who only have their words, has not proven evidence enough.

We know full well that not all suffering is readily visible. So what then? We are left with words. But words weave together a reality as good as the survivor is articulate and the observer (listener or reader) is attentive and informed. The discussion to follow continues to focus on how text and testimony invite doubt, stand to be overridden as subjective or self-serving. There is a power to seeing not found in words. As with all else, we remind ourselves that senses are imbricative and in conversation as: 'seeing comes before words … it is seeing which establishes our place in the surrounding world; we explain that world with words, but words can never undo the fact that we are surrounded

[133] John Vorhaus, 'Bringing People Down: Degrading Treatment and Punishment' (2021) 24 (3) *New Criminal Law Review* 436.

[134] Kelly (2015) 88.

[135] Hedi Viterbo, 'Torture's In/Visibility' in Lon Olson and Stuart Molloy (eds), *Interdisciplinary Perspectives on Torture* (Brill 2019): the value placed on of photographic and video documentation of torture which he claims to have 'facilitated the denial of certain evidence or aspects of torture'; Dauphinée (2007).

[136] Cohen (2001) 168–195.

[137] Viterbo (2014) 316.

[138] Cohen (2001) 168–95.

by it'.[139] This is not to relegate words but to complicate them, as I aim to in what follows.

6.4 TESTIMONY: SAYING SUFFERING

> Pain is an inner experience, and even those closest to a patient cannot truly observe its progress or share in its suffering … Absolute private certainty to the sufferer, pain may become absolute public doubt to the observer.[140]

> Verbally expressing pain is a necessary prelude to the collective task of diminishing pain.[141]

As with concepts, language both expands and limits capacity for recognition. The testimony-based advocacy of Amnesty International, as touched upon in Chapter 5, has long played an important role in building public sentiment to pressure states to act against torture.[142] The senses, as also evoked through text, have proven themselves to be powerful devices determining the degree of law's recognition – having long featured in the contemporary anti-torture field from its early days. Humanitarian movements have also been 'closely linked to visual and literary images of suffering and innocence', 'humanitarian narratives' and bodily similarity.[143] Expressions of victims, represented through written or spoken words, have been afforded a foundational (at least rhetorical) role here.[144] Yet, as with visuals, voices are also reduced through text (particularly as

[139] Ibid.

[140] DelVecchio Good (1994) 5.

[141] Scarry (1985) 9.

[142] As example of this was found in the *Greek Case*. See here for a comprehensive treatment: Kostis Kornetis et al (eds), *The 1969 'Greek Case' in the Council of Europe: A Game Changer for Human Rights* (Bloomsbury 2024).

[143] Lyndsey Stonebridge, *Writing and Righting: Literature in the Age of Human Rights* (OUP 2020) 25, 26, 31: 'Fiction names and shames: it makes us reflect on otherwise invisible suffering and injustice'. See also Lynn Hunt, *Inventing Human Rights: A History* (WW Norton 2008).

[144] I admit to not tending to the effects (and affects) of sound nor the question of translation in this chapter. For scholarship who is attempting to do this, see Drumbl and Fournet (2024). See also Maria Ristani, 'Sound Prisoners: The Case of the Saydnaya Prison in Syria' (2020) 1 (2) *Violence* 273–284 for how sound can be used to torture. See also Kate Herrity et al (eds), *Sensory Penalities: Exploring the Senses in Spaces of Punishment and Social Control* (Emerald 2021) to read how this approach has been taken up by prison scholars.

prominent international human rights courts and committees work on text-based evidence mainly without live hearings). Suffering has, however, come to be characterised as resistant to language, as 'the most private and least communicable of all',[145] with 'the vocabularies that are available for describing pain … inadequate in the face of feeling'.[146] Victim-survivors, it is true, have often (but not always) 'struggled to find words to describe their pain'[147] and, therefore, depended on others 'who are not themselves in pain'.[148] The limitations are amplified by legal processes desiring 'language to be more precise than it can be, particularly when it comes to describing and determining experience'.[149]

As will be borne out in the following discussion, there is a dangerous slippage here between difficulty and impossibility. That in treating the difficulty in saying or communicating suffering as an impossibility, a risk arises in internalising unattainable standards of knowing, for the victim-survivor, documenter or decision-maker. At its starkest, torture is presented with a propensity to destroy language, a position formulated by Elaine Scarry who wrote that[150]

> When one hears about another person's physical pain, the events happening within the interior of that person' s body may seem to have the remote character of some deep subterranean fact, belonging to an invisible geography that, however portentous, has no reality because it has not yet manifested itself on the visible surface of the earth. … its resistance to language is not simply one of its incidental or accidental attributes but is essential to what it is.[151]

In later work, Scarry found that 'philosophic and literary descriptions of such imagining show the difficulty of picturing other persons in their full weight and solidity'.[152] This difficulty of imagining, for her, helped

[145] Hannah Arendt, *The Human Condition* (University of Chicago Press 1958) 50.
[146] Ahmed (2014) 22.
[147] Boddice (2017) 96, discussing chronic pain.
[148] Richardson (2016) 2.
[149] Ibid.
[150] Scarry (1985) 3.
[151] Ibid 162.
[152] Elaine Scarry, 'The Difficulty of Imagining Other Persons' in Eugene Weiner (ed), *The Handbook of Interethnic Coexistence* (Continuum Publishing 1998) 40.

to injure and ignore: 'if other persons stood clearly visible to us, the infliction of that injury would be impossible'[153] and that 'the human capacity to injure other people is very great precisely because our capacity to imagine other people is very small'.[154] Améry, a survivor, too wrote that his suffering marked the limit of the capacity of language to communicate concluding that it would be 'totally senseless to try and describe here the pain' inflicted on him by Nazis:

> Was it 'like a red-hot iron in my shoulders', and was another 'like a dull wooden stake that had been driven into the back of my head'? One comparison would only stand for the other, and in the end we would be hoaxed by turn on the hopeless merry-go-round of figurative speech. The pain was what it was. Beyond that there is nothing to say.[155]

That torturous pain can only be truly known by the person with the lived experience (for whom it is interior, certain, effortless) not the observer (for whom it is difficult, doubtful, elusive as it cannot be adequately objectified, externalised and materialised), if at all, seems like a sensible position. This has been described as the 'doubleness of pain' given that pain is both certain and ungraspable, communicable and incommunicable.[156] There is certainly an asymmetry of appreciation of pain as we cannot share the first-hand perspective of the sufferer, it cannot be directly seen or touched. This unknowability works to disarm, to lower standard of proof for victim, but equally to emphasise uncertainty of the observer.

To be sure, Scarry and Améry's remains the most circulated and appealing position, unreflectingly and intuitively adopted by anti-torture actors – if nothing else but to underscore torture's destructive power. Others, however, have critiqued Scarry's position as a 'hyperbolic rendering of the subjectivist account of pain'.[157] The defeatist stance

[153] Ibid 42.
[154] Ibid 43.
[155] Améry (1980) 33.
[156] Käll (2013) 28–29.
[157] Timothy Vance Kaufman-Osborn, *From Noose to Needle: Capital Punishment and the Late Liberal State* (University of Michigan Press 2009). See also Samuel Moyn's critique in *Human Rights and the Uses of History* (2nd ed, Verso 2017) Chapter 8.

towards which Scarry leads, to 'assign the pain of torture to permanent unspeakability risks – however unintentionally – repeating the original violence'.[158] Darius Rejali, another scholar to weigh in on this discussion, has argued that the 'inexpressibility that matters politically is not the gap between the brain and the tongue, but between victims and their communities, a gap that is cynically calculated, a gap that shelters a state's legitimacy'.[159] So, for Rejali, it is about how victim-survivors are listened to that shapes the possibility of understanding their suffering.[160] Elizabeth Stanley, studying torture survivors in Timor-Leste, has similarly written that communication is not simply a struggle to find the language for the individual. Rather, she has found, it is also linked to 'the wider societal and institutional reticence to hear painful or chaotic stories that challenge common sense notions of state protection [as] victims may be discouraged from speaking out when there is little outlook for prosecutions, commissions, or other change'.[161]

That it is not simply the sufferer who cannot speak but also the other's ability to hear is evident in how courts have treated testimonies of victim-survivors with scepticism.[162] Many in fact are capable of articulating their suffering so the key issue becomes how this experience is 'named and categorized; how we see, hear, and name what is front of us'.[163] Ultimately, although often denied, observers can readily accept 'whatever the experiencing person says it is, existing whenever he or she says it does'.[164] There is the option of deferring to the victim-survivor who ultimately can best 'bear witness to the pain and its intensity'.[165] This is dismissed outright based on the scepticism built into legal processes that testimonial evidence is potentially self-serving. The establishment

158 Richardson (2016) 156.

159 Rejali (2007) 31.

160 Ibid 30.

161 Elizabeth Stanley, *Torture, Truth and Justice: The Case of Timor Leste* (Routledge 2009) 13.

162 Rob Boddice, 'Introduction: Hurt Feelings?' in Rob Boddice (ed), *Pain and Emotion in Modern History* (Palgrave 2014).

163 Tobias Kelly, 'Sympathy and Suspicion: Torture, Asylum, and Humanity' (2012) 18 *Journal of the Royal Anthropological Institute* 753–768; see also Kelly, *This Side of Silence* (2012) 12–13.

164 McCaffery as quoted in Boddice (2017) 45; see Vorhaus, 'Bringing People Down', 436.

165 Ingelse (2001) 209.

of facts are instead entrusted to narrow evidentiary processes – which in turn create 'epistemological and interpretive' problems to 'take seriously the empirical world of the body and its suffering even as they necessarily run up against the limits of their capacity to know that world and to render it in language'.[166] This is not to dismiss that our everyday language around suffering has become 'weightless' failing to move us to action.[167] The point is that there remains more work to be done in improving our capacity to communicate. This is evident with incremental or invisible suffering – which tasks us to make the unapparent 'insidious, yet unseen or imperceptible violence' appear through imaginative writing, 'making it accessible and tangible by humanizing drawn-out threats inaccessible to the immediate senses'.[168]

Metaphorical and creative thinking and writing is similarly advanced as a means to counter this difficulty. Many scholars, especially those with an orientation towards literature, have sought solace in metaphors. As there is 'no literal language' to describe suffering,[169] we tend to resort to 'metaphors – burning, searing, or stinging, for instance – or reliant on objects external to the body – cutting, piercing, crushing' [and] frequently calls for simile: pain must be likened to razor blades or needles'.[170] Metaphor has also been invoked in countering Scarry's thesis: as a 'lack of referential content makes pain even prone to destroying language, through the substitution of metaphor it can be made present as a palpable object'.[171] International law scholarship has also identified the significance of metaphorical language in its own object of inquiry – finding that metaphors are 'international law's scaffolding', helping 'categorize situations in doctrinal categories' and 'build a shared, tangible universe of legal meaning'.[172] Metaphors are thus characterised as a crucial *progressive* force aiding in 'relating, image-making and

[166] Sarat (2014) 66.

[167] Lyndsey Stonebridge, *Writing and Righting: Literature in the Age of Human Rights* (OUP 2020) 16.

[168] Rob Nixon, *Slow Violence and the Environmentalism of the Poor* (Harvard 2011) 15.

[169] David Biro, *The Language of Pain: Finding Words, Compassion, and Relief* (2010) 73.

[170] Richardson (2016) 2.

[171] Käll (2013) 23.

[172] Harlan Cohen, 'Metaphors of International Law' in Bianchi and Hirsch (2021) 222.

perspective-taking' and expanding imaginations as to 'alternatives and possibilities'.[173]

There is another sense-centric register that is at play here: it is time. The Bulgarian death penalty cases have already invoked this register in Chapter 3 in posing: how long did suffering last and was it long enough to amount to a violation? did it diminish over time? Far from a quantifiable scientific measure, time has been largely left to work intuitively and naturally.[174] In what follows, I turn to how advocates and adjudicators have acted on their varied senses of time particularly in looking for a temporal fit for events before them in assessing their veracity and gravity.

6.5 TEMPORALITY: TIMING SUFFERING

> Events do no occur in an instant, but over time. Every process implies duration. The act of torture might end, but its effects and affects always endure.[175]

> It is through the intensification of pain sensations that bodies and worlds materialise and take shape.[176]

Two 10-year-old boys abducted, tortured and murdered a two-year-old in the UK. The two were arrested and detained for about ten months pending their trial. The trial was primarily conducted as if it were an adult trial and led to the conviction and sentencing of the two older boys to eight years imprisonment. The two boys brought a case before the ECtHR arguing that, amongst other factors, the cumulative effect of the lengthy and intimidating trial, effectively as adults under the public eye, breached their right to be free from inhuman and degrading treatment. The majority of the judges rejected their case. Two partly dissenting

[173] Maks Del Mar, 'Metaphor in International Law: Language, Imagination and Normative Inquiry' (2017) 86 *Nordic Journal of International Law* 170, 189, 175.

[174] See Linda Berger, 'Creating Kairos at the Supreme Court: Shelby County, Citizens United, Hobby Lobby, and the Judicial Construction of Right Moments' (2015) *Scholarly Works Paper* 988, 157: 'kairos may be understood as a concept incorporating time (the most opportune time); space (the essential point in time that embodies the story or the concept); action (the author's use of the time and space); and fittingness (each of these matching up with the other)'.

[175] Richardson (2016) 164.

[176] Ahmed (2014) 24.

opinions focussed on the temporal framings used by the majority. The first dissent, in accepting the case as inhuman and degrading, critiqued how the majority split up the treatment into 'separate phases' in a manner which lost 'sight of the effect which the treatment in this case must have had on ... physical well-being and psychological balance'.[177] They, therefore, did not see the trial and sentencing of the two boys as separate, but instead as cumulative. The second minority similarly found that 'the uncertainty, which the two applicants have lived with since the day they were sentenced, that is for more than six years, has obviously caused them considerable distress'.[178] The gravity of the 10-year-old boys' suffering was dismissed by the majority through separating the experiences and events. Connecting, these minorities argued, ought to have lifted the suffering above the threshold amounting to a violation.

Such temporal registers (or frames) have pervaded the interpretation of torture's prohibition. Time has featured in a range of devices characterising the harm suffered at the hands of states and brought before international human rights courts and committees: 'act', 'period', 'duration', 'indefinite', 'uncertainty', 'imminence', 'prolonged', 'permanent', 'combination', 'composite', 'continuous', 'accumulation', 'short', 'isolated'. These notions have aided advocates and adjudicators in distinguishing between the prohibition's categories, that is, torture, inhuman and degrading treatment, and all that fails to fall under the purview of the prohibition, as below the 'minimum level of severity' (as incidental, trivial, unavoidable, inherent), and as 'lawful sanctions'. Time has been implicit in the evolving interpretation that presumes that certain harms will come to be recognised as violations with shifts in socio-political attitudes. It is time that Antonio Cassese singled out in explaining that 'unlike torture, which takes the form of single acts against an individual, [inhuman and degrading treatment] are the result of numerous acts and circumstances combined'.[179] This is because time is present in shaping assessments of causality (were the act and impact proximate in time and space?) and gravity (how long did the victim suffer?).

[177] *T v. UK* [1999] ECtHR 24724/94, joint partly dissenting opinion of Judges Ridruejo et al.

[178] Partly dissenting opinion of Judges Rozakis and Costa.

[179] Cassese (1996) 48.

There is, however, nothing on the face of international definitions of torture that suffering must arise from a singular or contained act. There is no temporal requirement, that is to say, severe pain need not be singular, cumulative, composite, combined,[180] or 'prolonged'.[181] Adjudicators have in principle established that 'permanent injury is not a requirement for torture'.[182] Pain need not be extreme, 'difficult for the subject to endure'.[183] These remain in the realm of principle as, when we turn to how time is registered, either implicitly or explicitly, during adjudication of individual torture claims – remaining an important proxy in assessing harms inflicted in certain practices. That torture need involve 'death, organ failure, or serious impairment of body functions', as advanced by the 'Bybee Memo', have been discredited. If not permanent suffering, then where has the line been drawn?

Time in framing a violation is an important yet largely implicit device in torture's adjudication, both in terms of how torture is imagined to happen and how it is understood to be substantiated. To variably emphasise proximity and continuity (or discontinuity or longevity), as in the opening illustration, can serve reasoning to establish severity, intentionality, proximity, veracity, causality. These concepts, as drawn from law more broadly, operate to serve how anti-torture actors imagine and evidence the harms before them. These concepts are assumed to be inextricable: causality is informed by proximity, gravity by longevity and so on. Complexities in combinations of facts (factual matrices), practices and subjectivities are readily accepted as defeating any meaningful reflection towards a minimum temporal rule (on say sleep deprivation) accounting

180 *Rodley and Pollard* (2009) 92; *Aydin v Turkey* [1997] ECtHR 57/1996/676/866 [86]; *Krnojelac* [2002] ICTY IT-97-25 Trial Chamber [182]: torture 'may be committed in one single act or can result from a combination or accumulation of several acts, which, taken individually and out of context, may seem harmless ... The period of time, the repetition and various forms of mistreatment and severity should be assessed as a whole'.

181 CAT, 'Concluding Observations on USA' (2006) CAT/C/USA/CO/2 [13].

182 *Prosecutor v. Brdjanin* [2004] ICTY IT-99-36-T [484]: *Prosecutor v Naletilic and Matinovic* [2006] ICTY IT-98-34 Appeal [300]: 'no rigid durational requirement is built into the definition'.

183 This is a formulation is found in the Torture Memos, see Robert Goldman, 'Trivializing Torture: The Office of Legal Counsel's 2002 Opinion Letter and International Law against Torture' (2004) 12 (1) *Human Rights Brief* 5.

for all victims in whatever the context. When the questions of *time* meet *space*, as they often do in cramped detention conditions[184] or lengthy prisoner transportation,[185] the task to extrapolate any generalisable principle becomes fraught. Causality between acts and impacts comes to the fore here. Causality is admittedly complex, especially where harms are invisible and incremental and not immediately manifest, non-linear and not continuous.

As mentioned, the principles of anti-torture law do not explicitly support Cassese's observation but its interpretive practices do. How suffering is *temporally* framed, splintered and fractured, the sequence of events that led to it or the length of the suffering it caused, has often been at the core of legal reasoning. The question often asked is 'how long' was the detainee detained incommunicado, questioned, isolated, sleep deprived, food and drink deprived, restrained, treated in hospital? This is effectively to ask: how long is long enough for the finding of a violation? Here as elsewhere,[186] time is revealed to be a significant device for 'ordering experience',[187] as a 'structuring logic' and a 'sense-giving dimension',[188] effectively as a register of recognition for the victim-survivor as for the observer – that a given experience merits action (or not).[189] As in the discussion of evidentiary certainty, the law and its actors fixate on how certain acts meet certain forms and thresholds – limiting the 'structural conditions' of recognition. In what

[184] *Mursic v. Croatia* [2016] ECtHR 7334 [172] finds an article 3 violation concerning 'the period of twenty-seven days (between 18 July and 13 August 2010) in which the applicant disposed of less than 3 sq. m of personal space'.

[185] *Guliyev v. Russia* [2008] ECtHR 24650/02 [64]: the ECtHR coupled time and space in finding inhuman treatment based on 'the duration of the journey, confined space, sleep deprivation, insufficiency of food and possibly inadequate ventilation and lighting'.

[186] In *Savca v. Moldova* [2016] ECtHR 17963/08 [27] the applicant argued that his months-long isolation across different centres violated article 3. The Court held that 'each period of detention referred to specific events … occurred on identifiable dates and … cannot therefore be construed as a "continuing situation"', in downgrading the harms at play.

[187] Rebecca R French, 'Time in the Law' (2001) 72 *Uni Colorado Law Review* 663, 693.

[188] Christine Morgenstern, 'Time, Civilisation and Ultimate Penalities' in Nicola Carr and Gwen Robinson (eds), *Time and Punishment: New Contexts and Perspectives* (Springer 2022) 37–39.

[189] Canning (2023) 48.

follows, I identify narrow and expansive temporal framings through 'proximity' and 'prolongation'.

6.5.1 PROXIMITY AS PROXY. Proximity is a central proxy in how suffering is assessed, with 'events that occur within a short duration of time are presumed to be causally related', relatively readily.[190] Torture is associated with intense suffering over a short period of time,[191] with beatings, falanka, electrocution, mock executions and rape, dominating over and above the cumulative. This emphasis is also present in the language of 'imminence' or 'immediacy' that can be readily found especially in cases involving the deportation of non-nationals in need of medical care[192] and those threatened by law enforcement authorities.[193] The less imminent, the more illusory their suffering is taken to be. Imminence is one legal concept, amongst others, that works to 'separate out or distance responsibility connections temporally', so that responsibility is not transferred across different actors across time.[194]

An example *par excellence* is *N v. UK* where 'N', a Ugandan national, was deported by the British authorities who knew that her human immunodeficiency virus (hiv) 'without antiretroviral drugs [her] condition would deteriorate rapidly and she would suffer illness, discomfort, pain and death within a year or two'. The British authorities emphasised, before the ECtHR, that N was not 'at the present time critically ill' and that the 'future' harms or the 'rapidity of the deterioration' involved 'a certain degree of speculation'. N's death would occur at another time and place – with distance and delay dissipating and discharging state responsibility. The lack of imminence were grounds enough to

[190] Liaquat Ali Khan, 'Temporality of Law' (2009) 40 *McGeorge Law Review* 55.

[191] Ergun Cakal, 'Registering Time in Recognising Torturous Harm: Figuring the Single, Plural and Historical in Torture's Adjudication' (2024) 33 (2) *Social & Legal Studies* 276.

[192] *D v. UK* [1997] ECtHR 30240/96; *N v. the UK* [2008] ECtHR 26565/05; *Paposhvili v. Belgium* [2016] ECtHR 41738/10.

[193] *Gäfgen v. Germany* [2010] ECtHR 22978/05 [103]; *El-Masri v. Macedonia* [2012] ECtHR 39630/09; *'Street Children' (Villagran-Morales et al.) v. Guatemala* [1999] IACtHR; see also Ergun Cakal, 'Perception, Practice and Proximity: Qualifying Threats As Psychological Torture in International Law' (2021) 31 (1) *Torture* 19.

[194] Veitch (2007) 78.

dismiss N's claim. Whilst a 'deathbed' scenario is no longer required by the Court, its logic in subsequent cases maintains the premium placed on imminence.[195] Distance in time and place, this logic has it, diffuses danger.

The meaning attached to the 'immediate' has also been scrutinised in a notable study on siege starvation.[196] This has compared 'kinetic [bombing] attacks on civilian populations [which] are characterized primarily by their immediate consequences' with the 'different trajectory' of siege starvation where '[r]ather than a moment of immediacy, it is a process of steady escalation, the pace of which can be described comparatively as "glacial"'.[197] As consequences from the outset seem 'uncertain and distant', the intentionality and in turn culpability involved in siege deprivation are less pronounced. There arises a deniability out of a[198]

> normatively meaningful difference between the gradual escalation of suffering in that process and the execution of the threat of a kinetic attack on civilians. ... In contrast, the continuation of a siege entails (at each stage) an escalation of suffering that is not only incremental in aggregate, but incremental for the affected individuals. Parts of the population are affected sooner and more acutely than others, but even for the hardest hit, the consequences develop over time. Irreversible impacts, such as

[195] Time since ill-treatment in a country of origin has been used against applicants at the risk of deportation in rejecting claims, requiring the risk of suffering to be 'foreseeable, personal, present and real' (CAT, General Comment 4 (2017) [11]). On such grounds, the CAT has occasionally rejected cases where the risk argued was 'so many years after the alleged events occurred' (CAT-C-64-D-680-2015 [15.6], CAT-C-40-D-309-2006 [8.5], CAT-C-41-D-285-2006 [7.5]), where 'time has elapsed' (CAT-C-40-D-293-2006 [10.6]), and where it was not established 'as to why the authorities would start being interested in him 15 years after the death of his brother' (CAT-C-58-D-609-2014 [8.7]). The ECtHR has also questioned or rejected medical documentation due to the delay in its production (that the victim took too long to be seen by a doctor): *Balogh v. Hungary* [2004] ECtHR 47940/99 [37]; *Gurepka v. Ukraine* [2005] ECtHR 61406/00 [35]: 'The sick leave certificate presented by the applicant as to his illness from 7 December 1998, that is 6 days after his release, does not constitute sufficient proof of a causal link with the alleged ill-treatment'.

[196] Tom Dannenbaum, 'Siege Starvation: A War Crime of Societal Torture' (2022) *Chicago Journal of International Law* 410–412.

[197] Ibid 410.

[198] Ibid 412.

> death or permanent health effects, occur not in an explosive instant, but through a cumulative and extended process, arising from the combination of the continuous series of decisions to persist with the siege and various intervening factors that may exacerbate or ameliorate its effects.

Distance is also wound up in omission. Denying medical treatment, or offering that which is inadequate, is a corollary scenario to aid us in explicating the emphasis on proximity. Although planned action to harm dominates the legal imaginary and satisfies some ephemeral need to identify evil on the part of the perpetrator, harmful omissions are quietly produced through a lack of material resources, institutional architecture and staff attitudes. Denial (or variably omission or inaction) allows 'the prisoner's body to do the prison's punitive work on its behalf'.[199] Violence through omission raises difficult questions, particularly in attributing responsibility: 'Who is to blame for compromised and compromising circumstances? Where can we locate agency or intentionality in order to identify someone blameworthy to hold accountable?'[200] Due to a lack of certainty, violence through inaction has been viewed as mattering less than that which is inflicted through action. In other words, 'deaths of those killed appear to matter more than the deaths of people allowed to die'.[201]

Narrow timeframes have served to divide and disconnect and present time as something other than inseparable or inextricably complex. 'Temporal stretching' (including less proximate facts), on the other hand, serve to enrich, complicate and visibilise and narrowing as dividing, fragmenting and eliding relevant considerations such as structural factors as pertaining to an event in question. The judicial discretion as to the broad or narrow timeframes applied to a given set of legal facts, how it *conditions, textures, focuses* or *structures* an event, it has been argued, 'conceals the politics of legal judgement'.[202] Treating time as an intuitive and implicit aspect of interpreting the crime of

199 Andrew M Jefferson and Ahmed Jalloh, 'Health Provision and Health Professional Roles under Compromised Circumstances: Lessons from Sierra Leone's Prisons' (2019) 19 (5) *Criminology & Criminal Justice* 585.

200 Ibid.

201 Ibid.

202 Tanzil Chowdhury, *Time, Temporality and Legal Judgment* (Routledge 2020) 11.

torture thus produces a high degree of legal indeterminacy.[203] The indeterminacy in that 'the same legal rules can produce different factual determinations' is held to gesture to how 'deeply political' these exercises just are[204] – as judges actively make choices about which timeframes to apply in a given case.

6.5.2 PROLONGATION AS PROXY. Prolongation is another central temporal proxy for understanding how advocates and adjudicators make sense of suffering. It has been present in the search for longevity of suffering (how long did it last?). Longer timeframes have aided judges in assessing suffering to have been inflicted over 'hours at a stretch',[205] having been sufficiently prolonged,[206] that impact remained with 'the passage'[207] or 'the passing' of time.[208] Psychologically oriented torturous practices, such as sleep deprivation and solitary confinement, present a particular example here. While legitimate uses of some psychological pressure are recognised, accusatorial, protracted or suggestive interviews overlayed with threats, manipulation and coercion are underscored as problematic, and depending on their 'degree, severity, chronicity and type, undue psychological pressure and manipulative practices' may be ill-treatment.[209] Doctrine has in fact been pushed to elaborate on

203 Tanzil Chowdhury, 'Time Frames and Legal Indeterminacy' (2017) 1 *Canadian Journal of Law & Jurisprudence* 57–76.

204 Ibid 7.

205 *Ireland v. UK* [1978] ECtHR 5856/72 [167].

206 *Kurt v. Turkey* [1998] ECtHR 15/1997/799/1002 [131]: 'the uncertainty, doubt and apprehension suffered by the applicant over a prolonged and continuing period of time caused her severe mental distress and anguish'; cf. *Arapkhanovy v. Russia* [2014] ECtHR 2215/05 [152]: 'there was no distinct long-lasting period during which the applicants sustained uncertainty, anguish and distress characteristic to the specific phenomenon of disappearances [therefore] the mental suffering endured by the applicants has not reached a dimension and character distinct from the emotional distress which may be regarded as inevitably caused to relatives of a victim of a serious human-rights violation'.

207 *AB and others v. France* [2016] 11593/12 [114].

208 *Cyprus v. Turkey* [2001] ECtHR 25781/94 [155]: pointing to how applicants' 'mental anguish did not vanish with the passing of time'.

209 UN SRT, Report (2016) A/71/298 [44]; Rejali (2007) 4–5: 'Moreover, torturers tend increasingly to use clean torture techniques in conjunction with each other. I call this tendency clustering. This clustering occurred first in the torture of modern democratic states in the early twentieth century and only rarely in authoritarian torture chambers'.

the duration concerning these practices more so than more physically overt practices such as beatings. Solitary confinement has been regulated temporally, with its prolonged (more than 14 or 15 days) and indefinite uses deemed to violate the prohibition. Sleep deprivation, or the provision of sleep for less than six hours over a twenty-four-hour period, has also been viewed as violating the prohibition.[210] Such suffering, therefore, has required prolongation before coming into the prohibition's view.[211]

States have also played into duration, arguing that it need be longer to be considered serious. The 'Bybee Memo' infamously qualified 'mental suffering' as needing to last for months or years before amounting to torture. The US has in fact had a history in playing with duration in practicing sleep deprivation. Identifying that the US Army Manual technically allowed for 40 hours of continuous interrogation, the CAT found that this effectively authorized sleep deprivation.[212] States have also emphasised short durations of act or impact before the ECtHR.[213] Prolongation is also present in establishing continuous suffering. The difficulty of the fragmented/continuous nature of enforced disappearances has been

[210] *Bagel v. Russia* [2016] ECtHR 37810/03 [70]; *Sadretdinov v. Russia* [2016] ECtHR 17564/06 [96].

[211] Richardson (2016) 55: 'Non-touch techniques, such as sleep deprivation, cannot be torture in the moment in which they occur … Their state as torture is always already deferred to a future potentiality'. Concerning 'enhanced interrogation technique'; UNSRT, Report (1997) E/CN.4/1997/7 [121]: '[e]ach of these measures on its own may not provoke severe pain or suffering' but when 'applied on a protracted basis of, say, several hours'. Rejali (2007) 4–5: 'torturers tend increasingly to use clean torture techniques in conjunction with each other. I call this tendency clustering'.

[212] CAT, Conclusions on USA (2014) CAT/C/USA/CO/3-5 [17].

[213] *Adam v. Slovakia* [2016] ECtHR 68066/12 [43]; *Lecomte v. Germany* [2016] ECtHR 80442/12 [83]; *Hinderberger v. Germany* [2010] ECtHR 28183/06, p. 8; *Gavrilovici v. Moldova* [2010] ECtHR 25464/05; *Staszewska v. Poland* [2010] ECtHR 10049/04 [57] 'the impairment of the applicant's health lasted for a period shorter than seven days …. The applicant did not need hospitalisation'; *Barakhoyev v. Russia* [2017] ECtHR 8516/08 [43]: 'Contrary to the Government's assertion, the absence of long-term health consequences cannot exclude a finding that the treatment is serious enough to be considered inhuman or degrading'; *Khlaifia and others v. Italy* [2015] ECtHR 16483/12, dissent of Judges Sajo and Vucinic 'a short duration may minimise the harm caused by those poor conditions, with the result that the measure falls short of the Article 3 threshold' [7]; *Corley and others v. Russia* [2021] ECtHR 292/06 43490/06 [103]; *Wainwright v. UK* [2006] ECtHR 12350/04 [36] ('relatively brief').

contrasted to the instantaneous offense consummated 'with a single blow'.[214] Judges have found it difficult to determine when it ceases and the nature of mental suffering it entails.[215] To emphasise that one period of isolation was interrupted upon a change of facilities, or to hold apart the harms inflicted during the trial and the sentencing phase, as we saw in the opening illustration, can serve to disconnect and downgrade what the victim experienced as compounding harms.

Prolongation as proxy is also apparent in widening the view to include contextual or systemic factors producing a specific instance of suffering (what else was relevant to the experience than the specific event in question?). To look at a wider history of a specific act may result in discovering chronic long-term causes or consequences not immediately visible after that act. Coercive control, for instance, is not a 'violent rupturc' but 'chronic rather than episodic' and has a 'cumulative effective', is a useful parallel here. These emerging concepts come up against conventional conceptualisations which take violence to be a 'perpetrator-centred, intentionality-centred, and time-specific' phenomenon,[216] or producing the 'exemplar image of violence [as] roughly that of deliberate physical acts of non-consensual force by a perpetrator occasioned against a subject'.[217] This can be said to disserve psychological suffering, which can have a relatively longer time horizon, as narrow frames are more suited to immediately and materially visible physical suffering. This figures widely in the critical scholarship examining 'the ways that the conventional

[214] *Heliodoro Portugal v. Panama* [2008] IACtHR [112]; separate opinion of Judge Garcia Ramirez [9]: 'In the hypothesis of the instantaneous offense, the consummation occurs once, "with a single blow", if you will allow me to use this expression. In the continuous crime (using a specific terminology), the unlawful conduct is fragmented over time: it begins and ceases, with unity of active and passive subjects and breaking the same norm'.

[215] Ibid, separate opinion [12]: 'The Court must obligatorily ask itself this question: when does a forced disappearance cease? [18] the deprivation of liberty can be differentiated from the violation of integrity, but it is also reasonable to suppose that the suffering of the victim of forced disappearance is maintained continuously (or of a continuing nature) while this extremely serious situation persists, with all the dangers, terror and stress that this implies'.

[216] Vittorio Bufacchi and Jools Gilson, 'The Ripples of Violence' (2016) 112 (1) *Feminist Review* 27, 33.

[217] Gabrielle Mardon and Louise Richardson-Self, 'Stuck in Suffering: A Philosophical Exploration of Violence' (2022) 48 (1) *Australian Feminist Law Journal* 113, 114.

legal preoccupation with causation narrows understandings of injury and liability' – where the devices of temporality and proximity loom large.[218] Judges are served by imminent connection between act and impact to draw a certain conclusion as to fact and responsibility, tending to 'individualize responsibility for injury in ways that obscure and direct attention away from exposing broad, systemic patterns'.[219] Impulses for convenience persist. Measurability becomes paramount.

Conceptualisations of 'agentless' though equally lethal accretive actions, inactions and impacts have spawned a strand of scholarship unto itself. One powerful concept in this vein has been Elizabeth Povinelli's 'letting die', through which she captures 'the everyday drifts toward death: one more drink, one more sore; one bad cold, bad food; a small pain in the chest'.[220] For Povinelli, these cannot compete with the spectacle: 'bodies in hoods, in naked piles, attached to real or fake electrodes' – and in their spectacular appearance creating the 'ontological necessity to respond ethically'.[221] So, '[w]hen the waters recede and the ground stops shaking, empathy also evaporates, as ethical sense settles back into doxic accounts of poverty and its causes and consequences'.[222] Empathic recognition is sourced at intensity of suffering. Psychological suffering on a longer temporal horizon fails to fulfill such a threshold of the temporally contained spectacle.

Lauren Berlant's work on 'eventness' also offers further insights here, on the cruddy, cumulative, chronic and corrosive. Whilst in the mess of reality it is 'hard to distinguish modes of incoherence, distractedness, and habituation from deliberate and deliberative activity', events are used to simplify and solve the problem of causality.[223] This is, Berlant finds, underpinned by the liberal intentional and autonomous

[218] McCann (2018) 9–10.

[219] Ibid.

[220] Elizabeth Povinelli, *Economies of Abandonment: Social Belonging and Endurance in Late Liberalism* (Duke University Press 2011) 145.

[221] Ibid 183.

[222] Ibid 182.

[223] Lauren Berlant, 'Slow Death (Sovereignty, Obesity, Lateral Agency)' (2007) 33 *Critical Inquiry* 754, 754. Elaine Crawley, 'Institutional Thoughtlessness in Prisons and Its Impacts on the Day-to-Day Prison Lives of Elderly Men' (2005) 21 (4) *Journal of Contemporary Criminal Justice* 350–363 can also be invoked here.

subject, exuding a militaristic and melodramatic view of agency. The concept of 'slow violence' also helps to explicate time as a threshold device. It captures less visible violence 'that occurs gradually and out of sight, a violence of delayed destruction that is dispersed across time and space, an attritional violence', that which is 'neither spectacular nor instantaneous, but rather incremental and accretive'.[224] Such temporal scales are conventionally not registered as violence – as violence is 'customarily conceived as an event or action that is immediate in time, explosive and spectacular in space, and as erupting into instant sensational visibility'.[225] Conventional conceptions of violence, as violations, are thus 'event focused, time bound, and body bound'.[226] A favourable and 'unequal attention' is afforded here to the bounds of the contained event.[227]

In all, as demonstrated through the values associated with proximity and prolongation, units of time law works with are varied. Framings and measures of time are principally presented as objective, linear and quantitative. Yet there is much that adjudicators do to aggregate or disaggregate, connect and disconnect, factual elements in building a narrative of a victim's experience. Factors can thus be singled out (and exceptionalised) to mark their worthiness (as extraordinarily important) or worthlessness (as insignificant outliers). In all these examples, time (or duration) normally frames the act or impact in question – delimiting what is to be assessed as a violation or not. Acts and events, and the suffering they entail, are usually viewed in isolation and not in combination or cumulation.[228]

The difference between how certain practices are associated with immediate and intense therefore severe suffering and those which are not becomes important here once again. It reveals that judges retain the discretion to use cumulative assessments notwithstanding 'however trivial

224 Nixon (2011) 2.

225 Ibid.

226 Ibid 3.

227 Ibid 2.

228 Maeve O'Rourke, 'Prolonged Impunity as a Continuing Situation of Torture or Ill-Treatment? Applying a Dignity Lens to So-Called "Historical" Cases' (2019) 66 (1) *Netherlands International Law Review.*

the isolated incidents might be'.[229] Torture might prove difficult to find because the hidden logic is that it requires serious enough singular acts and resists arguments of accumulation. Putting this together, time, far from a natural background dimension, is actively constructed, including by judges, who retain a wide and powerful discretion to accept broader or narrower temporal frames towards in/visibilising claims of harm.

6.6 CONCLUSION

> It is important to avoid essentializing, naturalizing, or sentimentalizing suffering. There is no single way to suffer; there is no timeless or spaceless universal shape to suffering. There are communities in which suffering is devalued and others in which it is endowed with the utmost significance.[230]

> The figure of the physical blow cannot describe the full spectrum of violence; indeed, no one figure can.[231]

Suffering is in the eye as the ear of the beholder. Suffering is also in the observer's sense of time, whether it was long enough or close enough between act and impact to prove causality. In this chapter, I have argued that sense-centric reasoning is a productive prism to examine how torturous suffering is being assessed in reality. It is implicated in every aspect of how torturous suffering is imagined and evidenced. It is a potential 'means through which unnoticed assumptions are illuminated, or how [they] direct attention to norms, commitments and inherent values that are otherwise ignored'.[232] It enriches understandings of how interpretive practices are embodied, towards 'building a fairer, more effective system'.[233] These improve our understanding (self-understanding) of how professionals 'screen, categorize and interpret information; influence

[229] *Levchuk v. Ukraine* [2020] ECtHR 17496/19 [80]. *Rochela Massacre v. Colombia* [136] 'the passage of time', *Caesar v. Trinidad and Tobago* [99]; *Miguel Castro-Castro Prison v. Peru* [333]; *Tibi v. Ecuador* [148].

[230] Kleinman and Kleinman (1996) 2.

[231] Butler (2020) 138.

[232] Abrams and Keren (2010) 2004.

[233] Susan A Bandes, Jody Lyneé Madeira, Kathryn D Temple and Emily Kidd White, 'Introduction' in Bandes et al (2021) 1.

[their] evaluations of the intentions or credibility of others; and help decide what is important or valuable'.[234] How professionals emotionally engage with a case, and reflect on that engagement, can illuminate our understanding of the stakes at play,[235] and help in cultivating 'a serious interest in lived experiences under the impugned law'.[236] Their *uses* are ultimately as good as their *users*.

There are several takeaway points made in this chapter: that senses are inescapable registers of cognition (sorting suffering); that senses condition and mediate between the individual and social; what is seen or can be said are socio-politically conditioned; what is imagined (conceptualised) as torture impacts its substantiation; and, that access and communication of suffering is complex but not impossible. I have also argued that what is left uncritically or easily accepted reveals how law's agents, in advocates and adjudicators, actively foreground certain harms as necessarily worthy of attention. Whilst these may be instrumental and inevitable to some degree, they also serve to foreclose a more critical consideration of emergent and non-physically overt harms. As sense-centric reasoning is shaped socially, culturally and politically, it packs the potential to reify preconceptions towards essentializing, pathologizing and paternalizing. They thus variably activate or deactivate concern and regard for others and mobilise predetermined notions of reality.

[234] Susan A Bandes and Jeremy A Blumenthal, 'Emotion and the Law' (2012) 8 *Annual Review of Law and Social Science* 161, 165.

[235] Ibid; Susan A Bandes (ed), *The Passions of Law* (New York University Press 1999) 7.

[236] Emily Kidd White, 'On Emotions and the Politics of Attention in Judicial Reasoning' in Amalia Amaya and Maksymilian Del Mar (eds), *Virtue, Emotion and Imagination in Law and Legal Reasoning* (Bloomsbury 2020) 110.

CHAPTER 7

Conclusion

> The making visible of what was previously unseen can sometimes be the effect of using a magnifying instrument ... But to make visible the unseen can also mean a change of level, addressing oneself to a layer of material which had hitherto had no pertinence for history and which had not been recognized as having any moral, aesthetic or historical value.[1]

7.1 RECOGNISING OUR RESPONSIBILITY

Suffering is 'defined, delimited, and determined by a legion of people not so much in pain as in power' – by advocates, academics and adjudicators rather than those who bear its brunt.[2] Immense and seemingly endless labour is exerted towards this very end. These actors, as this book has made clear, retain the power 'to establish a dominant way of construing events and to silence others, thus channelling and determining the outcome of legal proceedings'.[3] How they (read: we) understand suffering has informed where and how it has been looked for.[4] Legal (as much as medical) language, in the means and modes illustrated in the preceding pages, has helped 'construct social reality as much as they express it and are the crucial stakes of political struggle'.[5]

[1] Michel Foucault, *Power/Knowledge: Selected Interviews and Other Writings 1972–1977* (Pantheon Books 1980) 50–51.

[2] Boddice (2017) 44.

[3] Anne van Aaken and Jan-Philip Elm, 'Framing in and through Public International Law' in Bianchi and Hirsch (2021).

[4] Boddice (2017) 3: 'How we communicate – that is, the labels we give to pain – and how we conceptualise – that is, the ways in which we see pain, especially in others – are essential to the ways in which pain is experienced'.

[5] Pierre Bourdieu, *In Other Words: Essays Towards a Reflexive Sociology* (Polity 1994) 134.

Linguistic devices, namely concepts and categories of law and medicine, have 'contribute[d] to the production of the world, but only within the limits of their correspondence with preexisting structures'.[6] How acts of state violence are named have carried with it a normative or symbolic force, vying for stronger degrees of attention and condemnation in short supply. Naming has served as a signifier of power, not only the effective limits to state power, but more critically to the interpretive frames of actors. The interpretive script, that not everything can be called torture, has been codified onto the bracketing of dominant concepts and categories, as is often manifest in legal precedent.

Language has acted as a device of domination, inflicting symbolic violence in imposing dominant understandings and excluding alternatives.[7] This script constrains and controls possible actions for the present and will continue to do so unless somehow interrupted and interrogated. It is this dominance which gives rise to a responsibility necessitating rethinking and reflection. Researchers and practitioners alike rarely recognise their responsibility on this front and, to follow Veena Das, must come to understand that they occupy positions to enable 'private experiences of pain to move out into the realm of publicly articulated experiences of pain'.[8]

Instead of questioning the language with which they operate, however, the doctrinally committed have fixed their gaze on serving the law – on animating it. If only more evidence is brought before a legal process; if only the decision-maker is made to look at the evidence, as dictated by rules of interpretation, and so on. Without calling into question the operative framework, these actors have constructed and fortified a distorted reality. Unreflectingly believing in the beneficence of law and medicine has aided in neutralising the personally and politically oriented decisions of themselves and others alike. With their discretion left unscrutinised, crucial factors have remained concealed and unaddressed, with alternative readings foreclosed, exclusions naturalised and rendered invisible or irrelevant to consideration and contestation.

[6] Bourdieu (1987) 839.

[7] Boddice (2017) 44.

[8] Veena Das, *Critical Events: An Anthropological Perspective on Contemporary India* (1995) 193 as quoted in Kelly (2009).

Law, attributed a central role in redressing human suffering, equally packs the potential to legitimate (tolerate as to perpetuate) that same suffering. Law's force depends on the police and prisons, yet these mechanisms are simultaneously (and perhaps paradoxically) responsible for redressing excesses in law's name. International human rights law is very much implicated here too, responsible for 'sanitising' disputes around suffering into 'doctrinal debates, dry legal arguments, discussions of precedents and constitutional or statutory texts, arcane questions of whether the right procedural route has been followed so that we can get to the merits at all'.[9] Through positioning the workings of law as antithetical to state violence, much has been hidden from plain sight – with advocates and adjudicators discouraged 'to confront law's lethal character and the masking of its interpretive violence' and to 'ignore the bloody consequences of their authoritative acts and the pain those acts produce'.[10] This book has attempted to articulate a reckoning – at least in 'law and torture' research and practice.

Rejecting the sanitisation, the advocate and the adjudicator, and not simply the prison guard, must be seen as active (not merely passive) parts in the system of inflicting violence on the individual – with interpretive practices needing to be viewed as taking 'place in a field of pain and death' and as 'the engine of law's violence'.[11] Taking a judge's actions as contained to the courtroom and not as foreseeably mandating the transportation of an individual to their demise, judicial complicity and responsibility are distanced and vanish with other practices perpetuated.[12] The law, through such disconnections, reduces the dynamics between the deliverer and the recipient of the violence.[13]

These connections and clues, as unpacked in this book, have underscored how undue narrow interpretive practices prove blind to and silence context and exclude conditions in which suffering is produced – concealing 'the complex institutional and organizational context in

[9] Wald (1993) 82, 77.

[10] Sarat, 'Knowing the Suffering of Others' (2014) 1.

[11] Cover (1986) 1609.

[12] Veitch (2007) 88.

[13] Wald (1993) 82.

which torture occurs'.[14] As law is an exercise in normalisation, as it is simplification, simplicity becomes equated with certainty and quality – not with rigidity or reductivity. Doctrinal dominance readily dissolves when rigorously examined. A failure is revealed to more adequately understand the torture victim and torture's context, institutionally, situationally and ecologically. Beneath the seemingly settled surface of 'law and torture' research and practice brews a complex tension between subjectivity, objectivity, inclusivity, exclusivity and contextuality. The tension is explained away as borne out of the discretion necessitated by the difficulties in this terrain.

7.2 RETHINKING PRACTICE AND RESEARCH

Those who have come before to settle the law and torture terrain simply have not done the work to properly establish productive prisms to think through the pressing problems facing the field. Surely much has been produced – creating a path dependency to a point of redundancy. Those who have come before have conceivably caused harm by the omission of their doctrinal apertures. They should have done more to articulate reflected alternatives. I speak not only to research but also to the dominant anti-torture practice it feeds and frames. Lawyers and doctors have ended up asking and answering the same worn question: does something amount to torture or not? This is unquestionably important yet how it has been answered has fixated on the (law) book and the (victim's) body – devoid of due social, cultural and political contexts. Doctrine has failed to speak about the body in society in its complexity. Doctrine stands disconnected from such crucial contexts – from the everyday, the empirical and the ecological. In redressing this, I propose the rethinking of four distinct traits: *definition-centricity*, *case-fixity*, *act-specificity* and *context-reductivity*. Energies are precious on all fronts. I have written this book to redirect precious energies so that these conversations can be continued in new ways, to see that received stories are not repeated without due pause. I do not believe that repetition and reproduction will see torture's eradication, as the end to incremental doctrinal logics resembles a *cul-de-sac*.

[14] Rejali (2007) 163.

The impoverished[15] state of 'law and torture' research, at least, means that the potential to contribute is wide. Questions of definition, distinction, prohibition, prevention and redress can readily be approached in radical new ways to address the extant redundancy and circularity. So how should anti-torture practice and research look? What then is the approach needed? It is one which starts and ends in foregrounding political, evidential, emotional and temporal imaginaries, mobilities and pathways. It is one which reflects on 'negative moments or exclusions'.[16] These are productive entry points to counter the prevalent act-specificity and context-reductivity fixated on in practice and research. Such reflexive contextualisation might just lead us to a more desirable end, to better understanding the conditions under which torture is inflicted and can be inhibited. With this aim, I make three suggestions towards the kernel of a novel model: *embracing ecological and emotional registers; against hierarchy and selectivity*; and, *towards embedding and embodying.*

As a first-order priority, in asking how torturous suffering is made sense of by the survivor as well as the observer, the doctrinal (the official institutional scripts as manifest in the case law and related interpretive practices) needs to be reconnected to the empirical (its institutional and sociopolitical contexts). Torturous acts, impacts and their contexts need to be taken together, in their totality. A simple solution here is to better understand how anti-torture law (its processes) is *experienced* (emotionally and otherwise). This can be achieved through moving beyond doctrinal analysis to using interviews and participant observation – in courts but also in communities. The anti-torture movement, its modes and means (whether research or practice), will otherwise remain unquestionably top-down. It will continue to focus on national (parliaments, police and prisons) and international institutions (the UN and human rights courts) and on codified standards and how to further develop them. On one register, this prevailing approach is understandable. It is directed and when change is achieved it promises to pack power. It is convenient to think linearly and vertically. It expects the power to affect change down the line. *Top*-down, however, expects *trickle*-down. Yet, the

[15] I use 'impoverished' relative to other disciplines.

[16] Davies (2005).

top (say the UN) is often removed from what happens on the ground. This misses many essential accounts of how this power is felt or not – in homes, the street, the legal office and the clinic.

Two related fronts, where doctrinal brackets limit the range of conditions and contexts taken into consideration are most visible, relate to *time* and *space*. What happens out of the immediate proximity of the immediate act in law's vision struggles for recognition. Crucial patterns in perpetration are missed (say, what happened in a neighbouring police station six months before an act in question might well be instructive) – deemed and dismissed as extra-legal, inadmissible or non-justiciable before the eyes of the law. The question of what is afforded recognition needs to be critically scrutinised – not simply as expected silences and discontinuities. Suffering is produced both through actions and through silences and denials. Whilst it is unquestionably easier to document more direct infliction of state violence as evident in marks, this convenience (of training attention on actions first and inaction second) should not (as it often has) determine the significance of the indirect, implicit, insidious or structural. In failing this, one fails to understand that torturous suffering is not necessarily exceptional, explicit and elsewhere but here and everyday – in terms of both its infliction and inhibition.

Abstracted acts similarly stand to be contextualised, so should individuals isolated from their institutions be embedded and embodied. Individuals are conditioned and often controlled institutionally, towards extending complicity and culpability. While this risks denying their agency and might hamper the pursuit of individual accountability, the opposite (overlooking institutional condition and control) serves to perpetuate logics that disserve effective eradication. The fraught figure of 'THE torturer', giving heed to the 'bad-apple' theory, is a case in point.

As the individual should be better situated in their institution, respective state institutions must also be connected to each other – with parliaments, courts, police stations, prisons, state forensic authorities and ministries potentially acting in a chain of collaboration and complicity. Responsibility for torturous suffering is often shared across institutions but rarely connected. Institutional independence (e.g., that courts are autonomous) should not be presumed. It may be simpler for anti-torture actors to delimit their interventions to certain parts of the state apparatus, for example, working with prosecutors to reduce the use of pre-trial detention, but these delimitations encourage the notion that eradication can be achieved through knowledge exchange rather than broader sociopolitical change. All these signalled shifts may be methodologically challenging and resource intensive but these will generate new ideas for research and practice.

In this book, I have aimed to develop a simple but stark thesis: that doctrine fails to offer a full and genuine exploration of its objects of concern: torture, inhuman and degrading treatment and how they are understood in the practice and research concerned with infliction and inhibition. I have identified how doctrine and doctrinally framed anti-torture practice and research have missed and dismissed the complexities and context of the body, politics, science and society – including remaining oblivious to existing non-legal understandings. Dogma has deluded. It has deluded its disciples into thinking that dogmatic positions and premises are clearly defined and that its promises will be delivered upon. It has allowed little to no critique, restricting a truer view of grounded realities.

7.3 A FINAL NOTE

I end by returning to where I started: disillusionment. It remains, as does the problem: doctrine. I have posed a litany of questions and made some connections to context for myself, as for the reader, some to explicate and others to explain doctrinal dynamics. I must certainly occasionally have misconnected and missed. In defence of any detractors, I am merely starting out myself to push the envelope. Questions, at this stage, prove more useful than answers, offering some comfort even if fleeting. Fleeting as they unfurl and unravel one's frames and fundament. As with any disavowal of a belief or value system, the immediate feeling may be a combination of hollowness and hopelessness. I hope to have transferred to you, not my disappointments, despair and disenchantment, but instead a constructive critique, if nothing else, through equipping you with questions to direct at doctrine as you encounter and engage it wherever you may sit.

The dominance of law in anti-torture, as medicine, looks as though it is here to stay. Lawyers have long dominated central positions in the anti-torture field. Suffering is inflicted on victims, documented and argued by advocates before adjudicators. Adjudicators then assess as to verify and qualify the suffering, ruling as to assign responsibility and provide redress (or not). The position of the UN Special Rapporteur on Torture, which is a singularly significant standard-setting mandate, has been filled by a lawyer since its inception three decades ago, despite no formal requirement that this necessarily be so. The UN Committee against Torture and the Subcommittee for Prevention of Torture have been exceptions bringing in the occasional medical doctor or psychologist. These exceptions are ultimately made by the gatekeepers, the legally trained and doctrinally committed. The law and its actors' casting have been central. These actors have brought with them their impulse to reduce empirical complexities to the commensurable and have created silences and blind spots. The omissions, silences and blind spots conversely and complementarily revealed through this process become integral to law's operation – with its excess and aberrations not emerging as law's dysfunctions but rather, I would argue, its successful functions.

To be sure, I have not sought to substitute that which prevails with something of my own, except for such a critical stance. Neither have I aimed to dismantle doctrine's dominance in research and practice, but to mark a shift towards the critical. We all work with and within institutions, which necessitates collaboration. We relate, please, compromise and appease – inside our own institutions as well as outside (I myself operate in and between the university and an anti-torture NGO). In this, co-optation poses a real risk, never definitively resolved. So I do not pretend that this is any more than a start, an invocation to dive deeper, to explore outside of the bounds of our received frames, to more genuinely connect to context. The questions posed are presented to shield critical collaboration from slipping into co-optation. It will take much more than my rudimentary reflections in these pages to do damage more than a dint of disavowal. I do not pretend that I am 'there' yet nor that this piece of work entirely delivers on its promises. This is a modest attempt to move the conversation forward.

Doctrine, on the other hand, does do damage, insidiously (and perhaps at times inadvertently) invisibilising suffering at the hands of the state. This has been the primary charge I have made in this book. In appearing to push against the perpetrative state, doctrine also pulls away from due recognition of the victim-survivor's lived experience. As I have argued, doctrine holds out recognition of some experiences whilst it frustrates, excludes, conceals, legitimates so many others. The initial violence is perpetuated and sustained for the survivor as for the system. It is incumbent, therefore, for those waging the fight against torture with doctrinal means and modes to gauge its costs for the individual as for our institutions of protection. If you have found my text compelling enough to make it this far, I find it fair to say that you are also hereby implicated in this project. Complacency or doing any less is to be complicit.

Academia, as much as it has been a transformative space for me, is equally compromised. I continue to grapple with the abundance and varied f/utility of our words – how and when they affect change is beyond me. I do not pretend that this wordy work marks any watershed. So I make no claims to selflessness. The anti-torture field (practice and research) resists and tempers subversive voices, such as mine, well. I sometimes wonder why it has tolerated me. I do hope that I've helped the next thinker-on-the-precipice to embrace and make better sense of the doctrinal mess. It might be surprising to some (who do not know me) to not read of lofty wide-reaching aims – since the objects of study are unmistakably ominous and onerous (you read of torture no less!). I wouldn't be faithful to myself if I didn't strike this note of defeat. As long as faulty thoughts on torture prevail, I will remain hesitant to celebrate academic achievements. I write from the figurative periphery, purposefully messily and relatively powerless. To those who have arrived ready with their claims of my fragmenting and undermining hard-won achievements of the field, I ask to check their privilege and power and to extend the inkling of generosity to entertain ideas that may ring foreign and peripheral. This is not a textbook. It may be approached as a critical introduction but I advance it as an invitation for a reflective and reflexive reading of law's relation to torture, not a prescription to the ills I identify.

I have written this book on the premise that, if we know things in their complexity, we will be moved to change them with greater capacity. Although I am not interested in blame, I am in the recognition of responsibility through reflexivity. I am hopeful for such recognition to mobilise change. The task for those to come is to look beyond – to situate the book and the body in their contexts. Leaving this to social scientists, who do this better, will only leave lawyers and doctors stuck. If it is a question of competency, then retrain – unlearn, then learn again. It is imperative that those who dominate the core paradigms of anti-torture work reflect. Torture's eradication will simply not be realised in their absence.

Select Bibliography

Amaya, Amalia and Del Mar, Maksymilian (eds), *Virtue, Emotion and Imagination in Law and Legal Reasoning* (Bloomsbury 2020)

Amnesty International, *Combating Torture: A Manual for Action* (Amnesty International 2016)

Barnes, Jamal, *A Genealogy of the Torture Taboo* (Routledge 2017)

Başoğlu, Metin (ed), *Torture and Its Definition in International Law: An Interdisciplinary Approach* (Oxford University Press 2017)

Bentley, Lionel and Leo Flynn, *Law and the Senses: Sensational Jurisprudence* (Pluto Press 1996)

Berlant, Lauren, 'Slow Death (Sovereignty, Obesity, Lateral Agency)' (2007) 33 *Critical Inquiry* 754

Bianchi, Andrea and Moshe Hirsch (eds), *International Law's Invisible Frames: Social Cognition and Knowledge Production in International Legal Processes* (Oxford University Press 2021)

Biswas, Shampa and Zahi Zalloua (eds), *Torture: Power, Democracy and the Human Body* (University of Washington Press 2011)

Boddice, Rob, *Pain: A Very Short Introduction* (Oxford University Press 2017)

Butler, Judith, *Frames of War: When Is Life Grievable?* (Verso 2009)

Butler, Judith, *The Force of Non-Violence* (Verso 2020)

Cakal, Ergun, 'Assessing (and Making Sense of) Severity: Conceptualising and Contextualising Torture's Core' (2022) 91 (2) *Nordic Journal of International Law* 284–309

Cakal, Ergun, 'At the Threshold of Justiciable Violence: Configuring and Contesting Torture's Production' (2024) 20 (2) *Law, Culture and the Humanities* 355–372

Cakal, Ergun, 'Befogging Reason, Undermining Will: Understanding Sleep Deprivation as Torture and Other Ill-Treatment in International Law' (2019) 29 (2) *Torture* 11–22

Cakal, Ergun, 'Cruelty and Corpo-reality: Connecting Technologies and Practices Integral to Torture's Infliction and Investigation' (2022) 14 (3) *Journal of Human Rights Practice* 1021–1037

Cakal, Ergun, 'Debility, Dependency and Dread: On the Conceptual and Evidentiary Dimensions of Psychological Torture' (2018) 28 (2) *Torture* 15–37

Cakal, Ergun, 'Isolating Children in Detention: Cautioning International Comparison' (2023) 48 (3) *Alternative Law Journal* 166–171

Cakal, Ergun, 'Law and Torture: Contemporary Legal Scholarship on Torture, from the Doctrinal to the Critical' (2023) 25 (5) *International Community Law Review* 397–425

Cakal, Ergun, 'Perception, Practice and Proximity: Qualifying Threats as Psychological Torture in International Law' (2021) 31 (1) *Torture* 19–36

Cakal, Ergun, 'Registering Time in Recognising Torturous Harm: Figuring the Single, Plural and Historical in Torture's Adjudication' (2024) 33 (2) *Social & Legal Studies* 276–296

Cakal, Ergun, 'Sensing Suffering: On Common-Sense and Compassion in the Legal Imagination and Recognition of Torture' (2022) 10 (3) *London Review of International Law* 337–366

Cakal, Ergun, 'Torture and Progress, Past and Promised: Problematising Torture's Evolving Interpretation' (2023) 19 (2) *International Journal of Law in Context* 236–254

Canning, Victoria, *Torture and Torturous Violence: Transcending Definitions of Torture* (Bristol University Press 2023)

Cassese, Antonio, *Inhuman States: Imprisonment, Detention and Torture in Europe Today* (Polity Press 1996)

Celermajer, Danielle, *The Prevention of Torture: An Ecological Approach* (Cambridge University Press 2018)

Chowdhury, Tanzil, 'Time Frames and Legal Indeterminacy' (2017) 1 *Canadian Journal of Law & Jurisprudence* 57–76

Chowdhury, Tanzil, *Time, Temporality and Legal Judgment* (Routledge 2020)

Christie, Nils, *Limits to Pain* (Martin Robertson 1981)

Cohen, Stanley, *States of Denial: Knowing about Atrocities and Suffering* (Polity Press 2001)

Cover, Robert, 'Violence and the Word' (1986) 95 *Yale Law Journal* 1609

Dannenbaum, Tom, 'Siege Starvation: A War Crime of Societal Torture' (2022) *Chicago Journal of International Law* 410

Das, Veena (ed), *Violence and Subjectivity* (University of California Press 2000)

Davidson, Natalie, 'The Feminist Expansion of the Prohibition of Torture: Towards a Post-Liberal International Human Rights Law?' (2019–2020) 52 *Cornell International Law Journal* 109

Dayan, Colin, *The Law Is a White Dog* (Princeton University Press 2011)

Dayan, Colin, *The Story of Cruel and Unusual* (MIT Press 2007)

DelVecchio Good, Mary-Jo (ed), *Pain as Human Experience: An Anthropological Perspective* (University of California Press 1994)

Dewulf, Steven, *The Signature of Evil: (Re)Defining Torture in International Law* (Intersentia 2011)

Edwards, Alice, 'The "Feminizing" of Torture under International Human Rights Law' (2006) 19 *Leiden Journal of International Law*

Evans, Malcolm, *Tackling Torture: Prevention in Practice* (Bristol University Press 2023)

Evans, Malcolm and Jens Modvig (eds), *Research Handbook on Torture: Legal and Medical Perspectives on Prohibition and Prevention* (Elgar 2020)

Farrell, Michelle, 'The Marks of Civilisation: The Special Stigma of Torture' (2022) 22 *Human Rights Law Review* 1

Fassin, Didier and Estelle D'Halluin, 'The Truth from the Body: Medical Certificates as Ultimate Evidence for Asylum Seekers' (2005) 107 *American Anthropologist* 597

Fassin, Didier and Richard Rechtman, *The Empire of Trauma: An Inquiry into the Condition of Victimhood* (Princeton University Press 2009)

Fineman, Martha and Anna Grear (eds), *Vulnerability: Reflections on a New Ethical Foundation for Law and Politics* (2013)

Fitzpatrick Peter, *The Mythology of Modern Law* (Routledge 1999)

Garland, David, *Punishment and Modern Society: A Study in Social Theory* (Clarendon Press 1993)

Hajjar, Lisa, 'Does Torture Work? A Sociolegal Assessment of the Practice in Historical and Global Perspective' (2009) 5 *Annual Review of Law and Social Science*

Heri, Corina, *Responsive Human Rights: Vulnerability, Ill-Treatment and the ECtHR* (Hart 2021)

Jensen, Steffen et al, 'Torture and Ill-Treatment Under Perceived: Human Rights Documentation and the Poor' (2017) 39 *Human Rights Quarterly* 393

Kaufman-Osborn, Timothy Vance, *From Noose to Needle: Capital Punishment and the Late Liberal State* (University of Michigan Press 2009)

Kelly, Tobias, 'Recognizing Torture: Credibility and the Unstable Codification of Victimhood' in Steffen Jensen and Henrik Rønsbo (eds), *Histories of Victimhood* (2014)

Kelly, Tobias, 'Sympathy and Suspicion: Torture, Asylum, and Humanity' (2012) 18 *Journal of the Royal Anthropological Institute* 753–768

Kelly, Tobias, 'The Struggle against Torture: Challenges, Assumptions and New Directions' (2019) 11 *Journal of Human Rights Practice*

Kelly, Tobias, 'The UN Committee against Torture: Human Rights Monitoring and the Legal Recognition of Cruelty' (2009) 31 (3) *Human Rights Quarterly* 777

Kelly, Tobias, *This Side of Silence: Human Rights, Torture, and the Recognition of Cruelty* (Penn Press 2012)

Kelly, Tobias et al, 'A Comparative Study of the Use of the Istanbul Protocol amongst Civil Society Organizations in Low-Income Countries' (2016) 26 (3) *Torture* 62

Kesper-Biermann, Sylvia, 'Security, Transnational Law and Emotions: The History of the Transnational Anti-Torture Regime from the Enlightenment to the 1984 United Nations Convention Against Torture' (Max Planck Institute for European Legal History Research Paper Series No 2018-01)

Khan, Paul W., *Sacred Violence: Torture, Terror, and Sovereignty* (University of Michigan Press 2008)

Kleinman, Arthur, Veena Das and Margaret M Lock (eds), *Social Suffering* (UC Press 1997)

Langbein, John, *Torture and the Law of Proof: Europe in the Ancien Régime* (University of Chicago Press 2006)

Mavronicola, Natasa, *Torture, Inhumanity, and Degradation under Article 3 of the ECHR: Absolute Rights and Absolute Wrongs* (Hart 2021)

Nowak, Manfred, Moritz Birk and Giuliana Monina (eds), *The United Nations Convention against Torture and Its Optional Protocol: A Commentary* (2nd ed, OUP 2019)

Oette, Lutz, 'The Prohibition of Torture and Persons Living in Poverty: From the Margins to the Centre' (2021) 70 (2) *International and Comparative Law Quarterly* 307

Oette, Lutz, *The Transformation of the Prohibition of Torture in International Law* (OUP 2024)

O'Rourke, Maeve, 'Prolonged Impunity as a Continuing Situation of Torture or Ill-Treatment? Applying a Dignity Lens to So-Called "Historical" Cases' (2019) 66 (1) *Netherlands International Law Review*

Parry, John T, "'Just for Fun': Understanding Torture and Understanding Abu Ghraib", (2005) 1 *Journal of National Security Law and Policy*

Parry, John T, 'The Shape of Modern Torture: Extraordinary Rendition and Ghost Detainees' (2005) 6 *Melbourne Journal of International Law* 516

Parry, John T, *Understanding Torture: Law, Violence, and Political Identity* (Michigan 2010)

Rejali, Darius, 'Modern Torture as a Civic Marker: Solving a Global Anxiety with a New Political Technology' (2003) 2 (2) *Journal of Human Rights*

Rejali, Darius, 'The Field of Torture Today: Ten Years on from Torture and Democracy', in Barela et al (eds), *Interrogation and Torture* (OUP 2020)

Rejali, Darius, *Torture and Democracy* (Princeton 2007)

Richardson, Michael, *Gestures of Testimony: Torture, Trauma, and Affect in Literature* (Bloomsbury 2016)

Rodley, Nigel and Matt Pollard, *The Treatment of Prisoners under International Law* (3rd ed, OUP 2011)

Sarat, Austin (ed), *Law, Violence, and the Possibility of Justice* (Princeton University Press 2001)

Sarat, Austin (ed), *Knowing the Suffering of Others: Legal Perspectives on Pain and Its Meanings* (The University of Alabama Press 2014)

Sarat, Austin (ed), *The Punitive Imagination: Law, Justice, and Responsibility* (University of Alabama Press 2014)

Sarat, Austin and Thomas Kearns (eds), *Law's Violence* (1992)

Scarry, Elaine, *The Body in Pain: The Making and Unmaking of the World* (OUP 1985)

Silverman, Lisa, *Tortured Subjects: Pain, Truth, and the Body in Early Modern France* (University of Chicago Press 2001)

Stanley, Elizabeth, *Torture, Truth and Justice: The Case of Timor Leste* (Routledge 2009)

Veitch, Scott, *Law and Irresponsibility: On the Legitimation of Human Suffering* (Routledge 2007)

Viterbo, Hedi, 'Seeing Torture Anew: A Transnational Reconceptualization of State Torture and Visual Evidence' (2014) 50 *Stanford Journal of International Law*

Vorhaus, John, 'Bringing People Down: Degrading Treatment and Punishment' (2021) 24 (3) *New Criminal Law Review* 436

Waldron, Jeremy, *Torture, Terror, and Trade-Offs: Philosophy for the White House* (OUP 2010)

Webster, Elaine, *Dignity, Degrading Treatment and Torture in Human Rights Law: The Ends of Article 3 of the European Convention on Human Rights* (Routledge 2018)

Wilkinson, Iain and Arthur Kleinman, *A Passion for Society: How We Think about Human Suffering* (UC Press 2016)

Winter, Yves, 'Violence and visibility' (2012) 34 *New Political Science* 195

Yildiz, Ezgi, *Between Forbearance and Audacity: The European Court of Human Rights and the Norm against Torture* (CUP 2023)

Index